YOUNG WINSTON

The first twenty-six years of Winston Churchill's
life were packed with more incident and
adventure than most men see in a lifetime. As a
lieutenant in the 4th Hussars, he served in India,
and in the Sudan he was present at the battle
of Omdurman. As a newspaper correspondent
he covered the Boer War, was taken prisoner,
and escaped. As a politician he laid the
foundations of his later career with his election
as Member of Parliament for Oldham in 1900.

Based on exclusive use of Sir Winston's letters
and papers, THE YOUNG CHURCHILL is a
shortened version of YOUTH: 1874-1900,
the first volume of WINSTON S. CHURCHILL.

THE YOUNG CHURCHILL

RANDOLPH S. CHURCHILL

Lancer Books New York

A Lancer Book

THE YOUNG CHURCHILL

is a shortened version of YOUTH: 1874-1900,
Volume One of WINSTON S. CHURCHILL

This book was published by arrangement with
Houghton Mifflin Company. Its large sale
in the hardcover edition makes possible
this inexpensive reprint.

Lancer Books, Inc., 1560 Broadway
New York, N.Y. 10036

CONTENTS

MAPS BY JOAN EMERSON

ACKNOWLEDGEMENTS

THE AUTHOR WISHES first to acknowledge his indebtedness to Her Majesty the Queen, who graciously gave permission for him to have access to the Royal Archives and to use other documents which are her copyright. For guidance in the selection of this material the author is grateful to Mr Robert Mackworth-Young, Librarian at Windsor Castle.

The author's main source is the papers in the Chartwell Trust established by Sir Winston Churchill in 1946, which he directed in 1960 should be placed at the author's disposal. The author records his thanks to the Trustees of the Chartwell settlement, Baroness Spencer-Churchill, Sir Leslie Rowan, Mr Jock Colville and Mr Anthony Moir, who have been most helpful in causing the papers to be sorted and arranged at the Public Records Office under the supervision of Mr Lionel Bell.

Acknowledgements are also due to those who have kindly allowed the author access to their Archives: Mr Ian B. Hamilton, Sir Shane Leslie, the Duke of Marlborough (Blenheim Papers), Mrs Edward Phillips, the Earl of Rosebery, the Marquess of Salisbury and Viscount Wimborne; the Trustees of Sir Aylmer Haldane; Birmingham University Library (Joseph Chamberlain), the Trustees of the British Museum (Balfour Papers), New York City Public Library (Cockran Papers), and the Director of Government Archives, Pretoria.

Copyright permission has also been kindly provided by the Trustees of the late Maurice Baring, the Marquis de Breteuil, Rear-Admiral Sir Anthony Buzzard, Mrs Norah Brown (Goodacre), Mr Peregrine S. Churchill, Miss K. M. Clegg, Brother Norwood Coaker, CR, Mr Angus Davidson, the Earl of Derby, Mr Henry Drummond-Wolff, Dr A. R. B. Haldane, Mr Charles James and Mrs F. L. Klin, Sir Frederic Johnstone, Dr C. F. Keuzenkamp, Mrs Janet Leeper and Mrs George Shield (Hamilton), Mrs Anita Leslie, Sir Shane Leslie, Pamela,

Countess of Lytton, the Duke of Marlborough, Mrs Terence Maxwell (Joseph Chamberlain), Mr Iain Murray (Aylesford), Sir Frederick Rawlinson, Lady Rayleigh (Blood), Viscount Runciman, Lady Tweedmouth, A. P. Watt & Sons, Lord Wigram (Colonel Neville Chamberlain), the Earl of Wilton and Mr Leonard Woolf. And also by the following publishers: Edward Arnold (*Reminiscences* by Lady Randolph Churchill), Blackwood (*How We Escaped from Pretoria* and *A Soldier's Saga* by Aylmer Haldane), Gale and Polden (*History of the Fourth Hussars* by David Scott Daniell), George G. Harrap (*Marlborough* by Winston S. Churchill), Hogarth Press (*The Development of English Biography* by Harold Nicolson), Hodder and Stoughton (*An Ambassador of Peace* by Lord D'Abernon), Methuen and Co (*The Relief of Ladysmith* by J. B. Atkins), John Murray (*Parliamentary Reminiscences and Reflections* by Lord George Hamilton), Odhams Press (*The River War, Savrola, Lord Randolph Churchill, The World Crisis, My Early Life, Thoughts and Adventures*, all by Winston S. Churchill), Weidenfeld and Nicholson (*Lord Randolph Churchill* by Robert Rhodes James). Also *Encounter* and *The Star*, Johannesburg.

The events recorded in these pages happened many years ago, and in some cases it has not been possible to trace the holders of copyright. Will any copyright holders who have been omitted please accept the author's apologies?

For reminiscences the author is indebted to Mr Humphrey Bingham, Baroness Spencer-Churchill, the late Mrs John Churchill, Mr. A. M. Davey of the University of South Africa, Brigadier Jack Gannon, Mr. Lewis C. B. Howard, Dr C. F. Keuzenkamp, Mrs Anita Leslie, Sir Shane Leslie, Pamela, Countess of Lytton, Dr Jan Ploeger, and the late Mrs Muriel Warde.

To the following the author expresses his thanks for reading the proofs and for tendering valuable advice: Hon Sir George Bellew, Mr R. A. Bevan, Mr Anthony Montague Browne, Mr Lionel Capstickdale, Baroness Spencer-Churchill, Mr Peregrine S. Churchill, Mr Winston S. Churchill, Mr Jock Colville, Colonel F. S. Corke, Mr Robert Rhodes James of All Souls, Sir Shane Leslie, Mr Robert Mackworth-Young, Hon Mrs Christopher Soames, Mr Robert Taylor of Nuffield College, Oxford, and Mr Ivan Yates.

Finally the author desires to express his indebtedness to the following who have assisted in sorting, assembling and studying the material: Mr Michael Wolff, who has from the beginning directed the research; Mr Andrew Kerr and Mr Martin Mauthner, who have been chiefly concerned with work on this volume; Mr Martin Gilbert of Merton College, Oxford, and Mr George Thayer, who have been more concerned with work on later volumes; and Mr Michael Molian. Also to his secretarial staff: Miss Eileen Harriman, archivist, and Miss Barbara Twigg, personal secretary; Mrs Trevor Adams; Mrs Margaret Bentley, Miss Lynette Parker, Miss Alice Golding, Miss Bettye Verran and Mrs Richard von Goetz. And to Mrs Robert Bevan, who assembled the illustrations and advised on their selection.

PREFACE

BROUGHT UP TO ADMIRE his grandfather, and daily growing throughout his youth and manhood in his love and veneration for his father, the author has long aspired to write a filial and objective biography. This is evidenced by two telegrams that passed in 1932 between the author, who had not yet come of age, and his father, who was lecturing in America.

RSC to WSC
(Stour Papers)

TELEGRAM

[27 February 1932]   72 Glebe Place
                                                                  Chelsea

Have been offered 450 pounds advance on substantial royalties for biography of you have you any objection to my accepting if I do it will naturally be unauthorised unofficial and undocumented my aim would be present political history last thirty years in light unorthodox fashion believe could produce amusing work without embarrassing you mummie looking very well all counting days to your return love

                                                                  R

WSC to RSC
(Stour Papers)
TELEGRAM

27 February 1932   Indianapolis

Strongly deprecate premature attempt hope some day you will make thousands instead of hundreds out of my archives most improvident anticipate now stop lecture pilgrimage drawing wearily final stage much love show mamma

                                                    FATHER

11

This sensible advice was naturally heeded, resulting in advantages to the family even more abundant than Mr Churchill had predicted.

In planning what will be a colossal work, I have been guided very much by the lectures which that master of biography, Sir Harold Nicolson, gave in 1927 and which were first published in 1928 in the Hogarth Lectures on Literature. In *The Development of English Biography*, Sir Harold points out that Izaak Walton revived the 'admirable practice of introducing original letters into the text'. He later says of Mason, who wrote the *Life and Letters* of Gray : 'He is said to have first conceived of this method on reading Middleton's *Cicero;* but he expanded it, and allowed the letters to tell their own story, introducing them only with short explanatory captions, or explaining them by sensible and vivid notes. "In a word," as he says, "Mr Gray will become his own biographer." ' Sir Harold also observes in the same series of lectures :

> For the *Life of Johnson* is a work of art, not merely in its actual excellence of outline, but in the careful adjustment of internal spaces. We have thus the absence of comment, or rather the very skilful interspacing of comment—the way in which Boswell first provides the evidence, and then, at a later period, confirms by comment the conclusion which the reader has already reached.

I have also been influenced by what Lockhart, the son-in-law and biographer of Sir Walter Scott, wrote :

> I have endeavoured to lay before the reader those parts of Sir Walter's character to which we have access, as they were indicated in his sayings and doings through the long series of his years—making use, whenever it was possible, of his own letters and diaries rather than of any other materials—but refrained from obtruding almost anything of comment. It was my wish to let the character develop itself.

I have also been fortified in my conception of my task by what Lockhart wrote to Scott's friend, William Laidlaw, '. . . that his sole object was to do Scott justice "or rather to let him do himself justice, by so contriving it that he shall be, as far as possible, from first to last, his own biographer . . ." ', thus echoing what Mason had written.

Churchill himself in prefacing the Life of his father wrote:

For a thing so commonly attempted, political biography is difficult. The style and ideas of the writer must throughout be subordinated to the necessity of embracing in the text those documentary proofs upon which the story depends. Letters, memoranda, and extracts from speeches, which inevitably and rightly interrupt the sequence of his narrative, must be pieced together upon some consistent and harmonious plan. It is not by the soft touches of a picture, but in hard mosaic or tessellated pavement, that a man's life and fortunes must be presented in all their reality and romance. I have thought it my duty, so far as possible, to assemble once and for all the whole body of historical evidence required for the understanding of Lord Randolph Churchill's career. Scarcely anything of material consequence has been omitted, and such omissions as have been necessary are made for others' sakes and not his own. Scarcely any statement of importance lacks documentary proof. There is nothing more to tell. Wherever practicable I have endeavoured to employ his own words in the narration; and the public is now in a position to pronounce a complete, if not a final, judgement.

And even earlier, writing to his mother:

WSC to Lady Randolph

EXTRACT

31 March [1898]   Camp Peshawar

. . . As to the Biographer—who may investigate another human wretch's life—I would say as Oliver Cromwell did to Sir Peter Lely—'Paint me as I am' and thereupon was painted wart and all. . . .

With the wealth of material which has been entrusted to the author about a man who was in his own lifetime widely saluted as a patriot, a hero and a genius, it would scarcely be possible to write a dull book. Nonetheless the epic of his life, the innumerable activities in which he was involved, the vast number of personalities with whom he was brought into conflict or contact or with whom he transacted business, have presented the author with problems and decisions often of a tortuous complexity. What to put in? What to leave out? What to relegate to appendices? These have not been easy questions to answer. After much thought and consultation the author decided upon the following method :

To assemble the body of relevant and original and unpublished documents and letters in one or two independent appendix volumes as companions to each volume of the main work; to compile these first, and to use them as the raw material from which each volume of the main work was to be written. The general reader may rest assured that each volume of the main work will contain all that is most interesting and exciting in the life of Sir Winston Churchill, while the student and historian who wish to have access to the full documentation will find it readily available in the Companion Volume or Volumes to the main work, as each Companion comes from the press.

Every effort has been made in this volume and will be made in succeeding volumes of the main work to spare the reader the distraction of otiose footnotes which might have disfigured the pages : to avoid what Mr John Betjeman has called the 'rash of foot and note disease'. Whenever it has been possible without interrupting the flow of the narrative, references have been incorporated in the text. When no references are given it should in general be assumed that the information comes from Sir Winston's papers in the Chartwell Trust which have been carefully sorted and catalogued by the Public Records Office and which will eventually be available to students of the period. Spelling has for the most part been corrected and brought up to date except where it has been thought desirable to retain the 'period flavour' of the original. In the case of the subject of the biography, however, his original spelling and punctuation is preserved until he comes to manhood at the age of twenty, on the death of his father, after which obvious slips are corrected. Addresses and dates have been standardized. Where square brackets are used in letters or quotations it should be understood that they contain inter-

14

polations by the author; round brackets, where they occur,
are those of the original writer.

RANDOLPH S. CHURCHILL

Stour
East Bergholt
Suffolk
April 1966

SHORT BIOGRAPHIES

OF THE

PRINCIPAL CHARACTERS

TO BE BROUGHT BEFORE THE READER IN THIS VOLUME

B A L F O U R Arthur James (1848–1930); eldest son of James Maitland and Lady Blanche Cecil, second daughter of 2nd Marquess of Salisbury. Succeeded his uncle, 3rd Marquess of Salisbury, as Prime Minister 1902–5 and leader of the Tory Party 1902–11. Conservative MP for Hertford 1874–85, for Manchester East 1885–1906, for City of London 1906–22. For a time a member with Lord Randolph Churchill of the Fourth Party. President of Local Government Board 1885–6; Secretary for Scotland 1886–7; Chief Secretary for Ireland 1887–91; Leader of the House and First Lord of the Treasury, 1891–2, 1895–1905. Succeeded WSC as First Lord of the Admiralty 1915; Foreign Secretary 1916–19; Lord President of the Council 1919–22, 1925–9. Earl 1922.

B A R I N G Hugo (1876–1949); sixth son of 1st Baron Revelstoke. Lieutenant 4th Hussars, in India with WSC. Served in Boer War (severely wounded), and in First World War (wounded). Married 1905 Evelyn Harriet, widow of 2nd Baron Magheramorne, second daughter of 8th Earl of Shaftesbury.

B A R N E S Reginald Walter Ralph (1871–1946); son of Prebendary R. H. Barnes of Stoke Canon, near Exeter. He and WSC were fellow-subalterns in the 4th Hussars and they went to Cuba in 1895. Major-General and KCB 1919.

B E A C O N S F I E L D 1st Earl of—see D I S R A E L I.

BLANDFORD Albertha Frances Anne (Bertha), Marchioness of (1847–1932); sixth daughter of 1st Duke of Abercorn and Louisa Jane, daughter of 6th Duke of Bedford. She had seven brothers, and was one of seven sisters, all of whom married into the peerage. She married in 1869 George Charles, Marquess of Blandford (qv below), eldest son of 7th Duke of Marlborough (qv). This marriage was dissolved in 1883; the decree nisi was awarded five months before her husband succeeded to the dukedom, but was not made absolute until four months after. However, she preferred to retain the style of Marchioness of Blandford, though by 1896 she was one of five ladies then living who were or had been entitled to the style of Duchess of Marlborough. The others were Jane, widow of 6th Duke; Fanny, widow of 7th Duke; Lily, widow of 8th Duke; and Consuelo, wife of 9th Duke.

BLANDFORD George Charles, Marquess of (1844–92); eldest son of 7th Duke of Marlborough (qv), whom he succeeded 1883 and brother of Lord Randolph Churchill (qv). Married (1) 1869, Albertha (qv above), daughter of 1st Duke of Abercorn; (2) 1888 at the Tabernacle Baptist Church, New York, Lilian Warren (Duchess Lily), widow of Louis Hammersley and daughter of Cicero Price, Commodore US Navy. Succeeded as 8th Duke in 1883.

BLOOD Bindon (1842–1940); son of W. B. Blood, of County Clare, and a descendant of the celebrated Colonel Thomas Blood, who attempted to steal the Crown Jewels from the Tower of London in 1671. As Major-General commanding Malakand Field Force 1897 he afforded WSC opportunities for active service. KCB 1896, GCB 1909. Retired as General 1907.

BRABAZON John Palmer (1843–1922); son of Major H. Brabazon of County Mayo, and Eleanor Ambrosia, daughter of Sir W. H. Palmer, 3rd Bart. Served in Grenadier Guards and 10th Hussars; appointed to command 4th Hussars 1893. Later commanded 2nd Cavalry Brigade in South Africa. Major-General and KCB 1911.

BRETEUIL Henri Charles Joseph le Tonnelie, Marquis de (1848–1916); son of Alexandre Charles Joseph de Breteuil and Charlotte Fould, daughter of Napoleon III's finance minister, Achille Fould. Served with distinction in Franco-Prussian War. Member of Chamber of Deputies 1877–92, sat as a conservative and monarchist, and was noted as an authoritative speaker on finance matters and foreign affairs. Close friend of Lord and Lady Randolph.

CASSEL Ernest Joseph (1852–1921); born at Cologne, youngest son of Jacob Cassel, a small banker. In 1869 came to England, where he amassed a vast fortune: he became an intimate friend of the Prince of Wales, later King Edward VII, and of Lord Randolph Churchill. Knighted 1899.

CHAMBERLAIN Joseph (1836–1914); eldest son of Joseph Chamberlain, a boot and shoe manufacturer, and Caroline, daughter of Harry Harben, a provision merchant. Made a substantial fortune as screw manufacturer in Birmingham; three times Mayor of Birmingham 1873–5, MP 1876–1914. President of the Board of Trade under Gladstone 1880–5, and President of the Local Government Board 1886, when he left the Liberal party on the issue of Home Rule and allied himself with Tories as Liberal Unionist. Secretary of State for Colonies 1895–1903, when he left the Tory government to campaign for imperial preference. Three times married; one son (Austen) became Chancellor of the Exchequer and Foreign Secretary, the other (Neville) Chancellor of the Exchequer and Prime Minister.

CHURCHILL John Strange Spencer- ('Jack') (1880–1947); younger brother of WSC. Born in Dublin 4 February 1880; educated at Harrow; served in the South African War where he was wounded and mentioned in despatches, and in First World War at Gallipoli. By profession a stockbroker. He married in 1908 Lady Gwendeline Bertie (1885–1941), daughter of 7th Earl of Abingdon.

CHURCHILL Lady Randolph Henry Spencer- ('Jennie') (1854–1921); mother of WSC and Jack Churchill. She was born on 10 January 1854 in Brooklyn, New York, second daughter of Leonard Jerome (qv), and married (1)

Lord Randolph Churchill (qv below); (2) on 28 July 1900 Captain George Cornwallis-West, whom she divorced 1913; (3) 1919 Montagu Porch.

CHURCHILL Lord Randolph Henry Spencer- (1849–95); father of WSC and Jack Churchill (qv). Born in London 13 February 1849, third but second surviving son of 7th Duke of Marlborough. Educated Eton and Merton College, Oxford. He married 15 April 1874 Jennie Jerome. MP for Woodstock 1874–85, and for South Paddington 1885–95. Secretary of State for India 1885–6; Chancellor of the Exchequer and Leader of the House of Commons July–December 1886. He died in London 24 January 1895.

COCKRAN William Bourke (1854–1923); American lawyer and politician. Born in County Sligo, he went to America in 1871. Democratic Member of Congress for New York 1891–5, 1904–9, 1920–3.

CROMER Evelyn Baring, 1st Earl of (1841–1917); sixth son of Henry Baring MP, a member of the family of merchant bankers, and Cecilia, daughter of Admiral William Windham. British Agent and Consul-General in Egypt 1883–1907. Baron 1892, Viscount 1899, Earl 1901.

CURZON George Nathaniel (1859–1925); eldest son of Reverend Alfred Curzon, 4th Baron Scarsdale, and Blanche, daughter of Joseph Senhouse of Netherhall. Viceroy of India 1899–1905. Earlier, Tory MP for Southport 1886–98; Under-Secretary of State for India 1891–2; Under-Secretary of State for Foreign Affairs 1895–8. Later Lord Privy Seal 1915–16; Lord President of the Council 1916–19; Foreign Secretary 1919–24. Married (1) 1895 Mary, daughter of Levi Leiter of Washington, DC, who died in 1906; (2) 1917 Grace, daughter of J. Monroe Hinds of the United States and widow of Alfred Duggan of Buenos Aires. Created Baron Curzon of Kedleston (Irish Peerage) 1898; Earl Curzon of Kedleston, Viscount Scarsdale and Baron Ravensdale 1911; Marquess Curzon and KG 1921.

DISRAELI Benjamin (1804–81); son of Isaac D'Israeli, author and literary critic. Twice Prime Minister,

1868, 1874–80; Tory MP for Buckinghamshire 1847–76. Wrote more than a dozen novels, the last, *Endymion*, published in 1880. Created Earl of Beaconsfield 1876; KG 1878.

E L G I N Victor Alexander, 9th Earl of and 13th Earl of Kincardine (1849–1917); eldest son of 8th Earl, Viceroy of India 1862–3, and of Lady Mary Louisa, eldest surviving daughter of 1st Earl of Durham. He himself was Viceroy of India 1894–8 while WSC was serving there, and later Secretary of State for the Colonies when WSC became Under-Secretary in 1905. His grandfather, 7th Earl, salvaged in 1801 the marble frieze of the Parthenon (now known as the 'Elgin Marbles'), later acquired by the British Museum where it can still be seen to great advantage.

E V E R E S T Elizabeth Ann (1833–95); born in Kent. Children's nurse, first with Rev Thompson Phillips of Carlisle, then with Lord Randolph Churchill 1875–93. Nicknamed by Winston and Jack 'Woom' or 'Woomany'.

F I N C A S T L E Alexander Edward, Viscount (1871–1962); eldest son of 7th Earl of Dunmore. Major 16th Lancers; served with Sudan Field Force 1896; ADC to Viceroy of India 1895–7; served with Malakand Field Force and ADC to Sir Bindon Blood 1897 (VC, despatches three times). Published *A Frontier Campaign* 1898. In Boer War he raised and commanded Fincastle's Horse (despatches); and in World War I (DSO, despatches four times) was wounded twice. Succeeded as 8th Earl of Dunmore 1907.

F R E W E N Clara (1850–1935); eldest daughter of Leonard Jerome (qv). She married Moreton Frewen (qv); they had two sons, and a daughter, Clare, who married Wilfred Sheridan, a descendant of Richard Brinsley Sheridan, eighteenth-century playwright and politician. Clare Sheridan achieved fame as a sculptress and as a traveller in North Africa.

F R E W E N Moreton (1853–1924); son of Thomas Frewen MP, of Northiam, Sussex, and Helen Louisa, daughter of Frederick Homan, of County Kildare. Married

1881 Clara (qv above), eldest daughter of Leonard Jerome. A knowledgeable if unlucky student of economic affairs, he was the author of a number of works on bi-metallism. MP for North-East Cork, 1910–11.

GLADSTONE William Ewart (1809–98); fourth son of Sir John Gladstone, 1st Bart, and Anne, daughter of Andrew Robertson, Provost of Dingwall. Three times Chancellor of the Exchequer and four times Prime Minister, 1868–74, 1880–5, 1886, 1892–4. Liberal MP for Newark, Oxford University, South Lancashire, Greenwich (1868–80) and Midlothian (1880–95). Author of numerous works on religious and philosophical topics.

GUEST—see **WIMBORNE**.

HALDANE (James) Aylmer Lowthorpe (1862–1950); eldest son of Daniel Rutherford Haldane and Charlotte, daughter of James Lowthorpe, of Welton Hall, Yorks. Joined Gordon Highlanders 1882; served in India and South Africa with WSC. He was in command of the Chieveley armoured train when he and WSC were captured and imprisoned in Pretoria. KCB 1918; retired as General 1925.

HAMILTON Ian Standish Monteith (1853–1947); born in Corfu, the son of Col Christian Hamilton and Corinna, daughter of 3rd Viscount Gort; he married 1887 Jean, daughter of Sir John Muir, 1st Bart, and Lady Muir. Commanded 3rd Brigade, Tirah Campaign, 1897–8. Served in South Africa, 1899–1901, where he took part in the defence of Ladysmith, and later commanded one of the mobile columns described by WSC in *Ian Hamilton's March*. At the battle of Majuba Hill 1881 received a wound in his wrist which afflicted his left arm for the rest of his life. Commanded Mediterranean Expeditionary Force 1915, which attempted to capture the Gallipoli Peninsula. KCB 1900; General 1905.

JAMES Henry (1828–1911); lawyer and politician, befriended Lord and Lady Randolph and later WSC. Liberal MP for Taunton 1869–85, for Bury 1885–6. Twice Attorney-General under Gladstone 1873–4, 1880–5. With Chamberlain and Hartington left Liberal party and became

Liberal Unionist (MP for Bury 1886–95). Chancellor of Duchy of Lancaster 1895–1902. Knighted 1873; created Baron James of Hereford 1895.

JEROME Clara (1825–95); wife of Leonard Jerome (qv below), whom she married in 1849, and mother of Clara (Frewen), Jennie (Spencer-Churchill) and Leonie (Leslie) (qv). Youngest daughter of Ambrose Hall, a member of New York State Assembly, and Clarissa, daughter of David Willcox, whose father and grandfather had been blacksmiths in Dartmouth, Massachusetts. Lived for many years in Paris with her three daughters. After they were married she settled in England and died at Tunbridge Wells.

JEROME Leonard Walter (1817–91); husband of Clara Jerome (qv), fifth son of Isaac Jerome of Pompey, New York, and Aurora, daughter of Reuben Murray, of Connecticut. First a lawyer and small-town newspaper proprietor, he came to New York in 1855 and became a successful stockbroker and financier, and for a period principal proprietor of the *New York Times*. American Consul in Trieste 1851–2. A keen yachtsman, founder of the American Jockey Club and a patron of the opera.

JEUNE Mary Susan Elizabeth, Lady (1845–1931); daughter of Keith Stewart Mackenzie of Seaforth and Hannah, eldest daughter of James Hope-Vere of Craigie Hall. Married (1) 1871 John, second son of 2nd Baron Stanley of Alderley (d. 1878); and (2) 1881 Sir Francis Jeune 1st Bart, later 1st and last Baron St. Helier, President of the Probate Divorce and Admiralty Division of the High Court. Celebrated London hostesss who befriended WSC.

KINSKY Count Charles (1858–1919); son of Ferdinand, seventh Prince Kinsky, and Marie, Princess Liechenstein. Friend and admirer of Lady Randolph. Served in Austro-Hungarian diplomatic service, first in London and later at Brussels and Paris. A great sportsman and rider to hounds, he rode his own horse Zoedone to victory in the Grand National of 1883. Married 17 January 1895 Elisabeth, Countess Wolff Metternich, and succeeded as Prince 1904.

KITCHENER Horatio Herbert (1850–1916); second son of Lieutenant-Colonel Henry Horatio Kitchener of Cossington, Leicestershire and his first wife Anne Frances, daughter of the Rev John Chevallier, vicar of Aspall, Suffolk, who kept a lunatic asylum there and became a noted agriculturist. Commissioned in the Royal Engineers, he was Sirdar of the Egyptian Army 1892–9, planning and executing the campaign that ended in the Battle of Omdurman 1898 and led to the reconquest of the Sudan. Chief of Staff to Lord Roberts (qv) in South Africa, 1899–1900; Commander-in-Chief 1900–2; Commander-in-Chief India 1902–9; British Agent and Consul-General, Egypt 1911–14; Secretary of State for War 1914–15. Drowned in HMS *Hampshire* on way to Russia. KCMG 1894, KCB 1896, Baron 1898, Viscount and OM 1902, Earl (Kitchener of Khartoum) 1914, KG 1915.

KNOLLYS Francis (1837–1924); second son of General Sir William Knollys, and Elizabeth, sister of Sir Edward St Aubyn 1st Bart. Private Secretary to the Prince of Wales from 1870, continued to serve in that capacity on the Prince's accession as Edward VII in 1901, and to King George V until 1913. KCMG 1886. Baron 1902 and Viscount 1911.

LANSDOWNE Henry Charles Keith, 5th Marquess of (1845–1927); elder son of Henry, 4th Marquess of Lansdowne and Emily Jane Mercer, Baroness Nairne in her own right. Under-Secretary for War 1872–4; Under-Secretary for India 1880; Governor-General of Canada 1883–8; Viceroy of India 1888–94; Secretary of State for War 1895–1900; Foreign Secretary 1900–5. Married 1869 Maud Evelyn Hamilton, daughter of 1st Duke of Abercorn and sister of Albertha, Marchioness of Blandford (qv).

LESLIE Leonie Blanche (1859–1943); youngest daughter of Leonard and Clara Jerome (qqv), favourite aunt of WSC. Educated in France, she married 1884 John, only son of Sir John Leslie, 1st Bart, of Glaslough, County Monaghan. Their son, John Randolph Shane (born 1885), was a godson of Lord Randolph.

MARJORIBANKS Edward (1849–1909); eldest son of Dudley, 1st Baron Tweedmouth, whom he succeeded 1894. Married 1873 Lady Fanny Spencer-Churchill, third daughter of 7th Duke of Marlborough. Liberal MP for Berwick 1880–94, Chief Whip 1892–4; Lord Privy Seal and Chancellor of Duchy of Lancaster 1894–5, First Lord of the Admiralty 1905–8, Lord President of the Council 1908. His son Dudley (1874–1935) was at Harrow with Winston, joined Royal Horse Guards 1895; married 1901 Muriel, eldest daughter of W. St John Brodrick, at that time Secretary of State for War.

MARLBOROUGH Charles, 9th Duke — see **SUNDERLAND**.

MARLBOROUGH Frances Anne Emily ('Fanny'), Duchess of (1822–99); first daughter of Charles, 3rd Marquess of Londonderry, by his second wife, Frances, daughter and heiress of Sir Henry Vane-Tempest, Bart. She married John Winston, Marquess of Blandford (later 7th Duke of Marlborough, qv below), in 1843, and had five sons and six daughters. Only two of the sons (Lord Blandford, the eldest, and Lord Randolph, the third) survived their early childhood.

MARLBOROUGH John Winston, 7th Duke of (1822–83); eldest son of George, 6th Duke of Marlborough and Jane, eldest daughter of 8th Earl of Galloway. Father of Lord Randolph Churchill and grandfather of WSC. Tory MP for Woodstock 1840–5 and 1847–57, when he succeeded to the dukedom. Lord President of the Council 1867–8; Viceroy of Ireland 1876–80. Married 1843 Frances Anne, daughter of 3rd Marquess of Londonderry (qv above).

MILBANKE John Peniston (1872–1915); eldest surviving son of Sir Peniston Milbanke, 9th Bart, whom he succeeded in 1899. Came to Harrow (The Head Master's House) 1886, left December 1889, but remained close friend of Winston. Joined 10th Hussars through Militia 1892; won Victoria Cross during Boer War. Killed in action commanding Sherwood Rangers at Hill 70, Gallipoli. His younger brother Mark was at The Head Master's 1888–92; an artist, his early sketches were published in *The Harrovian;* later he exhibited at the Royal Academy.

MILNER Alfred (1854–1925); son of Dr Charles Milner of London and Mary, daughter of Major General Ready, Governor of the Isle of Man. A brilliant administrator, he was Under-Secretary for Finance in Egypt at the age of thirty-five; and Chairman Board of Inland Revenue at thirty-eight. High Commissioner for South Africa 1879–1905. Member of War Cabinet without Portfolio 1916–18, Secretary of State for War 1918–19, Secretary of State for Colonies 1919–21. KCB 1895, Baron 1901, Viscount 1902.

MINSSEN Bernard Jules (1861–1924); modern languages master at Harrow 1891–1921. Winston stayed with him and his parents at his home in Versailles, 1891–2.

MORIARTY Louis Martin (1855–1930); Army Class master at Harrow, where he also taught Classics and French, and was a housemaster, 1889–1917.

PLOWDEN Pamela Frances Audrey (born 1874); daughter of Sir Trevor John Chichele Chichele-Plowden and Millicent Frances, daughter of General Sir C. J. Foster. As a young girl accompanied her father to Hyderabad, where he was the Resident. Married 1902 Victor, 2nd Earl of Lytton.

ROBERTS Frederick Sleigh (1832–1914); born at Cawnpore, son of General Sir Abraham Roberts and Isabella, widow of Major Hamilton Maxwell. Won VC in Indian Mutiny 1858 (his son won a posthumous VC in South Africa). Exponent of the 'forward policy' on the Indian frontier, led the march from Kabul to Kandahar which resulted in the pacification of Afghanistan 1880. Lord Randolph Churchill, as Secretary of State for India, was instrumental in his appointment as Commander-in-Chief, India 1885–93. Field Marshal and C-in-C Ireland 1895–9. Commander-in-Chief, South Africa 1899–1900. KCB 1879, GCB 1880 and Bart 1881, Baron Roberts of Kandahar 1892, Earl Roberts of Kandahar and Pretoria, and KG 1901.

ROOSE Robson (1848–1905); third son of Francis Finley

Roose. An eminent and well-connected physician who practised in London and Brighton and attended Lord Randolph Churchill and his family.

ROSEBERY Archibald Philip, 5th Earl of (1847–1929); son of Lord Dalmeny (d. 1851) and Catherine, daughter of 4th Earl Stanhope. Succeeded his grandfather 1868. Friend of Lord Randolph at Oxford and later of WSC. Secretary of State for Foreign Affairs 1886 and 1892–4; Leader of Liberal Party, Prime Minister 1894–5. Racehorse owner: won the Derby 1894, 1895, and 1905. Married 1878 Hannah, only child and heir of the Austrian Baron Meyer Amschel de Rothschild, who died 1890.

SALISBURY Robert Arthur Talbot, 3rd Marquess of (1830–1903); three times Prime Minister 1885–6, 1886–92, 1895–1902. Second son of 2nd Marquess of Salisbury and of Frances Mary, only daughter of Bamber Gascoyne MP. Conservative MP for Stamford 1853–68; Secretary of State for India 1866–7 (resigned in protest against Disraeli's reform bill). Succeeded his father 1868. Secretary of State for India 1874–8, Foreign Secretary 1878–80, 1885–6, 1887–92 and 1895–1900.

SOMERVELL Robert (1851–1933); English master at Harrow 1887–1911, and Winston's first form master. He also taught History and Classics. He was Bursar of the School 1888–1919 and Housemaster 1904–11.

SUNDERLAND Charles Richard John, Earl of ('Sunny') (1871–1934); courtesy title of eldest son of Marquess of Blandford (qv) whom he succeeded 1892 as 9th Duke of Marlborough. Became close friend of his cousin WSC. Served with Queen's Own Oxfordshire Hussars, staff captain with Imperial Yeomanry in South Africa. Paymaster-General of the Forces 1899–1902, Under-Secretary of State for the Colonies 1903–5; Joint Parliamentary Secretary to the Board of Agriculture and Fisheries 1917–18. Married (1) 1895 Consuelo, daughter of Commodore William Vanderbilt of New York (marriage dissolved 1921), (2) 1921 Gladys, daughter of Edward Parke Deacon of Boston.

W A L E S Albert Edward, Prince of (1841–1910); eldest son of Queen Victoria, whom he succeeded as King Edward VII 22 January 1901. Married 1863 Princess Alexandra (1844–1925), daughter of King Christian IX of Denmark.

W E L L D O N James Edward Cowell (1854–1937); son of Rev Edward Welldon, sometime Master at Tonbridge School. Educated Eton and King's College, Cambridge. Headmaster of Harrow, at the age of thirty-one 1885–98; WSC was in his house. Chaplain in Ordinary to the Queen 1892–8. Bishop of Calcutta and Metropolitan of India 1898–1902; Canon of Westminster 1902–6; Dean of Manchester 1906–18; Dean of Durham 1918–33.

W I L S O N Lady Sarah Isabella Augusta (1864–1929); eleventh and youngest child of 7th Duke of Marlborough. Married 1891 Gordon Chesney Wilson (1865–1914), Royal Horse Guards, eldest son of Sir Samuel Wilson MP, and was besieged with him in Mafeking.

W I L T O N Laura Caroline, Countess of (1842–1916); youngest daughter of William Russell, Accountant-General of the Court of Chancery, who was a great-grandson of 4th Duke of Bedford. Married (1) 1862 Seymour John Grey Egerton (1839–98), younger son of Thomas 2nd Earl of Wilton, who succeeded 1885 his elder brother Arthur as 4th Earl. She married (2) 1899 Sir Frederick John William Johnstone (1841–1913), 8th Bart. Befriended Winston when he was at Harrow, and called herself his 'Deputy Mother'.

W I M B O R N E Cornelia Henrietta Maria, Lady (1847–1927); eldest daughter of 7th Duke of Marlborough, aunt of WSC. Married 1868 Sir Ivor Bertie Guest, 2nd Bart, who was created 1880 1st Baron Wimborne. When young, WSC frequently stayed at their house near Bournemouth with his first cousin Ivor (1873–1939) who succeeded as 2nd Baron 1914 and was created Viscount 1918.

W O L F F Henry Drummond (1830–1908); born in Malta : only child of Rev Joseph Wolff and Lady Georgiana, daughter of Horatio (Walpole), 2nd Earl of Oxford. Married 1852 Adeline, daughter of Walter Sholto-Douglas. Conservative MP Christchurch, Hants 1874–8, MP for

Portsmouth 1880–5. With Lord Randolph Churchill, John Gorst and Arthur Balfour, formed the Fourth Party. Founder, with Lord Randolph, of the Primrose League. Ambassador at Madrid 1892–1900. GCMG 1878, PC 1885, GCB 1889.

W O O D (Henry) Evelyn (1838–1919); son of Rev Sir John Page Wood, 2nd Bart, rector of St Peter's Cornhill, London, and Caroline, daughter of Admiral Sampson Michell. Midshipman 1852. Served in Crimean War, in trenches before Sebastopol. Transferred to Army 1855; served Indian Mutiny 1857; VC 1859. Adjutant-General 1897–1901. KCB 1879, GCMG 1882, GCB 1891. Field Marshal 1903. His sister, Katherine, was married first to Captain W. H. O'Shea and, after being divorced, to Charles Stewart Parnell.

1

BIRTH

WINSTON LEONARD SPENCER-CHURCHILL was born at Blenheim Palace in Oxfordshire on 30 November 1874. His father was Lord Randolph Churchill, second surviving son of the 7th Duke of Marlborough and Frances, a daughter of the 3rd Marquess of Londonderry. Winston's mother, Jeannie Jerome, was the second of the four daughters, three of whom were still living, of Mr and Mrs Leonard Jerome of New York City. It had been intended that the child should be born at the young couple's new London house, 48 Charles Street, Mayfair; but the birth was two months premature—hence Lady Randolph Churchill's Blenheim confinement. Lady Randolph's mother was in Paris at the time with her eldest daughter Clara; Lord Randolph hastened to send her the news:

Lord Randolph to Mrs Leonard Jerome

Monday 30 [November 1874]   Blenheim Palace
12.30 p.m.   Woodstock

Dear Mrs. Jerome,

I have just time to write a line, to send by the London Dr to tell you that all has up to now thank God gone off very well with my darling Jennie. She had a fall on Tuesday walking with the shooters, & a rather imprudent & rough drive in a pony carriage brought on the pains on Saturday night. We tried to stop them, but it was no use. They went on all Sunday. Of course the Oxford physician cld not come. We telegraphed for the London man Dr Hope but he did not arrive till this morning. The country Dr is however a clever man, & the baby was safely born at 1.30 this morning after about 8 hrs. labour. She suffered a good deal poor darling, but was vy plucky & had no chloroform. The boy is wonderfully pretty so everybody says dark eyes and hair & vy healthy considering its prematureness. My mother &

Clementine have been everything to Jennie, & she cld not be more comfortable. We have just got a most excellent nurse & wet nurse coming down this afternoon, & please God all will go vy well with both. I telegraphed to Mr. Jerome; I thought he wld like to hear. I am sure you will be delighted at this good news and dear Clara also I will write again tonight. Love to Clara.

Yrs affty
RANDOLPH S. C.

I hope the baby things will come with all speed. We have to borrow some from the Woodstock Solicitor's wife.

Lady Camden (Clementine) was the daughter of the 6th Duke of Marlborough by his second wife, so that she was an aunt of Lord Randolph's, though only a year older. She had married in 1866 the future 3rd Marquess Camden and had borne him four children, but was widowed in 1872. She became one of the godparents of the newly arrived baby.

Thirty years later the child whose premature arrival had caused such a commotion at Blenheim and in Woodstock gave this description of his birthplace and its history when writing his father's Life :

The cumulative labours of Vanbrugh and 'Capability' Brown have succeeded at Blenheim in setting an Italian palace in an English park without apparent incongruity. The combination of these different ideas, each singly attractive, produces a remarkable effect. The palace is severe in its symmetry and completeness. Nothing has been added to the original plan; nothing has been taken away. The approaches are formal; the wings are balanced; four equal towers maintain its corners; and the fantastic ornaments of one side are elaborately matched on the other. Natural simplicity and even confusion are, on the contrary, the characteristic of the park and gardens. Instead of that arrangement of gravel paths, of geometrical flower beds, and of yews disciplined with grotesque exactness which the character of the house would seem to suggest, there spreads a rich and varied landscape. Green lawns and shining water, banks of laurel and fern, groves of oak and cedar, fountains and islands, are conjoined in artful disarray to offer on every side a promise of rest and shade. And yet there is no violent contrast, no abrupt dividing-line between the wildness and freshness of the garden and the pomp of the architecture.

The whole region is as rich in history as in charm; for the antiquity of Woodstock is not measured by a thousand years, and Blenheim is heir to all the memories of Woodstock. Here Kings—Saxon, Norman, and Plantagenet—have held their Courts. Ethelred the Unready, Alfred the Great, Queen Eleanor, the Black Prince loom in vague majesty out of the past. Woodstock was notable before the Norman conquest. It was already a borough when the Domesday Book was being compiled. The park was walled to keep the foreign wild beasts of Henry I. Fair Rosamond's Well still bubbles by the lake. From the gate-house of the old manor the imprisoned Princess Elizabeth watched the years of Mary's persecution. In the tumults of the Civil Wars Woodstock House was held for King Charles by an intrepid officer through a long and bitter siege and ravaged by the victorious Roundheads at its close. And beyond the most distant of these events, in the dim backward of time, the Roman generals administering the districts east and west of Akeman Street had built their winter villas in this pleasant temperate retreat; so that Woodstock and its neighbourhood were venerable and famous long before John Churchill, in the early years of the eighteenth century, superimposed upon it the glory of his victories over the French.

Whether ancestry or environment play the greater part in influencing the character and destiny of human beings has long been disputed and is still an open question. The degree of influence must vary from case to case. It is diverting to speculate why such care is devoted to the breeding of dogs and horses while the human race prefers to reproduce itself in a largely indiscriminate and haphazard fashion. More than fifty years later, when Winston was writing his magnificent history of John, Duke of Marlborough, he set down a careful account of the origins of the Churchill family :

Besides attending to his son's education Winston [John's father] in his studious leisure bethought himself often of his pedigree and his arms. His researches into genealogy have produced as good an account of the origin of the Churchills as is likely to be required. He traced his 'Lyon Rampant, Argent upon a Sable coat,' to Otho de Leon, Castelan of Gisor, 'whome we call our common ancestor'. The said Otho had two sons, Richard and Wandrill, Lord of Courcelle, 'whose youngest son came into England with William the Conqueror'. After re-recounting conscientiously several generations, Winston rested with confidence upon 'John . . . Lord of Currichill, or as 'tis in divers records Chirechile, since called Churchill in Somersetshire,' whose son, Sir Bartholomew de Churchill, 'a man of great note in the tyme of King Steven, . . . defended the castle of Bristow against the Empress Maud and was slaine afterward in that warr.' In the time of King Edward I, after the Barons' War, the lordship of Churchill was seized by the Crown and given to some favourite, whose posterity continued in possession till 'nere about Henry VIII, his tyme.' After passing through the hands of a family of the name of Jennings . . . it was sold eventually in 1652 to a Sir John Churchill, sometime Master of the Rolls, 'and had come to my son in right of his wife, had it not been so unfortunately alianated by her said father.'

All this was very fine, but when, descending these chains, we come to John, 'ancestor of the present Churchills of Munston, and Roger, who by the daughter of Peverell, relict of Nicholas Meggs, had issue Mathew, father of Jaspar, my grandfather,' we enter a rather shady phase. Edward Harly rudely asserts 'that John Churchill's great grandfather was a blacksmith who worked in the family of the Meggs,' and certainly, as his great-great great-grandfather married a Mrs Meggs, this seems very suspicious and even disquieting. In any case, there are strong grounds for believing that John's grandfather solidly improved the fortunes of this branch of the Churchill family. He was a practising lawyer, a deputy registrar of Chancery as well as member of the Middle Temple, and lawyers were a prosperous class at this date.

Another streak of blood, strange and wanton, mingled in the child John's nature. His grandmother, Lady Drake, was herself the daughter of John, Lord Boteler, who had married the sister of George Villiers, Duke of Buckingham, the favourite of James I and Charles I. Some students have amused themselves in tracing all the men —some of the greatest and wickedest in our history—who have descended from George Villiers, father of Buckingham. They are said to have repeatedly produced, across the centuries, the favourites, male and female, of kings and queens; and Chatham, and Pitt, as well as Marlborough, bear the distinction of this taint or genius.

When at length, at the end of her life, Sarah, Duchess of Marlborough, read—tardily, for it had been kept from her—Lediard's history of the Duke, she made the following extremely up-to-date comment upon this part of the subject : 'This History takes a great deal of Pains to make the Duke of Marlborough's Extraction very ancient. That may be true for aught I know; But it is no matter whether it be true or not in my opinion. For I value nobody for another's merit.'

Be this as it may, students of heredity have dilated upon this family tree. Galton [in his *Hereditary Genius*], cites it as one of the chief examples on which his thesis stands. Winston himself has been accounted one of the most notable and potent of sires. Had he lived the full span, he would have witnessed within the space of twelve months his son gaining the battle of Ramillies and his daughter's son [the Duke of Berwick and Alba] of Almanza; and would have found himself acknowledged as the progenitor of the two greatest captains of the age at the head of the opposing armies of Britain and of France and Spain. Moreover, his third surviving son, Charles, became a soldier of well-tried distinction, and his naval son virtually managed the Admiralty during the years of war. The military strain flowed strong and clear from the captain of the Civil Wars, student of heraldry and history, and champion of the Divine Right. It was his blood, not his pen, that carried his message.

An older strain and one equally potent in Winston's blood was that of the Spencers. The Spencers are first heard of in the latter part of the fifteenth century. They were then Warwickshire shepherds whose flocks were to prove the foundation of the family fortune. By 1504 John Spencer had risen sufficiently in the world to obtain a grant of arms. He owned large estates at Wormleighton in Warwickshire, and later at Althorp in Northamptonshire. He was knighted by Henry VIII and Winston was descended from him in direct male descent through fifteen generations.

In 1603 the Spencer of the day, fourth in direct descent from the first Sir John Spencer, was made a baron, and it was his grandson, the 3rd Lord Spencer, who married Lady Dorothy Sidney at Penshurst in 1639. She was the celebrated 'Sacharissa' of Waller's poems. The 3rd Lord Spencer was created Earl of Sunderland in 1643 by Charles I. Within a few months he was to die, with his great friend Lord Falkland, at the Battle of Newbury.

'Sacharissa' was the chatelaine of Althorp during her son's minority of nineteen years. Her son, the 4th Lord Spencer and 2nd Earl of Sunderland, succeeded to Althorp in 1662 when he came of age. 'Sacharissa' Sidney had taken great pains to ensure that her son was a staunch Protestant, and while at Oxford he early gave proof of his attachment to the Reformed Church by joining William Penn, founder of the State of Pennsylvania, in a demonstration in Tom Quad in Christ Church against the wearing of surplices, which had recently been enjoined upon the authorities by King Charles II. Penn and some others were rusticated, and Sunderland left the University in sympathy with his friends. In 1665 he married Lady Anne Digby, daughter of the 2nd Earl of Bristol, and grand-daughter of the 4th Earl of Bedford. She was a striking beauty and also heiress to the great estates of her brother, the 3rd Earl of Bristol, who died in 1698.

While Cromwell ruled in England, Sunderland had travelled widely in Europe. After the restoration of Charles II he was appointed Ambassador first at Madrid at the age of thirty-one and then at Paris. He thus had the opportunity, which he embraced, of becoming a discerning patron of the arts. He acquired that splendid collection of pictures to which every succeeding generation of the family has had the good sense to add works by the leading artists of their day. He was a powerful minister who filled numerous offices under Chârles II, James II, and even William III. These various appointments under three different sovereigns could not have been achieved by a man who did not have a marked flexibility of character and principle.

He was succeeded in 1702 by his second and only surviving son Charles, who as Lord Spencer had three years before in 1699 married Lady Anne Churchill as his second wife. His first wife was Lady Arabella Cavendish, daughter and co-heiress of the Duke of Newcastle, who had died in 1698.

Charles Spencer, 3rd Earl of Sunderland, was to play a great role in politics during the lifetime of his father-in-law. After a career of lively political intrigue, during which he held many offices, he was First Lord of the Treasury from 1718 to 1721. It was the third son of this marriage who in 1733, at the age of twenty-six, inherited Blenheim and the Marlborough dukedom from his aunt, Henrietta, Countess of Godolphin and, by Special Remainder, Duchess of Marlborough. This boy, another Charles, had meanwhile become 5th Earl of Sunderland and had succeeded to Althorp in 1729 on the death of his elder brother.

Under a family compact made many years before, Charles vacated Althorp to his brother Jack, eighteen months younger, when he inherited the dukedom and Blenheim. Their grandmother Sarah, the old Duchess, disapproved of them both because of their extravagance, but Jack was her favourite and to him she left most of the family property, pictures and treasures which were not entailed with Blenheim. Thus it is that the finest family pictures and plate are today at Althorp and not at Blenheim. In the same way, the immensely valuable estates at Wimbledon and St Albans, together with several millions of cash, were alienated from the senior branch of the family. She further alienated from the Marlborough dukedom such trophies as the sword of Ramillies and Marlborough's campaign maps to another daughter who was married to the Duke of Montagu, whose heiress, Elizabeth, married the 3rd Duke of Buccleuch. These treasures now repose at Boughton in Northamptonshire.

By contrast with the cadet branch of the Spencer family, the holders of the Dukedom who succeeded Marlborough were somewhat undistinguished for several generations. Charles, 3rd Duke of Marlborough and 5th Earl of Sunderland, it is true, had an honourable career in the Army, commanded a brigade of foot guards at the Battle of Dettingen, the last battle at which a King of England, George II, was personally in command, and became Lord Privy Seal and Master General of the Ordnance. His son George succeeded as 4th Duke at the age of twenty, and remained the occupier of Blenheim for fifty-eight years until his death in 1817. It was he who employed Capability Brown in the 1760s and commissioned Reynolds and Romney to paint portraits of his family. Indeed, many of the pictures that made the Blenheim collection one of the most renowned in Europe were acquired by him or by younger members of his family. This was the most splendid time the Palace knew; when George III visited Blenheim in 1786 he was prompted to remark 'We have nothing to equal this.'

Spencer remained the family name of the Dukes of Marlborough until 1817 when Royal Licence the 5th Duke, shortly after he succeeded to the dukedom, changed it to Spencer-Churchill. The arms were quartered, the first and fourth quarters for Churchill, the second and third for Spencer, and were surmounted by two crests, a lion for Churchill, and a griffin's head for the Spencer family. In more recent times the Churchills have tended to drop the Spencer from their surname.

The 5th and 6th Dukes lived up to their age's reputation for profligacy and were noted for nothing so much as for their extravagance, which ruined the family. Gronow, the celebrated writer of reminiscences of the early nineteenth century, relates an astonishing story of how the 6th Duke, before he had succeeded and when he was still Marquess of Blandford, produced, while travelling in his coach, fifty £1,000 notes which he said he had borrowed. 'You see, Gronow,' he explained, 'how the immense fortune of my family will be frittered away; but I can't help it; I must live. My father inherited £500,000 in ready money and £70,000 a year in land; and in all probability when it comes to my turn to live at Blenheim I shall have nothing left but the annuity of £5,000 a year on the Post Office.' After he became Duke 'he lived in one remote corner of his magnificent Palace, a melancholy instance of extravagance'.

His son, John Winston, was left vastly impoverished by the folly of his predecessors. He devoted himself to politics, sat in the House of Commons for some fifteen years as Member for Woodstock and, after his succession as 7th Duke, became Lord President of the Council and a member of Lord Derby's third cabinet and of Disraeli's first cabinet for nearly two years. The great family talent, however, which had lain largely fallow during all these years and which had only burgeoned in the cadet Spencer branch, was not to erupt until Lord Randolph Churchill, younger son of the 7th Duke, entered Parliament in 1874.

When Winston was born his father was twenty-five. Lord Randolph had been the Conservative Member for the family seat of Woodstock for nine months but he had so far done little more in the House of Commons than make his maiden speech. His speech did not excite great interest but prompted an amiable letter from the Prime Minister to Lord Randolph's mother which has been published in Winston's *Lord Randolph Churchill*. But Disraeli also wrote the same day what was perhaps a more objective letter to the Queen:

Benjamin Disraeli to Queen Victoria
(Royal Archives)

EXTRACT

22 May 1874   2 Whitehall Gardens
                                              S.W.

. . . Tonight, there was an amusing debate respecting making Oxford a military centre. Mr Hall, the new Conservative member for Oxford city, made a maiden speech, of considerable power and promise—a fine voice, a natural manner, and much improvisation. While he was sitting down, amid many cheers, Lord Randolph Churchill rose and though sitting on the same side of the House upheld the cause of the University against the city, and answered Mr Hall.

Lord Randolph said many imprudent things, which is not very important in the maiden speech of a young member and a young man, but the House was surprised, and then captivated, by his energy, and his natural flow, and his impressive manners. With self control and study he might mount. It was a speech of great promise. . . .

*   *   *   *   *

Winston's mother, Lady Randolph, was twenty at the time of his birth. She was a woman of exceptional beauty in an age of famous beauties. They glittered around the circle of the Prince of Wales and they continued to glimmer after his accession to the throne as King Edward VII in 1901.

Lady Randolph's father, Leonard Jerome, was a financier of great drive and ability who in 1855 had settled in New York, where he joined the stock exchange and became a partner in a brokerage business with William R. Travers. He won and lost several large fortunes in the course of a daring and brilliant career. He was active in politics, serving for about eighteen months as American Consul in Trieste; and for a period he was the principal proprietor of the *New York Times*. But his name is best remembered as a founder of the American Jockey Club and a patron of the American turf. He built the race track in the Bronx, New York City, which was named Jerome Park after him. He was also a generous benefactor of the arts, particularly of opera, and an ocean-racing yachtsman. He was the fifth of seven sons of Isaac Jerome, whose great-grandfather Timothy had, along with other Huguenot families, sailed from the Isle of Wight to America in 1710.

Leonard Jerome married in 1849 Clarissa Hall, whose elder sister Catherine had married, five years before, Leonard's younger brother Lawrence. Clarissa, known after marriage as Clara, was a noted beauty in her day: a woman of good but expensive tastes, she spent most of her time in Europe, chiefly in Paris, after she had accompanied her husband to Trieste in 1851–2. She was the daughter of Ambrose Hall, a member of the New York State Assembly, whose family were settled in Connecticut before 1650. Her mother, Clarissa Willcox, was the grand-daughter of Eleazur Smith, of Dartmouth, Massachusetts, and Meribah (no maiden name recorded), who is believed to have been an Iroquois Indian. At least two of Leonard's forebears fought against the British in the American War of Independence; one great-grandfather Samuel Jerome served as a sergeant in the Berkshire County Militia; another great-grandfather, Major Libbeus Ball of the 4th Massachusetts Regiment, was with Washington at Valley Forge and fought in the Mohawk Valley.

Leonard's Jerome's marriage to Clarissa Hall was to produce four daughters: Clara born 1850, Jennie (1854), Camille (1855), who died at the age of seven, and Leonie (1859).

Lord Randolph had met his future wife at a reception

38

and dance at Cowes in August 1873. The original invitation
to Mrs Jerome and her daughters is preserved :

To meet
Their Royal Highnesses the Prince and Princess of Wales
and
Their Imperial Russian Highnesses the
Grand Duke Cesarewitch and Grand Duchess Cesarevna
Captain Carpenter and the officers of H.M.S. 'Ariadne'
request the honour of the Company of
MRS & MISSES JEROME
On board, on Thursday, August 12th, from 3.30 to 7.30 pm
DANCING
Boats will be in attendance at the R.Y.C. Landing Place.

R.S.V.P.

Afterwards Jennie wrote on her invitation card between
the lines, immediately below *To meet,* one word,
Randolph.

It seems on both sides to have been love at first sight—
both were hot-blooded and impetuous. Lord Randolph in
particular sought to brush aside all suggestions of delay
either by his father, the Duke, or by his brother Blandford,
or by Mr Jerome. Mr Jerome was at first overjoyed at the
news his daughter Jennie and his wife had sent to New
York. He wrote :

Leonard Jerome to Jennie Jerome

EXTRACT

11 September [1873]   Union Club

. . . I must say I have been very happy all day. I have
thought of nothing else. I telegraphed your mother immediately that I was 'delighted' and that I would arrange £2000
per year for you which she says in her letter will do.
I cannot imagine any engagement that would please me
more. I am as confident that all you say of him is true as
though I knew him. Young, ambitious, uncorrupted. And
best of all you think and I believe he loves you. He must.
You are no heiress and it must have taken heaps of love

to overcome an Englishman's prejudice against 'those horrid Americans'. I like it in every way. He is English. . . .

This last was of prime importance to Mr Jerome. Earlier he had written to Jennie : 'You know my views. I have great confidence in you and still greater in your mother and any one you would accept and your mother approves I could not object to Provided always he is not a Frenchman or any other of those Continental cusses.'

The Duke, on the other hand, had his reservations : 'My father and mother', Lord Randolph wrote to Mrs Jerome, 'have been very much taken by surprise & find it difficult to convince themselves of the reality & probable permanence of our feelings for each other.'

The Duke revealed that Lord Randolph's impetuosity was not the only cause of his doubts.

Duke of Marlborough to Lord Randolph
(Blenheim Papers)

31 August [1873]   Guisachan

My dearest Randolph,

It is not likely that at present you can look at anything but from your own point of view but persons from the outside cannot but be struck with the unwisdom of your proceedings, and the uncontrolled state of your feelings, which completely paralyses your judgement; never was there such an illustration of the adage *'love is blind'* for you seem blind to all consequences as regards your family & blind to trouble you are heaping on Mamma and me by the anxieties this act of yours has produced. I do but write the expression of my constant thoughts when I say this, that you must not think me unkind for telling it to you.

Now as regards your letter I can't say that what you have told me is reassuring. I shall know more before long but from what you told me & what I have heard this Mr J. seems to be a sporting, and I should think vulgar kind of man. I hear he drives about 6 and 8 horses in N.Y. (one may take this as a kind of indication of what the man is). I hear he and his two brothers are stock brokers, one of them bears a *bad* character in commercial judgement in *this* country, but which of them it is, I do not know, but it is evident he is of the class of speculators; he has been bankrupt once; and may be so again; and when we come to think of N.Y. speculators & their deeds look at Fiske and *hoc genus omne*.

Everything that you say about the mother and daughters is perfectly compatible with all that I am apprehensive of about the father & his belongings. And however great the attractions of the former they can be no set off against a connection shd it so appear wh no man in his senses could think respectable. I can say no more at present till I have seen you, & get some further replies to enquiries I have set on foot. I am deeply sorry that your feelings are so much engaged; and only for your own sake wish most heartily that you had checked the current before it became so over-powering.

May God bless and keep you straight is my earnest prayer.

Ever your affectionate father
MARLBOROUGH

Lord Randolph's determination to marry Jennie some-what mollified the Duke but he continued to be obstinate. Lord Randolph reported to Mrs Jerome on 30 September 1873 'that taking into consideration the suddenness & rapidity of the attachment formed he [the Duke] said he wld give his consent if we were of the same mind a year hence'. Lord Randolph succeeded in bearing down his father who agreed that the marriage might take place as soon as the General Election, due to be held soon, was over and Lord Randolph had been elected for the family borough of Woodstock. The election took place on February 3, and Lord Randolph defeated the Liberal candidate George Brodrick, polling 569 votes against 404.

Further complications were soon to arise about the marriage settlement. Lord Randolph was receiving £1000 a year as a result of a settlement made by the Duke shortly before the election. Mr Jerome, as we have seen, was very willing to settle £2000 a year on his daughter : this income was to be derived from a settlement of £40,000 consisting of a house in New York on the corner of Madison Avenue and 26th Street. The Duke's solicitors at first suggested that the settlement should be raised to £50,000 on the grounds that 'it was not usual to give trustees power to make investments which yield 5%'. British solicitors and trustees at that time thought that all trustee settlemens must be confined to gilt-edged securities which produced between $2\frac{1}{2}$ and 3 per cent per annum. A more serious objection to Mr Jerome's plans was now raised. Mr Jerome intended that the £2000 be paid to his daughter : the Duke of Marlborough would have none of this. 'Such a settlement', wrote the Duke's solicitor, Frederick L. Capon, to Lord Randolph on February 25, 'as far as Lord Randolph is personally concerned cannot be considered as any settlement at all, for . . . Miss Jerome is made quite independent [of Lord Randolph Churchill] in a pecuniary point of view, which in my experience is most unusual, & I think I might add in such a case as the present without precedent—and His Grace desires it to be distinctly understood that in accepting Mr Jerome's proposal you have done so in direct opposition to his [the Duke's] views & wishes and solely upon your own responsibility.'

As a compromise it was suggested that Lady Randolph should be given 'pin money', first £300, then £500, then £600, and that the residue of the £2000 should be paid to Lord Randolph. In the end Mr Jerome agreed that half the allowance of £2000 a year should be paid to his daughter and half to Lord Randolph.

Even then the matter was not finally resolved. Mr Jerome had wanted to leave the disposal of the capital sum of £50,000 to be entirely at the discretion of Lady Randolph should she die before Lord Randolph. Now this was changed so that the apportionment of the £50,000 was to be decided, in the event of there being children, between Lord Randolph and Lady Randolph, or, if no apportionment was made, for the sum to be divided equally between the children. If there were no children and Lady Randolph died before Lord Randolph, half the £50,000 was to be paid to Lord Randolph and the other £25,000 to Lady Randolph's family.

On 14 April 1874 Lord Randolph was able to report to his mother : 'Things are all going now as merrily as a marriage bell. I expect the settlements over tonight and they will be signed tomorrow'. And the Duke wrote from London on the same day :

42

EXTRACT

14 April [1874]   London

My dearest Randolph,

I must send you a few lines to reach you tomorrow, one of the most important days of your life, & which I sincerely pray will be blessed to you & be the commencement of a united existence of happiness for you & for your wife. She is one whom you have chosen with less than usual deliberation but you adhered to your love with unwavering constancy & I *cannot* doubt the truth & force of your affection: and now I hope that as time goes on, your two natures will prove to have been brought, *not* accidentally, together: may you both be 'lovely & pleasant in your lives' is my earnest prayer. I am very glad that harmony is again restored, & that no cloud obscures the day of sunshine but what has happened will show that the sweetest path is not without its thorns & I must say ought not to be without its lesson to you. . . .

On April 15 Lord Randolph and Jennie Jerome were married at the British Embassy in Paris by the Reverend Dr Edward Forbes in the presence of Mr and Mrs Jerome, the Marquess of Blandford (Lord Randolph's elder brother) and Mr Francis Knollys, private secretary to the Prince of Wales.

2

IRELAND

LORD AND LADY RANDOLPH and their newly born son, Winston, spent the Christmas of 1874 with the Marlboroughs at Blenheim and two days later on December 27 the baby was baptised in the chapel of Blenheim by the Duke's chaplain, the Reverend Henry William Yule. On their return from their honeymoon Lord and Lady Randolph had lived for three months in Curzon Street until their short lease had expired at the end of July 1874. Early in the New Year they moved into the house they had rented in Charles Street. Shortly after their return to London, Mrs Everest, who will play a striking role in these pages, was engaged as Winston's nanny. Lord and Lady Randolph gave themselves up to the delights of the London season and Lord Randolph does not seem to have been particularly attentive to his parliamentary duties. Indeed, in the course of the year, he only made two speeches, the first defending John, Duke of Marlborough, against the sneers of some Irish members : and the second defending the family borough of Woodstock which he had the honour of representing in the House of Commons.

Winston was later to give some account in his Life of Lord Randolph of the style in which his father and mother lived in Charles Street :

> . . . they continued their gay life on a somewhat more generous scale than their income warranted. Fortified by an excellent French cook, they entertained with discrimination. The Prince of Wales, who had from the beginning shown them much kindness, dined sometimes with them. Lord Randolph's college friend, Lord Rosebery, was a frequent visitor. . . . But in the year 1876 an event happened which altered, darkened, and strengthened his [Lord Randolph's] whole life and character. Engaging in his brother's quarrels with fierce and reckless partisanship, Lord Randolph incurred the

deep displeasure of a great personage. The fashionable world no longer smiled. Powerful enemies were anxious to humiliate him. His own sensitiveness and pride magnified every coldness into an affront. London became odious to him. The breach was not repaired for more than eight years, and in the interval a nature originally genial and gay contracted a stern and bitter quality, a harsh contempt for what is called 'Society', and an abiding antagonism to rank and authority. If this misfortune produced in Lord Randolph characteristics which afterwards hindered or injured his public work, it was also his spur. Without it he might have wasted a dozen years in the frivolous and expensive pursuits of the silly world of fashion; without it he would probably never have developed popular sympathies or the courage to champion democratic causes. . . .

At the time when Winston wrote his father's Life thirty years later he probably did not know the full details of the event which caused Lord Randolph's temporary exile in Ireland. Moreover, so far as he knew the facts, they could hardly at that time be presented to the public. The 'great personage' had now become, at the time of writing, King Edward VII. Many accounts have appeared of Lord Randolph's quarrel with the Prince of Wales but none of them has been complete. Here it is proposed to put down all the details that are known, for it is important that the causes which led Winston and his parents to spend three years in Dublin are understood.

On 11 October 1875 the Prince of Wales left England on a tour of India. Among those who accompanied the Prince were the Earl of Aylesford and his brother-in-law Colonel Owen Williams of the 'Blues'. Aylesford had, as Lord Guernsey, married Edith Williams in January 1871, just ten days before he succeeded to the earldom. Although he was only twenty-six when he went to India, he had already acquired a reputation which earned him the nickname of Sporting Joe. He owed this not only to his activities on the turf, where he was known for his perseverance rather than for any success, but also to the fact that he was a man of violent disposition and extravagant tastes with a fondness for pugilism, cock-fighting, and the pleasures of the notorious Cremorne Gardens.

The Prince of Wales, Lord and Lady Randolph, Lord Randolph's elder brother Blandford and the Aylesfords had all been part of the same social group. For many months before the events that must now be described, Blandford had become very susceptible to the charms of Lady Aylesford. While the Royal party was away in India Blandford moved his horses to stables near Packington, the Aylesford seat in Warwickshire, and took up his residence in a nearby inn. Early in 1876 Lady Aylesford volunteered news of her infidelity to Lord Aylesford who was still in India. On receipt of this letter Aylesford at once telegraphed to his mother to send for his two children from Packington Hall and to keep them until his return to England : 'a great misfortune has happened'. Word was sent to his brother-in-law Owen Williams, who had just left the Royal party on his way home to be with his wife Fanny, who was seriously ill. Aylesford's mother complied with her son's directions and the young Lady Aylesford then wrote the following poignant letter which came to light in a subsequent legitimacy case in the House of Lords :

Lady Aylesford to Dowager Countess of Aylesford
(Copy: Minutes of Evidence, House of Lords 1 July 1885)

Friday night [?25 February 1876]   [Packington Hall]

Dear Lady Aylesford,
    By the time this letter reaches you I shall have left my home for ever. Guernsey knows of this, which will account for his telegram to you. I do not attempt to say a word in self defence, but you can imagine I must have suffered much before I could have taken such a step; *how* much it would be impossible to tell you, but it is the only reparation I can make to Guernsey, and he will now have the opportunity of getting rid of one who he has long ceased to care for. You do not know, you never can know, how hard I have tried to win his love, and without success, and I cannot live uncared for. I do not ask you to think kindly of me; I know you could not do it, but for God's sake be kind to the children, and do not teach them to hate their wretched mother, let them think I am dead, it will be the best. I heard from Minna [Aylesford's sister Lady Anne Murray] the

46

other day, but never answered her letter; she will know why.

You have always been most kind to me, and it is the last word I shall ever say to you; do not be offended if I thank you for all your kindness and tell you how very wretched it makes me feel to think that I should have brought such sorrow and disgrace upon you all. Oh! Lady Aylesford, if it is possible, try and forgive me, as you hope for forgiveness. I know that Guernsey does not care for me, therefore, I do not think he will feel my loss, and perhaps may be glad to be free; but what it costs me to leave my children I cannot tell you, and I cannot bear to think; that they will be cared for I know, as you will be a mother to them, but my God I shall *never* see them again, it is like being dead and yet alive. I could not give orders about the children; they, therefore, know nothing, so please give the necessary orders yourself. I have left the diamonds with James, and as regards the things belonging to me, I have written to him to send them, and they will be forwarded to me. I wrote to Madge [sister of Lady Aylesford, and wife of Sir Richard Williams-Bulkeley] to come to me today. I have told her all as I have told you; she has just returned to town, and I am left alone completely broken-hearted. I bring this letter to town myself. I would have seen you, but feel that perhaps you would rather not see me. God bless you, dear Lady Aylesford, and for the last time farewell, and try not to think too hardly of

EDITH

At this stage Lord Randolph intervened in a dramatic and perhaps inexcusable way. He believed that a divorce would not only cause grave scandal but also that it would not be in the best interests of Blandford and his wife and four children. Furthermore he had reason to believe that the Prince of Wales himself had shown attentions to Lady Aylesford and he felt that his brother Blandford was being made a scapegoat. Moreover Aylesford had spread the Prince's strictures on Blandford all over London. Accordingly he took it upon himself to call on the Princess of Wales. He was accompanied by a young newly created peer, Lord Alington. They pointed out to the Princess that it would be undesirable for divorce proceedings to be instituted and they asked her to tell the Prince to stop Aylesford continuing with his divorce plans. At the same time, Lord Randolph let it be widely known that he had in his possession certain letters which the Prince of Wales had written to Lady Aylesford; and Sir Charles Dilke recollected that he said: 'I have the Crown of England in my pocket.' Thus he was espousing in ardent fashion the cause of his brother —not always to the satisfaction of Blandford himself who was still intent on divorce and re-marriage.

The Queen was furious: 'What a dreadful disgraceful business,' she wrote to the Prince of Wales, 'and how unpardonable of Lord Alington to draw dear Alex into it! Her dear name should never have been mixed up with such people. Poor Lord Aylesford should not have left her. I *knew* last summer that this was going on. Those Williamses are a bad family.' The whole affair was now getting so out of hand that it was essential to call in the aid of the Prime Minister, Disraeli. Where Hartington and Lansdowne, great Lords of the Whig and Tory parties, had failed, it was hoped that the subtle Jew would succeed. He did. To Disraeli the Queen caused her Lady of the Bedchamber, the Marchioness of Ely, to write: 'The Queen says you are so kind—so full of tact and judgement, Her Majesty feels you will manage this perfectly.'

The Prince of Wales, who was still in India, had of course now been fully informed. He was incensed. He wrote a furious letter from India to one of his courtiers, Lord Hardwicke, Master of the Buck Hounds. Lord Randolph replied: 'I can only understand His Royal Highness' letter to you as a demand for an apology or a meeting. If I have acted indiscreetly or have been guilty of the slightest disrespect to Her Royal Highness the Princess of Wales by approaching her on so painful a subject I must unreservedly offer their Royal Highnesses the Prince of Wales and Princess of Wales my most humble and sincere apologies. This is the only apology which circumstances warrant my offering. With regard to a meeting no-one knows better than his Royal Highness the Prince of Wales that a meeting between himself and Lord Randolph Churchill is definitely out of the question. Please convey this to his Royal Highness.'

The threat of a duel between the Prince of Wales and Lord Randolph caused the highest personages in the land to meet in secret confabulation. In due course the Prime

Minister, the Lord Chancellor, Lord Cairns, and Lord Hartington, the arbiter of all social questions at the time, drafted a formal apology which Lord Randolph, some months later, reluctantly signed, but with an ungracious addendum which was to make it unacceptable to the Prince.

In the meantime the Prince of Wales had left India, though he did not hasten his return to England, spending a few agreeable weeks on the Continent while matters were sorted out. On his arrival in London he made it quite clear that not only would he not meet the Randolph Churchills at any house in London but that he would himself not go to any house where they were received. One staunch friend alone resisted the cut. When the Prince of Wales reproached Mr John Delacour, a Yorkshire country gentleman, for seeing too much of 'the Randolph Churchills', Delacour replied : 'Sir, I allow no man to choose my friends.' For a young and socially ambitious bride like Lady Randolph it was indeed a sombre edict of the Prince's. Nor was life for the young Member for Woodstock any more palatable. It was under these circumstances that Disraeli offered to the Duke of Marlborough the post of Viceroy of Ireland which the Duke had already refused several times in preceding years. The purpose of this project was that Lord Randolph should be the Duke's private secretary. But there were objections to this : if Lord Randolph were paid it might mean that he would have to give up his seat in the House of Commons. Eventually it was decided that Lord Randolph should act as unpaid private secretary. In view of the animosity of Court and Society, which Lord and Lady Randolph had only temporarily escaped by taking a summer trip to America, it seemed best to leave the country as gracefully as possible.

The Duke, although he refused to see his son or his family humilated at the hands of the Court, was reluctant to leave Blenheim and involve himself in the discomforts and the expenses that the Viceroyalty in Dublin would involve. Though he appreciated Lord Beaconsfield's good intentions (Disraeli was elevated to an earldom in the midst of these transactions) the Duke protested vehemently against not being made a member of the Cabinet (he had been included in 1867–8) if he took up the appointment in Dublin. Worse still, he felt slighted that the Chief Secretary for Ireland, Sir Michael Hicks-Beach, was to be included in the Cabinet while he was excluded. Lord Beaconsfield showed himself to be a skilful negotiator, and the Duke after a show of resistance saw that it was in the best interests of himself and of his family that he should go to Ireland. 'He always did,' as Winston was later to remark, 'whatever Lord Beaconsfield told him to do.' And many years later the Duchess had to concede : 'The Viceroyalty was a great success and Lord Beaconsfield used to congratulate me on his foresight'.

Blandford was eventually divorced by his wife in 1883. Aylesford emigrated to America in 1882 and bought 27,000 acres at Big Springs, Texas, where he was 'exceedingly popular' with the cowboys, and where he died of dropsy and hardening of the liver, shortly before his thirty-sixth birthday in 1885. Lady Aylesford, who was five years older than Aylesford, survived him by twelve years. She and Blandford lived together for some time and she gave birth to a son Bertrand in Paris in 1881. But though he was free to do so, Blandford never married her : instead, he married in 1888 the American widow of Mr Louis Hammersley. Lady Aylesford however was not quite forgotten : on her death in 1897 a wreath was sent to her funeral by the Prince and Princess of Wales.

To clear the way for the Duke of Marlborough's entry into Dublin, it was necessary to dispense with the services of the incumbent viceroy, the Duke of Abercorn. This again involved some embarrassment since Bertha, the aggrieved wife of Blandford, was herself the daughter of the Duke of Abercorn. So the change-over between the two Dukes was very much a family affair and Lord Beaconsfield handled it with his usual address.

The Marlboroughs travelled to Dublin early in January 1877 to take up the Duke's new appointment.

Already the movement for Home Rule, led by Isaac Butt, was gaining ground; but though 59 Home Rulers had been elected to Westminster in the election of 1874, they made little progress by Parliamentary methods and the young member for County Meath, Charles Stewart Parnell, returned at a by-election in 1875, was soon to assert himself as the leader of a more militant faction among the Irish. At this time too, the first cargoes of cheap wheat were coming across the Atlantic to Europe. Within two years the unprotected agricultural industry of Britain suffered its worst depression since the 1840s: in England, with most of its population in urban areas, the cheap food at least favoured the majority; in Ireland, largely a farming community, this was aggravated by the failure of the potato crop 1877–9, which led to ruin and famine and opened the way to agrarian revolt and the terrorism that accompanied it.

Among the numerous retinue which accompanied the Viceroy to Dublin was Winston's nanny, Mrs Everest, who until her death in 1895, when Winston was twenty, was destined to be the principal confidante of his joys, his troubles, and his hopes. It was not until after the death of Mrs Everest and of Lord Randolph that there opened that period of warm-hearted eager companionship between mother and son which was to prove so valuable to both.

Winston's mother from the earliest days exercised an exceptional fascination for him. She died in 1921 at the age of sixty-seven. Nine years after her death, in *My Early Life,* Winston evoked his own childhood memories of those days in Ireland:

My picture of her in Ireland is in a riding habit, fitting like a skin and often beautifully spotted with mud. She and my father hunted continually on their large horses; and sometimes there were great scares because one or the other did not come back for many hours after they were expected.

My mother always seemed to me a fairy princess: a radiant being possessed of limitless riches and power. She shone for me like the Evening Star. I loved her dearly— but at a distance.

Lord D'Abernon, the celebrated Edgar Vincent, international banker in Turkey, Ambassador in Berlin, and an arbiter of fashion, in his memoirs etched this portrait of Lady Randolph as she was during those Irish days:

I have the clearest recollection of seeing her for the first time. It was at the Viceregal Lodge at Dublin. The Viceroy was on the dais at the farther end of the room surrounded by a brilliant staff, but eyes were not turned on him or on his escort, but on a dark, lithe figure, standing somewhat apart and appearing to be of another texture to those around her, radiant, translucent, intense. A diamond star in her hair, her favourite ornament—its lustre dimmed by the flashing glory of her eyes. More of the panther than the woman in her look, but with a cultivated intelligence unknown to the jungle. Her courage not less great than that of her husband—fit mother for descendants of the great Duke. With all these attributes of brilliancy, such kindliness and high spirits that she was universally popular. Her desire to please, her delight in life, and the genuine wish that all should share her joyous faith in it, made her the centre of a devoted circle.

In *My Early Life* Winston was subsequently to recall, though not with perfect accuracy, what he then remembered about his childhood days in Dublin : the Little Lodge, about a stone's throw from the Viceregal, where he lived; the riflemen in Phoenix Park; the burning down of the Theatre Royal; the unveiling by his grandfather the Viceroy of the Gough statue : 'A great black crowd, scarlet soldiers on horseback, strings pulling away a brown shiny sheet, the old Duke, the formidable grandpapa, talking loudly to the crowd.'

Winston was very young at the time of the sojourn in Ireland; but indirectly, through their influence on Lord Randolph, the years in Ireland proved important. Fox-hunting all over Ireland with his young wife Lord Randolph obtained a keen insight into the country and its inhabitants. As secretary of his mother's Famine Fund campaign he gained invaluable knowledge of the life of the poor. His work as private secretary to his father brought him in further contact with all of the many extremes of political thought and the ruddy pool of rebellion. He visited London quite frequently and attended the House of Commons, though he did not make many speeches. In September 1877, however, he excited the annoyance of the Tory party and embarrassed his father by making a speech in his constituency at Woodstock, at the dinner of the local agricultural and horticultural Show, in which he berated the Government for their policy in Ireland : 'I have no hesitation in saying that it is inattention to Irish legislation that has produced obstruction [in the House of Commons]. There are great and crying Irish questions which the Government have not attended to, do not seem to be inclined to attend to and perhaps do not intend to attend to'. Lord Randolph's father the Duke wrote to Sir Michael Hicks-Beach, the Chief Secretary : 'The only excuse I can find for Randolph is that he must either be mad or have been singularly affected with local champagne or claret'.

Except for such interludes this was the period which afforded scope for repose and meditation and it was certainly in this period that Lord Randolph's powers first came to fruition. All this early training, all this new-found knowledge in Ireland was to prove invaluable to him when he became the protagonist in the fight against Mr Gladstone's Home Rule Bill. His understanding of Irish politics enabled him in 1886 to assure Parnell that he would not be a member of any Government which renewed the Irish Coercion Bill. On this Parnell volunteered that in that case the Tory party would receive the Irish vote in England. In 1886 Gladstone was able to secure the Irish vote for the Liberals because of his support for Home Rule, but the Tories swept the country because of the adhesion of the English electorate to an anti-Home Rule platform. This too was the period in which he brooded much upon the injustices, as he thought them, that society had meted out to himself and his wife; and he acquired the fierce and sometimes bitter driving force which, in the next decade, was to carry him within a hair's breadth of the summit of power.

3

ASCOT

EARLY IN 1880 Lord and Lady Randolph together with Winston and his brother Jack, who had been born in Dublin on February 4, returned to England to face the General Election which took place in April. Lord Randolph successfully held the family seat, Woodstock, by 60 votes, though his majority was reduced by 105. In the country as a whole Lord Beaconsfield's Government went down to defeat and so the Duke of Marlborough's term as Viceroy came to an end. Mr Gladstone and the Liberals returned to Parliament 106 stronger than the Tories and with an overall majority against Tories and Irish combined of 46. Mr Gladstone seemed supreme. The political situation in the Parliament of 1880 was later to be vividly described by Winston in his *Lord Randolph Churchill*.

. . . The position of the Conservative Party, upon the other hand, was weak and miserable in the extreme. The sympathies and the intellect of the nation were estranged. Lord Beaconsfield, the only man who could touch the imagination of the people, was withdrawn from the popular assembly. Many of the Tory strongholds—family boroughs and the like—were threatened by approaching Redistribution. The Front Opposition Bench, cumbered with the ancient and dreary wreckage of the late Administration, was utterly unequal to the Government in eloquence or authority. The attendance of Conservative members, as in all dispirited Oppositions, was slack and fitful. Outmatched in debate, outnumbered in division, the party was pervaded by a profound feeling of gloom. They had nothing to give to their followers, nothing to promise to the people; no Garters for Dukes, no peerages for wealth, no baronetcies or knighthoods or trinkets for stalwarts. Although the new spirit created by Disraeli—*Imperium* abroad, *Libertas* at home—still lived in the Tory party, it had been profoundly discouraged by the results of the election; and many of those who swayed Conservative counsels could think of no plan of action except an obstinate but apathetic resistance to change. . . .

What political prophet or philosopher, surveying the triumphant Liberal array, would have predicted that this Parliament, from which so much was hoped, would be indeed the most disastrous and even fatal period in their party history? Or who could have foreseen that these dejected Conservatives in scarcely five years, with the growing assent of an immense electorate, would advance to the enjoyment of twenty years of power? It needed a penetrating eye to discover the method, and a bold heart first to stem and finally to turn the tide. Who would have thought of breaking up the solid phalanx of Liberalism by driving in a wedge between the Radicals and the Whigs; or dreamt of using the Irish to overthrow the great apostle of reconciliation between peoples; and who without the audacity of genius would have dared to force the Conservative party to base the foundations of their authority with confidence upon the very masses they dreaded and to teach those masses to venerate and guard the institutions they had formerly despised? . . .

This was the political background against which Winston was to live the four sensitive years of his life between the ages of five and nine. On their return to London Lord and Lady Randolph moved into a new house at 29 St. James's Place, next to that of Sir Stafford Northcote, Lord Randolph's nominal leader in the House of Commons. A few months later Northcote was to write in his diary:

I asked him [Beaconsfield] whether Randolph Churchill was forgiven yet in high quarters. He said he was all right so far as the Queen was concerned, but that the Prince of Wales had not yet made it up with him; which Lord B thought very unfair, as he and Hartington had been called in as umpires and had decided that Randolph should make an apology (which was drawn up by Cairns) under the full impression that the matter was to end there, but the Prince having got the apology, still kept up the grievance, but nothing, said the Chief, will help Randolph into favour again so much as success in Parliament. The Prince is always taken by success.

Though after their return from Ireland the general cut by London society was progressively relaxed it was to be another three years before Lord and Lady Randolph were to be reconciled with the Prince of Wales; but eventually Beaconsfield's prophecy was to be fulfilled.

It is from Blenheim that we have Winston's first known letter to his mother.

Winston to Lady Randolph

[Postmark 4 January 1882]   [Blenheim]

My dear Mamma

I hope you are quite well I thank you very very much for the beautiful presents those Soldiers and Flags and Castle they are so nice it was so kind of you and dear Papa I send you my love and a great many kisses

Your loving

Winston

St James's Place was to be Winston's home for the next two years; then after Lord and Lady Randolph had again visited the United States, the family moved to 2 Connaught Place.

Winston's school days were the only unhappy part of his life. His pugnacious and rebellious nature never adapted itself to discipline. The neglect and lack of interest in him shown by his parents was remarkable, even judged by the standards of late Victorian and Edwardian days. His letters to his mother from his various schools abound in pathetic requests for letters and for visits, if not from her, from Mrs Everest and his brother Jack. Lord Randolph was a busy politician with his whole interest absorbed in politics; Lady Randolph was caught up in the whirl of fashionable society and seems to have taken very little interest in her son until he began to make his name resound through the world. It will later be seen how neglectful she was in writing to him when he was for three years a subaltern in India and when his father and Mrs Everest were dead. His brother Jack, more than five years younger, could not be a satisfactory correspondent and Winston was to feel exceptionally lonely and abandoned.

Yet his love for his mother never abated. Hesketh Pearson recalls that Bernard Shaw said of his mother : 'Her almost complete neglect of me had the advantage that I could idolize her to the utmost pitch of my imagination and had no sordid disillusioning contacts with her. It was a privilege to be taken for a walk or a visit with her, or on an excursion.'

These comparable circumstances may suggest a similar explanation of Winston's extravagant adoration of his own neglectful mother.

Winston was later to write the story of his schooldays and, as it is impossible to improve upon his own account, considerable extracts from *My Early Life* follow :

The School my parents had selected for my education was one of the most fashionable and expensive in the country. It modelled itself upon Eton and aimed at being preparatory for that Public School above all others. It was supposed to be the very last thing in schools. Only ten boys in a class; electric light (then a wonder); a swimming pond; spacious football and cricket grounds;

two or three school treats, or 'expeditions' as they were called, every term; the masters all M.A.'s in gowns and mortar-boards; a chapel of its own; no hampers allowed; everything provided by the authorities. It was a dark November afternoon when we arrived at this establishment. . . .

I was taken into a Form Room and told to sit at a desk. All the other boys were out of doors, and I was alone with the Form Master. He produced a thin greeny-brown, covered book filled with words in different types of print.

'You have never done any Latin before, have you?' he said.

'No, sir.'

'This is a Latin grammar.' He opened it at a well-thumbed page. 'You must learn this,' he said, pointing to a number of words in a frame of lines. 'I will come back in half an hour and see what you know.'

Behold me then on a gloomy evening, with an aching heart, seated in front of the First Declension.

Mensa	a table
Mensa	o table
Mensam	a table
Mensae	of a table
Mensae	to or for a table
Mensa	by, with or from a table

What on earth did it mean? Where was the sense in it? It seemed absolute rigmarole to me. However, there was one thing I could always do : I could learn by heart. And I thereupon proceeded, as far as my private sorrows would allow, to memorize the acrostic-looking task which had been set me.

In due course the Master returned.

'Have you learnt it?' he asked.

'I think I can *say* it,' I replied; and I gabbled it off.

He seemed so satisfied with this that I was emboldened to ask a question.

'What does it mean, sir?'

'It means what it says. Mensa, a table. Mensa is a

noun of the First Declension. There are five declensions. You have learnt the first singular of the First Declension.'

'But,' I repeated, 'what does it mean?'

'Mensa means a table,' he answered.

'Then why does mensa also mean o table,' I enquired, 'and what does o table mean?'

'Mensa, o table, is the vocative case,' he replied.

'But why o table?' I persisted in genuine curiosity.

'O table,—you would use that in addressing a table, in invoking a table.' And then seeing he was not carrying me with him, 'You would use it in speaking to a table.'

'But I never do,' I blurted out in honest amazement.

'If you are impertinent, you will be punished, and punished, let me tell you, very severely,' was his conclusive rejoinder.

Such was my first introduction to the classics from which, I have been told, many of our cleverest men have derived so much solace and profit. . . .

How I hated this school, and what a life of anxiety I lived there for more than two years. I made very little progress at my lessons, and none at all at games. I counted the days and the hours to the end of every term, when I should return home from this hateful servitude and range my soldiers in line of battle on the nursery floor. The greatest pleasure I had in those days was reading. When I was nine and a half my father gave me *Treasure Island*, and I remember the delight with which I devoured it. My teachers saw me at once backward and precocious, reading books beyond my years and yet at the bottom of the Form. They were offended. They had large sources of compulsion at their disposal, but I was stubborn. Where my reason, imagination or interest were not engaged, I would not or I could not learn. . . .

The school which Winston later discreetly camouflaged as St James's was St George's, at Ascot, and the headmaster was the Rev H. W. Sneyd-Kynnersley. Winston entered the school on 3 November 1882, five weeks after the beginning of term and some four weeks before his eighth birthday.

Maurice Baring, who arrived at St George's shortly after Winston, has left, recorded in his book *The Puppet Show of Memory,* published in 1922, the following impression which Winston had made upon the school :

> Dreadful legends were told about Winston Churchill, who had been taken away from the school. His naughtiness appeared to have surpassed anything. He had been flogged for taking sugar from the pantry, and so far from being penitent, he had taken the Headmaster's sacred straw hat from where it hung over the door and kicked it to pieces. His sojourn at this school had been one long feud with authority. The boys did not seem to sympathise with him. Their point of view was conventional and priggish.

The fact that Winston had not complained overmuch to his parents about this school, but complained about it bitterly later in *My Early Life*, might have inclined one to believe that in his fifties he was exaggerating the degrading conditions in which he found himself as a boy of eight. It is only necessary to read the Life of Roger Fry by Virginia Woolf to realize that this is a false assumption. Mrs Woolf quotes a number of letters which Fry wrote to his parents from the same school at the time. Fry describes how disagreeable it was as head boy to have the painful duty imposed on him of holding the other boys while they were being birched; but he does not make very much of it in his letters to his parents.

Boswell records that Dr Johnson said 'A schoolmaster is a man among boys, and a boy among men'. Winston was to be withdrawn after less than two years at the school. Mr Sneyd-Kynnersley did not long survive Winston's departure : he died of heart failure in November 1886 at the early age of thirty-eight.

* * * * *

The first two terms of 1884, Winston's last year at St George's, were a time of hectic and successful political activity on the part of Lord Randolph.

A Redistribution Bill was at this time going through Parliament. Under one of its provisions rotten and family boroughs like Woodstock were to be abolished. At the same time Lord Randolph announced that at the next General Election he would fight the Central Division of Birmingham, a city at that time represented in Parliament by three Liberal members, Joseph Chamberlain, John Bright and Philip Henry Muntz. The announcement that Lord Randolph was to carry the fight for Tory democracy into the very citadel of radicalism and that he was going to challenge John Bright and through him the mighty Joe himself on his home ground galvanized the Tory Party throughout the country. Lord Randolph overnight became the established hero and darling of Tory working men throughout the land and his name was on every political lip.

During the first six months of this year, Lord Randolph was also concerned in a lively fight for control of the National Union of Conservative Associations. This was the organization whose local branches, as today, did all the donkey work in the constituencies and got the vote out at election times. Then as now, however, all real political authority was concentrated in London at the Conservative Central Office. It was this latter body, known at the time as the Central Committee, which raised the money and, subject to the Party leader, exercised control over policy. Lord Randolph wished to increase his power inside the Party and to impose his own policies upon it. To this end he waged a double campaign—(1) to obtain the Chairmanship of the National Union and (2) to increase the powers of that body at the expense of the Central Committee. His second objective naturally aided his first. These tactics were extremely distasteful to the mandarins of the Party in London; they had installed on the National Union their tame protégés (notably Lord Percy, son and heir of the Duke of Northumberland) who saw to it that the body they controlled confined itself to loyal resolutions supporting what had been decided in London.

Lord Randolph triumphantly carried the day, gained a majority on the Council, and was elected its Chairman. The Central Committee in London was abolished and, though real power still remained in the Party leadership (at this time divided between Salisbury and Northcote, respectively leaders of the House of Lords and House of Commons), Lord Randolph obtained for the National Union what at least appeared on paper to be considerable new powers in shaping Party policy and management. He also obtained official recognition for the Primrose League;

this was a new organization which he and his friends had set on foot in memory of Lord Beaconsfield and to procure for the Party a vast body of voluntary canvassers, because the 1883 Corrupt Practices Act was to make illegal the employment of paid canvassers at election time. These were substantial gains. To the surprise and dismay of many of his supporters Lord Randolph did not press his fight against the leadership, but having attained recognition of his new position acted, at any rate temporarily, with an unwonted sense of responsibility. No documentary proof exists, but it seems likely that it was at this time that Lord Randolph came to some arrangement with Lord Salisbury as to the terms on which he would be prepared to join the next Conservative Government, which was to take office in the following years.

4

BRIGHTON

THE EXACT CAUSES which led Lord and Lady Randolph
to take Winston away from St George's at the end of the
summer term of 1884, and to send him in the middle of
the following term to what was to prove for Winston a
more agreeable school at Brighton, are not known. It is
believed that Mrs Everest saw the wounds of his birchings
and told his mother about it.

Apart from the sea air, Brighton had the advantage that
the family doctor, the celebrated Robson Roose, had at
that time his main practice there. The school was at 29 &
30 Brunswick Road, Hove, and there Winston came under
the jurisdiction of two elderly spinsters, the Misses Thomson. Winston was much happier there. As he later wrote :

> This was a smaller school than the one I had left. It was
> also cheaper and less pretentious. But there was an ele-
> ment of kindness and of sympathy which I had found
> conspicuously lacking in my first experiences. At this
> school I was allowed to learn things which interested me :
> French, History, lots of Poetry by heart, and above all
> Riding and Swimming. The impression of those years
> makes a pleasant picture in my mind, in strong contrast
> to my earlier schoolday memories.

Indeed his earliest letters to his mother say that he is
happy, ask for more stamps, confess to extravagance in the
purchase of a stamp album and ask for more money.

That winter Lord Randolph undertook a trip to India.
Though again there is no documentary evidence, it seems
likely that he did so partly to recover from a recent illness
but, more importantly, because Lord Salisbury had indicated to him that if he should form a government after the
next election Lord Randolph would be Secretary of State
for India.

*   *   *   *   *

Into the eighteen months from June 1885 to December 1886 was crowded the final crescendo, drama and tragedy of Lord Randolph's unique political career. Gladstone's Government, whose members were increasingly divided among themselves, almost courted defeat. It was not in the immediate interests of the Tories to bring the Government down. The Reform Bill of 1884 had given votes to two million more householders. The Queen would not have granted a dissolution to either party until the new electoral registers were ready, so that if the Tories were to defeat the Liberals in the House and Lord Salisbury were to be asked to form a Government he would be unable to go to the country to secure a majority until the late autumn of 1885. Nevertheless, five years of bitter opposition had built into the Tories an instinctive reflex action to grab at any opportunity of pulling down the Government. The occasion came on 8 June 1885 when on an unimportant amendment to the Budget concerning beer and spirits duties the Government was defeated by 12 votes and resigned forthwith.

Opinion was much divided among the Tory leaders as to whether Salisbury should agree to form a Government. The Queen was put in the embarrassing position of having to ask Gladstone whether, if Salisbury refused, he would carry on with his existing Cabinet. Mr Gladstone said that he would not. Lord Randolph did not help Salisbury much in his difficulties—he had never held office : he was not a Privy Councillor : he was only thirty-six : but some time before he had let Salisbury know that he could not join a Government in which Sir Stafford Northcote was the Leader of the House of Commons.

The Queen herself was shocked by Lord Randolph's obduracy and telegraphed to Salisbury : 'With due consideration to Lord R. Churchill, do not think he should be allowed to dictate entirely his own terms, especially as he has never held office before'. Lord Salisbury sought to see Lord Randolph before going to Balmoral to see the Queen, but Lord Randolph, despite all the pressure that was brought to bear on him, declined to do so and rested on his position. Lord Randolph won. Sir Stafford Northcote went to the House of Lords as the Earl of Iddesleigh, Sir Michael Hicks-Beach who had supported Lord Randolph in this crisis became Leader of the House of Commons, and Lord Randolph was sworn of the Privy Council and became Secretary of State for India and a member of the Cabinet in what was known as the Caretaker Government since it was only intended to hold office until the General Election could take place.

Salisbury must by now have begun to realize that Lord Randolph was going to be a difficult colleague; but he knew, and the Tory Party knew, that the following general election could not be won without the magic of Lord Randolph's eloquence, particularly now that two million electors had been newly enfranchised. Lord Randolph further emphasized his growing authority by ensuring that his political lieutenants did not go unrewarded. Sir Henry Drummond Wolff was sworn of the Privy Council and entrusted with an important mission to the Porte in Constantinople, while Mr Gorst entered the Government as Solicitor General. Mr Balfour needed no recommendation from Lord Randolph; he was Lord Salisbury's nephew, and he became President of the Local Government Board, but without as yet a seat in the Cabinet.

* * * * *

This is no place to speak of Lord Randolph's short but successful tenure of the India Office during which Burma was annexed to the Crown. Salisbury dissolved at the earliest possible moment and the election was held in November.

Lord Randolph was fighting against John Bright for the Central Division of Birmingham and thereby challenging the great Joe and his party manager Schnadhorst on their own ground.

Lord Randolph, who had been largely responsible for the Tory successes in the boroughs, had fought a valiant but unsuccessful fight in Birmingham against Bright but he was defeated by 4,989 to 4,216, a margin of 773. He had, however, availed himself of the offer of an admirer who had stood down in South Paddington in Lord Randolph's favour so that on the following day he was elected to the new Parliament, being returned by 1,706 votes.

The Liberals were sure that with the mighty prestige of Gladstone and two million new voters they would be triumphantly returned. In fact their majority compared with five years before fell by twenty. The figures were: Liberals 335, Tories 249, Irish Nationalists 86. It was clear that whoever undertook the Government of the United Kingdom would be dependent on the Irish vote. For the time being Lord Salisbury carried on but only a few weeks after the election, on December 15, Herbert Gladstone, the G.O.M.'s son and private secretary, flew the 'Hawarden kite' when he disclosed that his father had espoused Home Rule for Ireland. Mr Gladstone's denials were delphic. But Lord Salisbury's administration was eventually defeated at the end of January 1886 on an amendment concerning agricultural labourers in England. Lord Salisbury resigned: Gladstone formed his third Cabinet at the beginning of February and it quickly became apparent that he was going to introduce a measure of Home Rule which would involve a separate Parliament for Ireland. In embracing Home Rule he split the Liberal leadership from top to bottom. Though the rank and file of the Liberal Party remained faithful to Mr Gladstone, such party chieftains as Lord Hartington, Joseph Chamberlain and Mr Henry James broke with him and entered into a confederacy with the Tories.

Lord Randolph instantly perceived that Gladstone had played into the hands of the Tory Party. There was at this time no question of partitioning Ireland; and the project was that Ulster should come under a Dublin Parliament. Lord Randolph wrote to his great Irish friend, Lord Justice Fitzgibbon, on 16 February 1886: 'I decided some time ago that if the G.O.M. went for Home Rule, the Orange card would be the one to play. Please God it may turn out the ace of trumps and not the two.'

Lord Randolph travelled to Belfast, where on February 22 in the Ulster Hall he made the famous speech which for its effect upon the audience was, according to his son and biographer, 'one of the most memorable triumphs of his life'.

A few weeks later, in a letter to a Liberal Unionist, Lord Randolph wrote:

If political parties and political leaders, not only Parliamentary but local, should be so utterly lost to every feeling and dictate of honour and courage as to hand over coldly, and for the sake of purchasing a short and illusory Parliamentary tranquillity, the lives and liberties of the Loyalists of Ireland to their hereditary and most bitter foes, make no doubt on this point—Ulster will not be a consenting party : Ulster at the proper moment will resort to the supreme arbitrament of force; *Ulster will fight, Ulster will be right.*

This famous slogan became the watchword of Ulster; it pithily explains why Ulster is still part of the United Kingdom of Great Britain and Northern Ireland.

* * * * *

Gladstone's Government survived for four months in a precarious equipoise. Then, in June, on the Home Rule Bill, it was brought down by a majority of 30. Gladstone resigned. The Queen sent for Salisbury who asked for an immediate dissolution. A General Election took place in July, the Tories and Liberal Unionists being returned with a clear majority over all other parties of 118. The figures were :

Conservatives	316
Liberal Unionists	78
Liberals	191
Irish Nationalists	85

It had been Lord Randolph's victory. He had pioneered it, engineered it and executed it. His exceptional services to the Party had to be recognised. He was indispensable to it. He was appointed Chancellor of the Exchequer and Sir Michael Hicks-Beach, twelve years his senior, when offered the leadership of the House of Commons again, persuaded both Lord Salisbury and Lord Randolph that it would be absurd for him to have the job. Many years later Sir Michael Hicks-Beach put his views on this matter in writing :

I felt that Lord Randolph Churchill was superior in eloquence, ability and influence to myself; that the position of Leader in name, but not in fact, would be intolerable; and that it was better for the party and the country that the Leader in fact should be the Leader also in name; Lord Salisbury very strongly pressed me to remain, saying that character was of most importance, and quoting Lord Althorp as an instance; but I insisted.

Lord Randolph accepted Sir Michael's advice and became Leader of the House of Commons as well as Chancellor of the Exchequer. Sir Michael accepted Lord Randolph's advice and became Chief Secretary for Ireland.

Lord Randolph proved a highly successful Leader of the House. He was diligent in his attendance and by his ready grace and wit much facilitated the progress of Government business. He also showed a high degree of punctilio in his nightly reports to the Queen on the progress of business in the House of Commons. At the end of the first session of the new Parliament the Queen, who had no reason to love him, began to mellow. She wrote to Lord Randolph on September 22 : 'Now that the session is just over, the Queen wishes to write and thank Lord Randolph for his regular and full and interesting reports of the debates in the House of Commons, which must have been most trying. Lord Randolph has shown much skill and judgement in his leadership during the exceptional session of Parliament.'

*   *   *   *   *

While these stirring affairs were afoot Winston was still at Brighton. His letters show that he had followed his father's political fortunes with interest. Lord Randolph improved his own majority at South Paddington from 1,706 to 1,807.

Winston to Lady Randolph

[? 6 July 1886]   Brighton

My darling Mummy,

I hope you are well. Has Everest gone for her holiday yet? I should like you to come and see me very much. I am very glad Papa got in for South Paddington by so great a majority. I think that was a victory. I hope the Conservatives will get in, do you think they will?

Give my love to Jack and Everest.

With love and kisses I remain, Your loving son
WINSTON S. CHURCHILL

On October 3, Lord Randolph, without consulting the Prime Minister, made a fateful speech at Dartford before 14,000 people. He demanded closer links with Germany and Austria in countering Russian influence in the Balkans, a proposal quite out of tune with the Government's policy of friendship towards France and hostility towards the Turks. As for home affairs, he ran counter to party opinion in demanding procedural reforms in Parliament (including the closure by simple majority), increased expenditure on local government, improvements for agricultural labourers, and reductions in Government expenditure. The Dartford Programme, as it came to be called, created a sensation. Lord Randolph left on a short continental holiday 'secretly and silently' immediately afterwards but returned in time to repeat his manifesto to the National Union of Conservative Associations at Bradford on October 30.

* * * * *

Lord Randolph's resignation is chronicled in detail in the reminiscences of those who watched it. On December 20, accompanied by Lord George Hamilton, the First Lord of the Admiralty, he went to Windsor to dine and sleep. There he wrote a letter to Lord Salisbury in which he told the Prime Minister that in view of the fact that neither Lord George Hamilton nor W. H. Smith at the War Office were prepared to decrease their estimates for the coming year 'I cannot continue to be responsible for the finances'. Lord George Hamilton records in his Memoirs that he told Lord Randolph : 'You cannot send a letter like that to Salisbury. Won't you consult somebody?'

'No, I won't consult anybody.'

'Have you spoken to your mother the Duchess?'

'No.'

After dinner Lord Randolph had an audience of the Queen but said nothing to her. Later Winston was to write in his Life of Lord Randolph about the events of the following morning, December 21 : 'Both Ministers left Windsor and returned to London. Lord Randolph bought, as was his custom, a number of newspapers, but found that neither he nor Hamilton had any change. The train was about to start, and the bookstall keeper, who knew both his customers by sight, cried : "Never mind, my lord—when you come back next time will do." Lord Randolph

69

looked sideways at his companion and said, with a quaint smile, "He little knows I shall never come back".'

Sir Henry Drummond Wolff, who had returned from a mission to Egypt, now takes up the story:

On Tuesday [December 22] Lord Randolph Churchill received no answer from Lord Salisbury; neither did one arrive on Wednesday morning. On that day, however, Lord Randolph lunched at the Carlton with Mr W. H. Smith who said that he had received a communication from Lord Salisbury and plainly showed that it was considered that Lord Randolph's resignation had been accepted.

The same evening Lord Randolph dined with me at the Carlton and in the middle of dinner received a letter from Lord Salisbury. This he at once showed me, and it seemed to cut out all chance of a negotiation and to accept the resignation in the most positive manner.

On this, Lord Randolph wrote a letter to Lord Salisbury, which he sent down to Hatfield by Special Messenger, and it arrived there late—there being a ball going on.

Meanwhile, Lord Salisbury was host at the ball at Hatfield attended by, among others, the Duchess of Teck and her daughter, the future Queen Mary, and the Duchess of Marlborough, Lord Randolph's mother. Mr Rhodes James records that 'Lord Salisbury was talking to the Duchess of Teck in the middle of the ball at Hatfield shortly before half-past one in the morning of the 23rd when a red dispatch box was brought to him; excusing himself, he opened it, read the one letter that it contained, and then resumed the conversation with unbroken composure. The ball continued until the early hours; Salisbury told no one of the nature of the single letter in the dispatch box; he did not communicate with the Queen; he did not warn the editor of *The Times*; he simply went to bed. He was woken early by Lady Salisbury, who reminded him that they must get up to see the Duchess of Marlborough off, as she was catching an early train. "Send for *The Times* first," was the sleepy response. "Randolph resigned in the middle of the night, and if I know my man, it will be in *The Times* this morning." It was. The Duchess of Marlborough, to her intense indignation, was allowed to leave Hatfield without seeing either her host or hostess.'

At Connaught Place the scene that morning was recorded by Lady Randolph : :

When I came down to breakfast, the fatal paper in my hand, I found him calm and smiling. 'Quite a surprise for you,' he said. He went into no explanation, and I felt too utterly crushed and miserable to ask for any, or even to remonstrate. Mr Moore [his private secretary], who was devoted to Randolph, rushed in, pale and anxious, and with a faltering voice said to me, 'He has thrown himself from the top of the ladder, and will never reach it again!' Alas! he has proved too true a prophet.

It is agreeable to the historian that so many different accounts are in substantial harmony. That is not what usually happens. Lord Randolph's resignation proved fatal to his career and cast a gloom over the homes of his mother, his wife and his children. He nearly destroyed Lord Salisbury, who took eleven days to find a new Chancellor, but in the event Lord Randolph destroyed himself. Asked some years later why he did not bring Lord Randolph back, Lord Salisbury said, 'Have you ever heard of a man having a carbuncle on his neck wanting it to return?'

The small family at Connaught Place long nourished the hope that Lord Salisbury would relent and that Lord Randolph's political fortunes could be restored. Perhaps if Lord Randolph's health had not collapsed this might have happened; it was not to be.

Nearly five years later he was to write to his wife from Johannesburg: 'So Arthur Balfour is really leader—and Tory Democracy, the genuine article, at an end. Well, I have had quite enough of it all. I have waited with great patience for the tide to turn, but it has not turned, and will not now turn in time. In truth, I am now altogether *déconsidéré*. A little more than three years later Lord Randolph was dead.

* * * * *

Winston was to spend another four terms at Brighton.

Football, amateur theatricals, cricket, and Queen Victoria's Golden Jubilee were the dominating themes of his letters in the first half of the year.

That summer was taken up with Queen Victoria's Golden Jubilee and Winston was much looking forward to participating in the celebrations in London on June 21. When one of the Miss Thomsons sought to deny him this pleasure, Winston used all his powers of pleading to reverse her verdict:

Winston to Lady Randolph

[Postmark 11 June 1887]   [Brighton]

My dear Mamma,

Miss Thomson does'nt want me to go home for the Jubilee and because she says that I shall have no place in Westminster Abbey and so it is not worth going. Also that you will be very busy and unable to be with me much.

Now you know that this is not the case. I want to see Buffalo Bill & the Play as you promised me. I shall be very disappointed, disappointed is not the word I shall be miserable, after you have promised me, and all, I shall never trust your promises again. But I know that Mummy loves her Winny much too much for that.

Write to Miss Thomson and say that you have promised me and you want to have me home. Jack entreats you daily I know to let me come and there are 7 weeks after the Jubilee before I come home. Don't disappoint me. If you write to Miss Thomson she will not resist you, I could come home on Saturday to stay till Wednesday. I have got a lot of things, pleasant and unpleasant to tell you. Remember for my sake. I am quite well but in a torment about coming home it would upset me entirely if you were to stop me.

Love & kisses, I remain, Yours as ever, Loving son
WINNY

(Remember)

Winston to Lady Randolph

[June 1887]   [Brighton]

Dear Mamma,

I am nearly mad with suspense. Miss Thomson says that

she will let me go if you write to ask for me. For my sake write before it is too late. Write to Miss Thomson by return post please ! ! !

I remain Your loving son
WINNY

Winston's unremitting pertinacity seems to have prevailed.

His letters at this time give more detailed accounts of his work, a fact not perhaps unconnected with threats of a tutor in the holidays.

Winston to Lady Randolph

[? 8 July 1887]   [Brighton]

Dear Mamma,

I am in want of 5/- because Miss Kates Birthday Present has taken 5/- out of my Exchequer. I want 'Jess' or 'She' soon. Autographs for goodness sake. My darling I hope you don't intend to make my Holidays miserable by having a Tutor.

Love & Kisses
I remain, Your loving son
WINNY

Winston to Lady Randolph

[July 1887]   [Brighton]

My dear Mamma,

I am told that 'Mr Pest' is going to be my tutor in the Holidays. Now as he is a Master here and I like him pretty well I shall not mind him at all, on one condition viz. 'Not to do any work' I give up all other conditions except this one I never have done work in my holidays and I will not begin now. I will be very good if thi is not forced upon me and I am not bothered about it. When I am doing nothing I don't mind working a little, but to feel that I am forced

73

to do it is against my principles. Without this I might have very happy holidays.

Hoping you will grant this.

I remain, Your loving son
WINNY

During the summer of 1887 Lord Randolph sought the advice of his sister Fanny's husband—Edward Marjoribanks—as to a suitable public school for Winston. Marjoribanks had put his own son, only a few months older than Winston, down for Harrow and now he wrote on behalf of Lord Randolph to the newly arrived Headmaster, the Reverend J. E. C. Welldon. The latter replied on September 24 that it would be a pleasure for him to find room for Lord Randolph's son 'somewhere'. 'It is difficult to speak positively about vacancies; and my own house is terribly full. But with Lord Randolph's leave I will make an arrangement by which his son may go temporarily into a Small House and may then pass from it into my own house, or, at the worst, into some other Large House'.

Lord Randolph agreed that Winston should go to Harrow and Mr Welldon replied on October 4: 'I shall look forward with much pleasure to his coming, & I hope I may be useful to him, when he is here. You may rely upon my placing him in a House where his health will be carefully watched, if I cannot find room for him immediately in my own'.

The Churchills had been an Etonian family for six generations in direct descent from the 3rd Duke of Marlborough who went there about 1722, down to Lord Randolph who went there in 1862. It appears that the decision to send Winston to Harrow rather than to Eton was based upon the severe attack of pneumonia which Winston had suffered at Brighton, and the idea that Harrow-on-the-Hill would be more bracing and less injurious to his lungs than Eton surrounded by the fogs and mists of the Thames Valley. Quaintly enough, in the course of a long life, though frequently assailed by pneumonia, Winston never suffered from lack of lung power, either on the political platform or in the House of Commons.

Winston's last term at Brighton was devoted to preparations for the Harrow Entrance Examination—in between joining in the 'Theatre Rage'. 'Please', Winston wrote to his mother on 14 February 1888, 'ask Everest to send down all the things and Scenes connected with the Play "Aladdin" & the stage as soon as the 5 trap doors are made. Also please send me a bottle of Sperm oil for the 8 footlights. I am very ambitious to beat the others. Ask Auntie Leonie to be quick with Britannia & Fairies.'

When the day of the examination came, Winston's tentative optimism was sorely tested and began to evaporate. Looking back on the event forty-two years later, he wrote in *My Early Life*:

. . . I should have liked to be asked to say what I knew. They always tried to ask what I did not know. When I would have willingly displayed my knowledge, they sought to expose my ignorance. This sort of treatment had only one result: I did not do well in examinations.

This was especially true of my Entrance Examination to Harrow. The Headmaster, Mr Welldon, however, took a broad-minded view of my Latin Prose: he showed discernment in judging my general ability. This was the more remarkable, because I was found unable to answer a single question in the Latin paper. I wrote my name at the top of the page. I wrote down the number of the question 'I'. After much reflection I put a bracket round it thus '(I)'. But thereafter I could not think of anything connected with it that was either relevant or true. Incidentally there arrived from nowhere in particular a blot and several smudges. I gazed for two whole hours at this sad spectacle: and then merciful ushers collected up my piece of foolscap with all the others and carried it up to the Headmaster's table. It was from these slender indications of scholarship that Mr Welldon drew the conclusion that I was worthy to pass into Harrow. . . .

Winston's contemporary letters to his father and mother make it plain that his examination papers cannot have been quite so inadequate as he later persuaded himself and his readers to believe. Just as his greatest friend of later days, F. E. Smith, was wont to exaggerate the poverty of his youth, Winston was inclined to exaggerate his own early ignorance. Both no doubt subconsciously felt in later years that their brilliant successes would be enhanced, set against a sombre background of poverty and stupidity.

5

HARROW

WINSTON ENTERED HARROW on 17 April 1888.
Earlier Winston had expressed a desire to go into Crook-
shank's House, because he knew some boys there. But the
Headmaster himself, the Reverend J. E. C. Welldon, had
consented to take Winston into his own House, although he
was not able to promise immediate entry. So Winston was
sent to 'wait' in one of the Small Houses which was run by
H. O. D. Davidson. It was not until a year had passed, in
April 1889, that there was room for Winston in the Headmaster's.

Davidson, who was Winston's 'tutor' for most of his time
at Harrow even after he had moved into the Headmaster's
House, was an Old Harrovian, a keen player of games, a
kindly but conventional schoolmaster. Mr Welldon was a
different type. An Etonian, a great classical scholar, and a
fine preacher of sermons, he had been appointed Headmaster of Harrow in 1885, at the age of thirty-one. Winston
has described how Mr Welldon had looked in a helpful
manner on his entrance examination. Throughout his
school career Welldon showed infinite patience, and took
considerable pains with Winston; ever afterwards the two
retained an admiration for each other.

He had been placed in the bottom form of the School,
the third division of the Fourth Form, under the supervision
of Mr Robert Somervell. Few of his early companions in
his first form were to distinguish themselves greatly in after
life : though the father of one of them, Archibald John
Campbell Colquhoun, was for some years owner of Chartwell, near Westerham in Kent, destined to become
Winston's home for the last forty years of his life. As the
new boys were placed in alphabetical order, young Spencer-
Churchill found only two below him, so that he 'gained
no more advantage from the alphabet than from the wider
sphere of letters.' When these two disappeared 'through
illness or some other cause', he found himself at the bottom

of the school. Visitors to the school, anxious to catch a glimpse of the great Lord Randolph's son as he filed past the master at Bill, the Harrow roll-call, were frequently heard to remark : 'Why, he's the last of all'. Winston himself objected strenuously to appearing under the letter S. 'I am called, and written Spencer Churchill here and sorted under the S's,' he complained to his father in a postscript to a mid-term letter. 'I never write myself Spencer Churchill, but always Winston S. Churchill. Is it your wish that I should be so called? It is too late to alter it this term but next term I may assume my proper name.' Since it was Lord Randolph who ten years before had remarked 'how often we find mediocrity dowered with a double-barrelled name' it might have been supposed that Lord Randolph would have been in sympathy with his son's wishes. But neither the next term, nor in any subsequent term did either Winston or his brother Jack succeed in dropping the Spencer, and they continued to be listed under S in the school register.

It did not take Winston long to discover a way of rising above his lowly position. 'I am learning 1000 lines of Macaulay for a prize,' he wrote to his father on June 3. 'I know 600 at present.' And he added, with disarming candour : 'Any one who likes to take the trouble to learn them can get one, as there is no limit to the prizes'. Among the lines he chose to learn were Horatius from *The Lays of Ancient Rome*, and his capacious and retentive memory permitted him all his life to recite with gusto and relish the lines he learned when he was thirteen. The stirring patriotism these verses evoked abided with him for ever and were the mainspring of his political conduct. The Harrow School Songs also stirred his youthful patriotism. In 1940 the author accompanied his father to the first of those annual singings of the School Songs at Harrow which Churchill was to attend throughout the war and for some years thereafter. Driving back he said with lively emotion : 'Listening to those boys singing all those well-remembered songs I could see myself fifty years before singing with them those tales of great deeds and of great men and wondering with intensity how I could ever do something glorious for my country'.

Winston certainly took trouble, and persevered even when he found shortly before the day of recitation that it was 1200, and not 1000 lines he had to learn. His efforts were rewarded with a success which, he later recalled, was thought incongruous for one 'stagnated' in the lowest form. To the end of his career at Harrow his name in the school register carried after it the distinction of an italic *p* commemorating the fact that he had gained a prize in the Speech Room.

The summer term had not been however without its difficulties for the new boy. His housemaster had written earlier in the term:

12 July 1888   Harrow

Dear Lady Randolph Churchill,

After a good deal of hesitation and discussion with his form-master, I have decided to allow Winston to have his exeat: but I must own that he has not deserved it. I do not think, nor does Mr Somervell, that he is in any way *wilfully* troublesome: but his forgetfulness, carelessness, unpunctuality, and irregularity in every way, have really been so serious, that I write to ask you, when he is at home to speak very gravely to him on the subject.

When a boy first comes to a public school, one always expects a certain amount of helplessness, owing to being left to himself so much more in regard to preparation of work &c. But a week or two is generally enough for a boy to get used to the ways of the place. Winston, I am sorry to say, has, if anything got worse as the term passed. Constantly late for school, losing his books, and papers, and various other things into which I need not enter—he is so regular in his irregularity, that I really don't know what to do: and sometimes think he cannot help it. But if he is unable to conquer this slovenliness (for I think all the complaints I have to make of him can be grouped under this head, though it takes various forms); he will never make a success of a public school. As far as ability goes he ought to be at the top of his form, whereas he is at the bottom. Yet I do not think he is idle: only his energy is fitful, and when he gets to his work it is generally too late for him to do it well. I thought it wd do him good to spend a day with you, and have therefore let him go: but unless he mends his ways, he will really have to be heavily punished and I cannot help thinking he does not deserve any

79

special treat during the exeat! I have written very plainly to you, as I do think it very serious that he should have acquired such phenomenal slovenliness. At his age, very great improvement is possible if he seriously gives his mind to conquering his tendencies : but I am sure that unless a very determined effort is made it will grow upon him. He is a remarkable boy in many ways, and it would be a thousand pities if such good abilities were made useless by habitual negligence.

I ought not to close without telling you that I am very much pleased with some history work he has done for me.

I am afraid this is a very long letter, but my excuse must be my interest in the boy.

Believe me yours sincerely
H. O. D. DAVIDSON

Winston's other great interest at Harrow was the School Rifle Corps. A few days after he arrived at Harrow, on 3 May 1888, the school magazine, *The Harrovian,* carried an indignant letter from a correspondent Miles Harroviensis, complaining about the state of the Rifle Corps. He said that the Harrow Rifle Corps ought to have at least 200 members 'whereas we have scarcely over 100, the majority of whom are inefficient.' The correspondent went on to consider the reason for this 'lack of energy and interest' in the Corps. 'It is due mainly to the fellows who belong to it themselves. The majority of them join merely for the pleasure of going to Wimbledon, and think it monstrous if they are obliged to attend twenty drills in the Summer term. The consequence is that whenever the Corps makes its appearance the drilling is bad, the marching is slovenly, and it becomes the laughing stock of the rest of the School. That is why it is so difficult to get smart and influential fellows to join.'

Winston, at this time, was neither smart nor influential, but he joined the Corps straightaway and derived great pleasure from it.

*   *   *   *   *

During the spring term of 1889 Winston asked his father to remind Mr Welldon of his promise to take him into the Headmaster's House. This Lord Randolph did, and Welldon replied on 2 April 1889 that he would take Winston into his House the following term, explaining

. The plan of battle was as near as
I could make out) like this

Railway station for Heiley

Railway station for Harrow

ROMANS under Pat...

RIVER CHESS

centre...

Harrow defends.

If I have left him so long as I have in a Small House, the reason is only that in Davidson's opinion and, I may add, in my own it seemed to be best for him, as he was very much of a child, when he first came, to be under more personal care, than can well be given to a boy who is one of a large number. However, as it happens, I told Davidson a fortnight ago that I should like to take him into my own House next Term. He has some great gifts and is, I think, making progress in his work.

Mr Welldon also took the opportunity of dropping a hint to Lord Randolph that it might 'perhaps not be disagreeable' to him and to Lady Randolph to come some time in the summer and take 'at least the opportunity of seeing what Winston's school life is like.' It looks as if it was to be another six months, and altogether eighteen months after Winston had first gone to Harrow, before Lord Randolph first went down to see the school.

Winston supplemented Mr Welldon's broad hints with entreaties of his own, begging his father to come to Harrow for Speech Day.

Winston to Lord Randolph

[? 2 July 1889]   [Harrow]

My dear Papa,

I am writing to tell you all about Speech-day. If you take the 11.7 from Baker Street you can get to Harrow at 11.37. I shall meet you at the station with a fly, if I can get one.

The 'Speeches' begin at 12. But dont let the name hinder your coming. Speeches simply mean the Greek-English-French-German plays & the distribution of Prizes by Mr Welldon who makes a short speech to each of the prizemen.

I don't think that you will be asked to make a speech. In fact I should think it will be very improbable. I do hope both you & Mamma will come as last Speech day nobody came to see me & it was vy dull.

You have never been to see me & so everything will be new to you. Ducker is reserved specially for the visitor to look at. You will see the Vaughan Library—the Gymnasium—the Racquets Courts—My room—& other places.

Am going to school this morning, so I must say 'Good Bye' & Love & Kisses

Remain your loving son
WINSTON S. CHURCHILL
P.S. I shall be awfully disappointed if you don't come.

'Do try to get Papa to come', he wrote to his mother. 'He has never been.' But Lord Randolph did not go.

*　　*　　*　　*　　*

In the summer term Lord Randolph expressed his desire that Winston should go into the Army. No doubt he had been much impressed by the obvious enthusiasm with which Winston was describing his outings with the Rifle Corps.

Accordingly Winston joined the Army Class in September 1889. Until 1888, apart from a handful of bright fifth-formers who anyway usually went to Woolwich and not Sandhurst, it was the rule rather than the exception for candidates for the Army examination to spend six months or more at a London crammer's after they had left Harrow. It was to discourage this premature loss from the school of boys of sixteen and seventeen that Mr Welldon, as part of his far-reaching reforms in the curriculum of the school, had reconstituted the Army Class. Although boys still nominally belonged to their regular forms, they were taken away from the main stream of ordinary school instruction and given special lessons in those subjects which were dear to the hearts of the Civil Service Commissioners who were responsible for selecting entrants to Sandhurst, as to all branches of the Government Service. Not only did this involve extra lessons in the evenings and on half-holidays, but it also meant that it was difficult for an Army Class boy to rise high enough in his ordinary form to obtain a Remove at the end of the term. This was apt to prove frustrating to the boys and irksome to their parents. In Winston's case, it meant that he never in fact got out of the Lower School throughout his four and a half years at Harrow; though after three years he was no longer compelled to fag. Mr Wellsford and Mr L. M. Moriarty, the Army Class tutors, did not consider Winston good enough in Mathematics to pass into Woolwich, the Military Academy for cadets seeking commissions in the Royal Artillery or the Royal Engineers. It was thought best that he should try to pass into Sandhurst which catered primarily for the Infantry and Cavalry.

That term, Winston continued to do well at shooting and he began to learn to fence, as he himself said, with an eye to its being useful when he got into the Army. That term too, Lord Randolph paid his first recorded visit to Harrow. But from an academic point of view it seems to have been a bleak period for Winston. Quite early he was put on 'reports'—that is to say he had to obtain weekly reports on his work and show them to his tutor or to the Headmaster. 'Please do try and come on Thursday,' he wrote to his mother at the end of October, 'as I want you to jaw Welldon about keeping me on reports for such a long time'. It seems that Lady Randolph for once did as she was asked : but it was of no avail.

Winston was supposed to take the Preliminary Examination for Sandhurst in the summer of 1890, but at the last moment Mr Welldon decided that he was not yet ready for it, his geometrical drawing being considered his greatest weakness. Lady Randolph replied to this news :

Lady Randolph to Winston

Thursday 12 June 1890   2 Connaught Place

Dearest Winston,

I am sending this by Everest, who is going to see how you are getting on. I would go down to you—but I have so many things to arrange about the Ascot party next week that I can't manage it. I have much to say to you, I'm afraid not of a pleasant nature. You know darling how I hate to find fault with you, but I can't help myself this time. . . . In the first place your Father is very angry with you for not acknowledging the gift of the 5£ for a whole week, and then writing an offhand careless letter.

Your report which I enclose is as you will see a *very* bad one. You work in such a fitful unharmonious way, that you are bound to come out last—look at your place in the form ! Yr Father & I are both more disappointed than we can say, that you are not able to go up for yr preliminary Exam : I daresay you have a 1000 excuses for not doing so—but there the fact remains ! If only you had a better place in your form, & were a little more methodical I

84

would *try* & find an excuse for you. Dearest Winston you make me very unhappy—I had built up such hopes about you & felt so proud of you—& now all is gone. My only consolation is that your conduct is good, & that you are an affectionate son—but your work is an insult to your intelligence. If you would only trace out a plan of action for yourself & carry it out & be *determined* to do so—I am sure you could accomplish anything you wished. Your Father threatens to send you with a tutor off somewhere for the holidays—I can assure you it will take a great deal to pacify him, & I don't know how it is to be done. I must say I think you repay his kindness to you very badly. There is Jack on the other hand—who comes out at the head of his class every week—notwithstanding his bad eye.

I will say no more now—but Winston you are old enough to see how serious this is to you—& how the next year or two & the use you make of them, will affect your whole life—stop and think it out for yourself & take a good pull before it is too late. You know dearest boy that I will always help you all I can.

Your loving but distressed
MOTHER

Winston replied manfully:

Winston to Lady Randolph

[Postmark 19 June 1890]   [Harrow]

My darling Mummy,

I have not written till now because I can write a much longer letter. I will not try to excuse myself for not working hard, because I know that what with one thing and another I have been rather lazy. Consequently when the month ended the crash came I got a bad report & got put on reports etc etc. That is more than 3 weeks ago, and in the coming month I am *bound* to get a good report as I have had to take daily reports to Mr Davidson twice a week and they have been very good on the whole. . . . My own Mummy I can tell you your letter cut me up very much. Still there is plenty of time to the end of term and I will do my *very best* in what remains. I want to go in for my Preliminary & I will explain the whole thing to you.

If in your examination you succeed in passing any 3 of the 8 subjects you need only compete in those you failed in. Now I knew that if I worked at

       1 Geography
       2 French
       3 & English Dictation & Composition

I should pass in all these.
3. I knew that work however hard at Mathematics I could not pass in that. All other boys going in were taught these things & I was not, so they said it was useless.

Goodbye my own
With love I remain Your own
WINSTON S. CHURCHILL

Actually Winston was luckier than he, or even his teachers, realised. When he was at last allowed to take the Preliminary Examination for Sandhurst in November 1890 he was still only just above the Fourth Form, in Modern Third Shell. It was just in time. This was the last Preliminary Examination at which Latin was an optional subject : the new regulations made it one of the obligatory subjects—in place of English Essay. It is interesting to speculate on what might have happened if Winston had failed to pass his Preliminary Examination before the new rules took effect.

Winston passed in all his subjects. Of the twenty-nine candidates from Harrow, only twelve succeeded in doing that, and of these Winston was from much the lowest form. Two fifth-formers and his cousin Dudley Marjoribanks were among the six who passed in four out of five subjects; four boys passed in only three subjects; and six failed altogether. 'I have received very many congratulations from scores of boys and many masters,' Winston told his mother. 'Dudley has not spoken to me. Vive la joie ! ! He has not passed and is furious.' And Lady Randolph hastened to send a glowing, indeed an overglowing, account to her husband, who was on his way home from a visit to Egypt.

The year 1890, which had promised to be dispiriting and ended triumphantly, brought new interests to Winston in a number of other fields. That summer Lord and Lady

Randolph took Banstead, a small property at Newmarket. Lord Randolph, though he had bought his first horse at Newmarket while he was still Chancellor in October 1886, had only started taking an interest in racing after his resignation He was in partnership with Lord Dunraven, who, as Under-Secretary of State for the Colonies, was the only other Minister to resign at the same time as Lord Randolph. Some horses were entered in Lord Randolph's name, others in Lord Dunraven's. The horses were trained by R. Sherwood at St Gatien House, Newmarket. In his first season as an owner, 1887, Lord Randolph only had one winner in his colours of pink, chocolate sleeves and cap (these colours were later adopted by his son Winston) and that a nominal prize of £100.

However, between 1889 and 1893 either Lord Randolph or Lord Dunraven were always among the leading winning owners on the turf. Lord Randolph was elected a member of the Jockey Club in 1890 and during these years racing and family friends like Colonel North and Colonel Montagu, the trainer Sherwood and his younger son Bob, provided Winston and Jack with lively company.

Naturally, both Winston and Jack were enormously excited that they had a country house to go to having spent so many holidays in London or at the sea-side in boarding houses. Mrs Everest realized how much her two young charges welcomed the changes :

Mrs Everest to Lady Randolph
(Blenheim Papers)

1 January 1891   Banstead

My Lady,
   We arrived here safely at 3 o'clock yesterday & I am very sorry but I quite forgot to send you a telegram until we had got some way on the road here. I hope you got Master Winston's letter he wrote last evening. They are both so happy & delighted & in towering spirits. Mr Winston walked from Cheveley up to the house yesterday & said he had left all his bad throat in the train he feels nothing of it. They danced all evening & were out before breakfast this morning & have been out with the keeper the whole morning, killed 5 rabbits & frightened 50. They

have just had luncheon & gone off again. They do not need pressing to go out here. On the contrary now I have the trouble to get them to come in to their meals. But they are so happy & well today. The house is very comfortable & warm. The weather changed in the night & it has been thawing today—otherwise the pond is beautiful for skating. They were looking forward to it, but if the thaw continues they will be able to ride. I should like to keep Master Jack here until Mr Winston returns from Canford. Mr W could come up with Walter the boy. It is so much better for them than London. I am desired to enclose drawings of last night with their best love & kisses.

Your ladyship's obednt servant
E. A. E v e r e s t

At Banstead Winston built the Den. It was quite a large hut constructed, with the aid of a few of the men who worked on the estate, of mud and planks, and carpeted with straw inside. With his brother Jack, his cousins Shane Leslie and Hugh Frewen and the gardener's son and other children on the estate, Winston built intricate fortifications around it. The author is indebted to Sir Shane Leslie for some accounts of these activities. There was a moat and a drawbridge. The entrance to the Den was guarded by a large home-made elastic catapult which propelled green apples with great force at any target which hazarded in the vicinity, notably a cow which was occasionally hit. Winston now graduated from drilling his toy soldiers in Connaught Square to drilling his brother, his cousins and his other 'volunteers' in the field outside the Den and it was at the end of the drilling that he marched his troops across the drawbridge into the Den, raised the drawbridge and defended the citadel against all comers with the aid of his powerful catapult.

At school at this time, Winston suffered a good deal from toothache and had to make numerous visits to a succession of dentists some of whom were thought inadequate in their duties. He also suffered a strain which was evidently some form of incipient hernia and for which he consulted an eminent specialist in hernia surgery, Sir William MacCormac. Nearly sixty years later he had to undergo an operation for this complaint which involved an eight-inch scar across the belly. This he triumphantly survived.

In April 1891 Lord Randolph had sailed for a lengthy visit to South Africa in search of health and with the expectation of making some money for his wife and children. He was oblivious of the fact, but his family had by now begun to accept that he would never recover his health or restore his political fortunes.

During Lord Randolph's absence in South Africa a benefactress entered into Winston's life. She was Lady Wilton, a close friend of both Lord and Lady Randolph Churchill. It may be surmised that she comprehended the difficulties which Winston's parents had in coping with one whom they regarded as an awkward boy amid their social and political pre-occupations and circumscribed as they were by increasingly limited means—the result of their joint extravagances.

Lady Wilton, who was a daughter of William Russell, nephew of the 5th and 6th Dukes of Bedford, married in 1862 the youngest son of the 2nd Earl of Wilton, who somewhat unexpectedly succeeded as 4th Earl in 1885. He was a rich landowner principally around Manchester. She took Winston under her wing; she was a keen fisherwoman and often asked Winston to stay at her house, The Hatch, near Windsor, on her summer visits to England. She also seems to have tempted him to come and stay with her at her villa Le Nid in the south of France. This project does not seem to have been realized.

Like most boys and indeed most grown-ups Winston was usually short of money. He seems to have been exceptionally extravagant. His parents were somewhat capricious, but on the whole generous; and Winston had at least one regular source of revenue which was unknown to his parents. A typical ending to a letter from Lady Wilton is:

... Enclosed £2 with best love & a kiss

from yr Deputy Mother
Laura Wilton

While Lord Randolph was away in South Africa, Lady Randolph was increasingly caught up in the world of fashion and society, and was more and more surrounded by a competitive band of handsome 'young admirers, of whom the famous Count Kinsky was the most prominent. Winston seems to have resigned himself to seeing little of his mother; but naturally not wishing to feel 'left out of it' on those occasions, like Speech Day, when most boys are visited by their parents, he appealed to her to make other arrangements.

Jack had had mumps, and Winston showed a touching concern for him, which went as far as copying out for Jack's benefit one of Lord Randolph's quite lengthy letters from South Africa—all this, it should be remarked, at a time when the disparity in their ages was probably most marked, for Winston was already sixteen and Jack only eleven.

While Winston was at Brighton and at Harrow there were numerous references in their correspondence to Lady Randolph's 'Concerts'. She was a gifted amateur pianist, good enough to be in demand for charity concerts—and not merely on account of her social position.

Twice in rapid succession, Winston made references to 'Lord's'. The annual cricket match between Eton and Harrow, played early in July at Lord's cricket ground in London, was the occasion for a mid-term holiday. All boys at Harrow were allowed to go to Lord's for the cricket, and nearly all made the most of their opportunity and spent the rest of the holiday at home. Shortly before the 'Lord's' holiday Winston learned that he might be deprived of this treat.

Winston to Lady Randolph

[3 July 1891]   [Harrow]

My darling Mummy,

Please do all you possibly can for me. Think how unhappy I should be being left at Harrow when 90 out of every hundred boys are enjoying themselves. You promised me I should come. It is no special exeat but a regular holiday given in the Summer Term to every boy whose conduct has been such as to merit it. I was terribly frightened when I got your letter this morning. The Possibility of my not being able to come being to my mind entirely out of the question. Could you not ask Grandmamma Marlborough to let me stay with her (at least.)

I managed all right about Speech day (having taken the precaution of writing & of telegraphing). Mummy darling if you knew or had known how much I was looking forward to my 'Lords' I am sure you would have endeavoured to avoid that Engagement, or make some provision for my holiday.

It will be a poor time indeed for me if I have to go to Lords, Friday & Saturday as a Harrow boy & answer my name every 2 hours & not leave the ground etc (as 100 other unfortunates usually have to do).

My darling Mummy I am sure you have not been very much troubled about me this term. I have asked for no visits & I forfeited the pleasure of seeing you on Speech Day therefore I do hope you will endeavour not to disappoint me utterly with regard to July 11th & 12th.

Please do come down in any case on Tuesday [July 7].

I have many things to talk to you about which take so much longer to write than to tell. How is poor little Jack? I have written several times & sent several newspapers & books for him to read but I have recd. no answer; so I conclude he is not well enough to write. I have had Mumps so there is no danger for me.

Where is everybody?

No one has written to me to tell me any news for a long time. Where is Everest. Do try my Darling Mummy to please your

Loving son
WINSTON S. CHURCHILL

Lady Randolph to Winston

Sunday [5 July 1891]   Banstead

Oh! dear oh! dear what an ado!! You silly old boy I did not mean that you would have to remain at Harrow only that I cd not have you here, as I am *really* obliged to go to Stowe on Saturday. But I shall see you on Friday & can arrange something for you. I shall be at Aunt Clara's. Perhaps she can put you up too. I will write & let you know. I believe Jack is all right—so Everest writes—but he has not written to me tho' I sent him some fruit. I had a long letter from Papa in Johannesburg—in very good spirits & health. He sent his best love to you both—I suppose you write to him? The mail leaves Friday night.

Goodbye my darling. Write to Aldford Street [her sister Clara's house] where I go tomorrow.

Your loving
MOTHER

It seems that Winston prevailed.

EXTRACT

11 July [1891]   18 Aldford Street

. . . Winston is here and is sleeping at your mother's as
there is no room here. We spent the day at Lords yesterday
—very hot and tiring and Harrow is getting much the best
of it. Jack is too infectious with the remains of mumps to
be allowed up. They both have good reports, but Welldon
says W should have special help for the French this
summer. I am going to try and find a little governess (ugly)
who wants a holiday. Just to talk and read with him . . . As
you may imagine the whole town is in a ferment about the
German Emperor and Empress . . . The Emperor begins
his day at eight in the Park riding with half a doz ADCs
in uniform and he changes his clothes about five times a
day. Margot Tennant [*who three years later was to marry
Mr H. H. Asquith*] sallied forth yesterday on a prancing
steed determined to make his acquaintance and she did. . . .

The term after Winston had passed his Preliminary
Examination to Sandhurst was comparatively tranquil as
far as the demands made upon him by his masters were
concerned, but in the Summer Term, immediately after the
Lord's exeat, Mr Welldon raised the question of Winston
going abroad during the summer holidays in order to
perfect his languages.

Winston reacted forcibly and unequivocally.

Winston to Lady Randolph

[? 14 July 1891]   [Harrow]

My darling Mummy,

Mr Welldon told me last night that he had written to you
about my going to spend 'at least 4 weeks' in France. His
ideal of course is a 'family' one of his own 'specials'. I told
Papa when he came down that I ought (in Mr W's
opinion) to go, but he said 'utter nonsense, if you like I'll
get a German scullery maid for Banstead'. I'm sure you
would not like me to be away the greater part of the holidays with some horrid French Family. It would be perfectly
—— well unpleasant. Besides practically there is no hurry.
I have very nearly 3 years at the outside limit.

Furthermore Dudley is not going & he has 9 months less
than I. How can you expect me to work all the term & then
go to a filthy den all the holidays.

How frightfully dull it would be. I shouldn't see Jack nor
you, nor Everest at all. Of course it is (as says Welldon)
entirely in your hands. But I am sure you will not send me
to any such abominable drudgery with your free consent.

Even if the worst comes to the worst you could send me
to some of your friends & not to the 'respectable creatures'.
A governess would I am sure answer all the immediate

93

colloquial requirements. As Papa absolutely veto'ed the idea
& as I beg you to let me have a bit of fun.

I remain, Your loving son
WINSTON S. CHURCHILL

P.S. Really I feel less keen about the Army every day. I
think the church would suit me much better. Am well, safe,
& happy. About Fire works ask Count K.

Winston's suggestion of going into the Church does not
appear to have been seriously considered in one way or the
other though he was later briefly to refer in *My Early Life*
to this fugitive idea. Discussing what might have happened
if he had not passed his Army examination, he wrote: 'I
might have gone into the Church and preached orthodox
sermons in a spirit of audacious contradiction to the age'.

'I hope she will turn a deaf ear', wrote Winston to his
father in telling him of Mr Welldon's request. Lady Randolph went to see Mr Welldon and succeeded in persuad-
ing him to compromise at any rate for the summer holidays.
'He thinks', Lady Randolph reported to her husband on
July 24, 'that a good governess will do as well—and I think
so too if I can find the right kind—but if I can't I shall
have to send him away. Welldon gave me an excellent
account of him and said his next report would be very good
and he was most anxious to meet your views and get him to
Sandhurst next year—"a triumph for me and for the
boy". . . .'

A few days later Lady Randolph had changed her mind.
She wrote to Lord Randolph on July 29: 'I am trying to
arrange now to get a French tutor over from Cambridge 3
or 4 times a week and the other days Winston can prepare
lessons. He is quite alive to the necessity of working—he
has improved very much in looks and is quite sensible now'.

It was towards the end of August that Lady Randolph
succeeded in finding 'a rather nice young man from Cambridge'. There is no record as to whether or not the three
weeks of intermittent tutorials benefited Winston. But on
his return to Harrow towards the end of September Mr
Welldon showed that he was not entirely happy.

In that winter term of 1891, just before his seventeenth
birthday, Winston was instructed for his confirmation in the
Church of England.

EXTRACT

6 November 1891

. . . Winston is going in for his Confirmation. Perhaps it will steady him—Welldon wrote that Winston wished to become a candidate—I am afraid only because it will get him off other work ! . . .

We have seen how the term before he had, perhaps somewhat unthinkingly and prematurely, contemplated taking Holy Orders. We have no evidence as to how seriously he viewed the important event of confirmation. Certainly from manhood onward he was not a regular communicant; he was apt to say that what with the daily chapel prayers—twice on Sundays—imposed on him in his youth, he had built up a solid reserve of church attendance in his religious bank and that this, augmented throughout the years by attendances at christenings, marriages, funerals and memorial services, had amply fortified his bank balance. He would often quote with approbation Disraeli's comment that 'all sensible men are of the same religion' and Disraeli's reply when pressed by his interlocutor as to the nature of that religion : 'Sensible men never say'. Winston's first cousin, Sir Shane Leslie, who was ten years younger than he, recalls how after he had become a Roman Catholic in 1908 he had a long talk with Winston 'about religion of the church kind'. He recalled that Winston had said that he 'had been confirmed but Communion he had received once and never again'.

It is of interest that Sir Shane remembers the phrase 'religion of the church kind'. For though Winston was not religious in the literal sense of the word, namely 'being bound', like most serious-minded people he frequently speculated on the mysteries of the universe—why we were here, what we were supposed to be doing and where we were going. Frequently the author heard him say that he thought the reason we were here was to find out why; but that when we did find out, the world would come to an end, as we would have achieved our objective.

* * * * *

Winston's half-term report did not live up to the expectations aroused by the favourable opinion which Mr Welldon had expressed at the beginning of the term.

Reverend J. E. C. Welldon to Lady Randolph

24 November 1891   Harrow

Dear Lady Randolph,
    You will, I hope, forgive me troubling you with one more letter about Winston. It seems to me essential that he should make the best use of his coming holidays. He has worked better this term than before but he is fitful, and he will need all the marks that he can get. If you will let me, I should like to send him to a M. Elmering whose address is

9 Rue de la Ferme
Rouen.

    M. Elmering has had Harrow boys under his care before and has taught them well. Of course I must count upon his being willing to go and upon his working steadily when he is there; for I cannot exercise the same control over him in the holidays as in the term time, and it will be in his power to defeat the project made for his good, unless he is sensible. But I ought to say plainly that his chance of passing his examination for Sandhurst depends upon himself, and, sorry as I am to spoil the pleasure of his holidays, I cannot doubt that I am advising you in his true interest.

Believe me, Sincerely yours
J. E. C. WELLDON

'Welldon makes all the arrangements. I shall have to let him go,' Lady Randolph told Lord Randolph. Winston himself seemed by now conditioned to the idea of having to go abroad : 'But let me beg you', he wrote to his mother, 'No Family! No Family! Ugh!' There then began a long struggle over the next three weeks in which Winston showed himself a tenacious but unsuccessful fighter. 'I beg and Pray that you will not send me to a vile, nasty, fusty, beastly French "Family".' He was allowed to go to London for the wedding of his Aunt Sarah to Captain Gordon Chesney Wilson, but he had to return to Harrow almost immediately. 'It was very "bad luck" having to go just as the fun was commencing,' he wrote to his mother on November 22. 'It is still worse having to look forward to such a time as you and Welldon seem to be planning out for me next Christmas.' It appears that at least Winston, through Lady Randolph, had persuaded Mr Welldon to drop the Rouen 'family', for it was arranged that Winston should stay at the Versailles home of one of the French masters at Harrow, M. Minssen. But then arose the question—when should Winston go? Mr Welldon wanted him to lose no time in getting to France after term had ended. This meant spending Christmas away from home.

Winston to Lady Randolph

[? 6 December 1891]   [Harrow]

My darling Mama,
I had written a long letter to you but on second thoughts I decided not to send it. I hear Papa will be nearly a fortnight later coming back. Mr Welldon is in consequence very keen on my going to Paris straight from here. Darling Mummy, I shall think it will be very unkind and unnatural of you if you allow him to do me out of my Christmas. Out of all this school not 5 boys are going away at all and I believe Dudley is the only one who goes before Christmas.

Please dont *you* put pressure on me. Welldon got very angry last night when I told him I couldn't give up coming home. He said 'very well then you must give up the Army.' That is all nonsense. But Mummy don't be unkind and make me unhappy. I have firmly made up my mind not to go abroad till after the 27th. If you in spite of my entreaties force me to go I will do as little as I can and the holidays will be one continual battle. I am sure Papa would not turn me away from home at Christmas or indeed at any time. If you do all you possibly can to make things nice for me I will go after the 27th and return so as to have 4 days with Papa.

Please don't be unkind
Ever your loving son
Winston S. Churchill

Lady Randolph to Winston

Tuesday [? 8 December 1891]   London

Dearest Winston,

I was beginning to wonder why you had not written. My dear boy, I feel for you in every way & can quite understand your anxiety & desire to be at home for Xmas, but quite apart from other considerations, the tone of your letter is not calculated to make one over lenient. When one wants something in this world, it is not by delivering ultimatums that one is likely to get it. You are old enough not to play the fool, & for the sake of a few days pleasure, give up the chance of getting through yr exam : a thing which may affect your whole life. You can be quite certain my darling that I will decide for what is best, but I tell you frankly that *I* am going to decide not *you*. If you have to go, I shall see if it is possible to make it up to you in another way. I *count* on you helping me & not making a useless fuss. I will let you know what train I come by Thursday—until then bless you & work so that Papa may see a good report.

Yr loving
Mother

[? 9 December 1891]   [Harrow]

My darling Mamma,
    You say it is for you to decide. I am required to give up
my holidays—not you, I am forced to go to people who
bore me excessively—not you. You were asked to give up
a short part of the year to take me abroad—you promised
—refused & I did not press the point.
    I am very much surprised and pained to think that both
you & Papa should treat me so, as a machine. I should like
to know if Papa was asked to 'give up his holidays' when he
was at Eton.
    You blame me for being frank to you. You say that 'if I
want to gain my point, other methods than those dictated
by honour and honesty should be used.'
    Please do come down on Thursday, if possible for lunch
because if you come by the 3.30 & leave by the 4.37 it
does not give very much time.
    Please do have a little regard for my happiness. There
are other and higher things in this world than learning,
more powerful agents than the Civil Service Commissioners.

                              With Love & kisses I remain
                                     Ever your loving son
                              W I N S T O N   S.   C H U R C H I L L

    Lady Randolph went down to Harrow to pacify Winston
but then a new difficulty arose. To go to France on Monday, December 21, Winston would have to leave Harrow
before the end of term. When would Mr Welldon allow
him to come home?

                         Winston to Lady Randolph

[? 13 December 1891]   [Harrow]

My darling Mummy,
    I am afraid by your not answering my letter that you
are angry with me. I hope this is not so. If you want me

to go to France next holidays very much I suppose I shall have to go, but I can't help feeling very unhappy about it.

You will see that beggar won't let me out of his clutches much.

Do please write to Mr. Welldon and ask that I may be allowed to come home on the Friday night. It would mean a great deal to me. The difference of 1 night in 3 days holiday is most noticeable.

I am awfully low about it. First feeling I won't go & then that I must.

Woomany tells me that you were trying to make arrangements with Baron H. [Hirsch] for me. I expect this little French brute will spoil it all.

—— Welldon; he is the cause of all my misfortunes but for him I should be looking forward to as nice a holiday, & as merry a Christmas as I have ever had.

> Goodbye my darling Mummy,
> With much love & many kisses
> I remain, Ever your loving son
> WINSTON S. CHURCHILL

Lady Randolph to Winston

Tuesday [? 15 December 1891]   2 Connaught Place

Dearest Winston,

I have only read one page of yr letter and I send it back to you—as its style does not please me. I confess after our conversation the other day I did not expect you to go back on yr word, & try & make everything as disagreeable for yrself & everyone else as possible. My dear you won't gain anything by taking this line. Everything that I can do for you to make things as smooth & palatable as possible I will do—more I cannot promise. I don't think I can write to Mr Welldon again—but you can ask him to let you come Friday—& say that I shd be very glad if he wd let you.

> Yr loving
> MOTHER

Write to me a nice letter!

[? 17th December 1891]   [Harrow]

[*At the top of this letter Winston wrote: 'P.S. I send the other letter back that you may peruse it.' He then crossed it out.*]

My darling Mummy,
   Never would I have believed that you would have been so unkind. I am utterly miserable. That you should refuse to read my letter is most painful to me. There was nothing in it to give you grounds for rejecting it. I am glad however that I waited 3 hours before answering or I would have sent you something that would have startled you. I can't tell you how wretched you have made me feel—instead of doing everything to make me happy you go and cut the ground away from under my feet like that. Oh my Mummy!
   I made up my mind I would write no letter to you of any length in future as in my letters length I can perceive a [reason] for your not reading it. I expect you were too busy with your parties and arrangements for Christmas. I comfort myself by this. As to the style—it was rather good. A letter of mine to the Harrovian has recently been accepted & pronounced good.

IMPORTANT
READ THIS

I have got to tell you that the Frenchman wants to know what time he can come & see you on Friday. Please let me know by return of post, or tell Everest to if you feel very 'spiteful.'
   Darling Mummy—I am so unhappy but if you don't read this letter it will be the last you'll have the trouble to send back. I think you might keep your promise to me & write to W. [Welldon] Likely he'd let me go isn't it? (on my own recommendation).
   If you don't—I refuse to go to Paris till Tuesday though you will probably be so unkind that I shall be glad to get away.
   I am more unhappy than I can possibly say. Your un-

kindness has relieved me however from all feelings of duty. I too can forget. Darling Mamma if you want me to do anything for you, especially so great a sacrifice don't be so cruel to

Your loving son
WINNY

Winston to Lady Randolph

[? 18 December 1891]   [Harrow]

My darling Mummy,

Welldon whom I have just seen says 'I am going to let you go home for the Sunday and that's all.' He says one thing to you, but quite another to me. If he doesn't let me come home till Sat. I do hope you will let me have 2 or 3 more days. Darling Mummy, do attend to my letter. I am so wretched. Even now I weep. Please my darling Mummy be kind to your loving son. Don't let my silly letters make you angry. Let me at least think that you love me.—Darling Mummy I despair. I am so wretched. I don't know what to do. Don't be angry I am so miserable.

Please don't expect me to go on Monday if he doesn't let me come till then. Oh how I wish I had not believed him. How I have been tricked. I don't know what to do. Do please write something kind to me. I am very sorry if I have 'riled' you before I did only want to explain things from my point of view.

Good Bye my darling Mummy.
With best love I remain, Ever your loving son
WINSTON

For a boy of just seventeen Winston had fought a staunch rearguard action, but he was beaten. Authority, personified by his mother and the headmaster, prevailed:

Reverend J. E. C. Welldon to Lady Randolph

[Friday] 18 December 1891   [Harrow]

Dear Lady Randolph,

I am afraid Winston cannot leave School until tomorrow, but he shall come to you early then. Mr Minssen, who has received an invitation from Winston, is anxious to see you and would like to call upon you tomorrow at 12, if that were a convenient time for you. He would prefer tomorrow to Monday as he may wish to have some conversation with me after seeing you.

I have had two conversations with Mr Minssen and I shall talk to Winston once more today.

The arrangement seems eminently satisfactory. I am confident that Mr Minssen will be kind, careful and considerate but much depends upon Winston himself. Mr Minssen will do everything for him, if he is docile and industrious; but he will not let him waste his time and, if he is idle, he must be sent home.

It is, I think, essential that he should not accept invitations to any family where he will speak English, I want him to make as much progress as possible in French conversation.

He tells me Baron Hirsch's sons, with whom he hopes to ride speak English fluently; but if that were so, it would be a loss to him to be much with them. Mr Minssen will probably ask you not to let him accept more than three invitations a week, and it is clearly bad for him to be out alone at night. Mr Minssen will, if you wish, supply him with such pocket money as is necessary. It is, I fear, somewhat of an intrusion for me to enter into these details; but my excuse is that I have set my heart upon his passing into Sandhurst and he has no time to lose.

I fully believe he will go in a sensible and right spirit.

Sincerely yours
J. E. C. WELLDON

P.S. Just as I finished writing this letter, Winston came in to say you had asked to see Mr Minssen to-day.

Lady Randolph to Lord Randolph
(Blenheim Papers)

EXTRACT

[? 18 December 1891]   2 Connaught Place

. . . Winston comes home tomorrow and on Monday goes to Versailles. He starts with the French Master of Harrow with whose parents he is to stay. Mr Welldon has arranged all.

I can't tell you what trouble I have had with Winston this last fortnight he has bombarded me with letters, cursing his fate and everyone. Of course it is a great disappointment to him not being home for Xmas but he makes as much fuss as tho' he were going to Australia for 2 years. Welldon insisted on his going at once, otherwise he wd not have time enough there to derive any benefit from it.

I have just seen Mr Minssen the tutor in whose family he is going and I think I have arranged everything satisfactorily. . . .

Throughout those tempestuous weeks Mrs Everest, as always, tried to be a calming, comforting influence. 'If you have to go to France without coming home I will send or bring your big tweed coat & some Fine Flannel Shirts for you to sleep in those you wore at Banstead.'

Winston to Lady Randolph

Tuesday evening after post   18 Rue de Provence
[22 December 1891]   [Versailles]

My darling Mummy,

Fatigue, the passage, The strange food, The cold, home sickness, the thoughts of what was behind & what was before nearly caused me to write a letter which would have been painful to you. Now I am better & I think that I will wait here my month though not one day more. Today we went to the 'Bon Marché' in Paris. We spent 3 hours there. I bought a present for you, a blotting pad which I hope will give you as much pleasure to receive & it has me to buy; and for Jack I purchased something too, Also a 'Sachée' for Everest.

The food is very queer, But there is plenty, & on the whole it is good. There is wine & beer to drink. I have a room to myself but it is awfully cold. However with rugs overcoats, dressing gowns etc I managed to sleep.

Tomorrow I am going to ride, in my boots.

I have already made great progress in French. M. Minssen says I know far more than he thought I did. These people are very kind. Of course I would give much to return, if you wish it I will come tomorrow—but considering all things I am prepared to stay my month.

I don't know how to get to see Baron Hirsch I am afraid you have not written. I would like very much to go and see them.

If you cannot get skates made to fit me—send me a line to the effect that you wish me to have them and are willing.

Goodbye my darling Mummy
Read this to Jack
With love I remain Your loving son
WINSTON

Winston to Lady Randolph

Tuesday [29 December 1891] 11 o'clock   [Versailles]

My dear Mamma,

It seems to me that with you 'out of sight and out of mind' indeed. Not a line from anybody. You promised to write 3 times a week—I have recd 1 letter. There seems to be something wrong in the Postal arrangements between France & England as between Africa & London.

It is not at all kind of you, and, my darling Mummy, I am very unhappy about it. This is the 3rd letter I have written to you. I have also sent 2 to Jack and 3 to Everest. I wish you would try my mummy to fulfill your promise. Baron Hirsch may be in Jericho for all I know.

Please do something for
Your loving son
WINSTON S. CHURCHILL

The same day Mrs Everest wrote to express her delight at the sachet, which she had just received. As always she was solicitous about Winston's health. 'If you feel sick or feverish or stomach out of order get a Bottle of Eno fruit salt & take a tea spoon full in water. I should buy plenty of fruit & eat if I were you keep you *regular you know dear.*'

On 1 January 1892 the Marquis de Breteuil sent Winston a charming invitation asking him to propose himself any day for luncheon. Baron Hirsch also responded to Lady Randolph's instructions to write to Winston.

Winston to Lady Randolph

[? 13 January 1892]   [Versailles]

My darling Mummy,

Il faut que je vous explique quelque choses. You addressed your letter to me a Paris. Result sent back and again forwarded by Edney. I had not recd. a letter from you for a fortnight when it arrived.

I have had lots of invitations. Last Monday I went to M. de B. and B. Hirsch after. He took me to the morgue. I was much interested. Only 3 Macabres—not a good bag. It is freezing hard and I am going skating this afternoon. I make much progress and Minnsen and I get on capitally.

I want either to come home Monday and see Jack and go on to France with you and Papa or—to wait here for Papa. I don't mind much which only you might easily bring Jack here too; But I am of course counting, my Mummy, on you to fulfil your promise which was more than anything the reason of my coming here willingly.

I must remind you it was a regular promise. I am willing and happy to leave all in your hands only I do hope . . .

I have written to Papa. Please write to me by return of post.
Winston S. Churchill,
    18 Rue de Provence,
        Versailles,
            France.

                    With love and kisses I remain, Your loving son
                                                    WINNY

Lord Randolph to Winston

15 January 1892   2 Connaught Place

Dearest Winston,

I was very glad to get your letter this morning. I think I will not try and get you an extra week because really every moment is of value to you now before you go up for your examination in June. The loss of a week now may mean your not passing, which I am sure you will admit would be very discreditable & disadvantageous. After you have got into the army you will have many weeks for amusement and idleness should your inclinations go in that direction, but now I do pray you my dear boy to make the most of every hour of your time so as to render your passing a certainty.

I remember when I was going up at Oxford for 'final schools' I took something of an extra week & consequently altogether neglected what was called 'special subjects'. The result was that I just missed the First Class degree and only took a Second, & I have often thought since what a fool I was to lose the chance of a First for a few hours or days amusement. If you return Monday as I understand you will, we shall have a few days together before you return to Harrow, and after that the Easter holidays will soon be upon us, tho I must say I hope you will work like a little dray horse right up to the summer examination, only about four months off.

Your mother and I have just come back from Penn, Lord & Lady Howe's place where there was to have been a party for the Prince of Wales. Of course he could not come on account of the illness of the Duke of Clarence, & the party was broken up by the death of the poor Duke one of the saddest events I have ever known. Our party was naturally gloomy & dull. I shall stay on in London now and not go to Paris till Saturday week at the earliest. I think you must have had a novel & not unpleasant experience staying at Versailles. Hoping to see you back all safe Monday

> Believe me ever Your most affte father
> RANDOLPH S. C.

There was nothing Lady Randolph could do. 'Papa showed me his letter to you,' she wrote to Winston on the same day. 'He won't hear of yr asking for extra week. I am very sorry—but if you come home Monday you will have nearly a fortnight at home'.

The Summer term of 1892 was devoted to working for the Entrance Examination to Sandhurst—the 'Further' as distinct from the Preliminary Examination which Winston had passed in the winter of 1890. The Examination took place in July and in the middle of August Winston learned the result. He had failed. Out of 693 candidates he was 390th scoring 5100 marks; the minimum, at this Examination, for entrance into the Cavalry was 6457 and into the Infantry 6654.

Mr Louis Moriarty the Army Class tutor, to whom, Winston later acknowledged, he owed a great deal, sought to comfort him :

Louis Moriarty to Winston

EXTRACT

23 August 1892   [Harrow]

. . . I think your marks & place very creditable for your first try, and I think you will remember that I had estimated the marks at less. If you work earnestly & sensibly & above all keep it up through the term I think you will pass all right this winter. But remember that it is by no means a certainty, 1500 marks are a good deal to make in about 3 months. (The Exam is on 20th Nov I think) Lang who was only about 100 places out last December, & who since then had been working all day at Wren's, has failed I see. I think he would have been more likely to pass from here, as I am sure they over-crammed him. I am glad you are going to cram up your Euclid—there are marks to be made in that and I feel sure that your history might be more accurate, but I wish you were reading a few French novels (with a dictionary, & notebook for new words.) One can learn a lot of French like that, without apparent effort. . . .

Mr Welldon, however, was less pleased :

Reverend J. E. C. Welldon to Winston

10 September 1892   [Harrow]

My dear Churchill,

Thank you for sending me your marks, which have just

reached me. I shall have something to say to you about them when we meet. But I feel it to be essential that in coming back to school you should come resolved to work not by fits & starts but with regular persistent industry.

The grammatical foundation of your languages is so uncertain that you lose marks which other boys gain. You have therefore ground to make up as well as new ground to cover.

If I did not think you would be sensible I should wire your father to take you away from Harrow now and send you to a 'coach'. But all depends on yourself.

Sincerely yours
J. E. C. WELLDON

And Lord Randolph was also displeased :

Lord Randolph to Frances, Duchess of Marlborough

EXTRACT

[? September 1892]   Banstead

. . . I don't think Winston did particularly well in the army examination. He was 300 places off the successful candidates 1500 marks less than the lowest successful & 700 marks less than Dudley M. However he has had two vy kind and encouraging letters from his army class tutor & his mathematical master. His next try is on Nov 24th. If he fails again I shall think about putting him in business. I could get him something very good either through Natty [Rothschild] or Horace [Farquharson] or Cassel. . . .

At this time Lord and Lady Randolph with their family and servants moved to 50 Grosvenor Square and doubled up with Duchess Fanny. Both families were feeling the pinch. Lord Randolph had left 2 Connaught Place during the summer of 1892 and he gave up Banstead in October.

In September Winston returned to Harrow for what was to be his last term. Older boys at Harrow were, like the boys at Eton, allowed to have their own room but those who had brothers there could share a room with them.

Winston to Lady Randolph

[? September 1892]   [Harrow]

Dear Mamma,

We are now quite settled down. The room is very beautiful. We purchased in London sufficiency of ornaments to make it look simply magnificent.

Papa has written to Jack & says that you are better for the change. I rejoice.

I got my remove & when you come down to Harrow you will see yours truly in 'Tails'. Jack is getting on capitally though I think he finds he has plenty of work to do & that is rather hard.

One of our hampers was spoiled 'in trasitu' owing to the careless manner in which it was packed.

There is of course no more news except that we both send our love & I remain

Your loving son
WINSTON S. CHURCHILL

P.S. I hope you can read this & if so I hope you will not read it out for the amusement of those staying at Invermark. W S C

Lady Randolph was on her annual autumn round of the houses of her friends and relations in Scotland; but when she returned to London early in October she became gravely ill:

Lord Randolph to Winston

25 October 1892   50 Grosvenor Square

Dearest Winston & Jack,

Your dear mother was extremely ill yesterday & we were rather alarmed. But thank God to-day there is an improvement & the doctors are vy hopeful. I only got up to town this evening. I will keep you informed as to how yr dear mother progresses.

You will have heard of the very sad death of your poor Uncle Roxburgh who taken vy ill last Monday had to undergo an operation Saturday to which he succumbed.

You did not know him much but I was vy much attached to him & my poor sister Annie is quite heartbroken. Troubles accumulate just now. I pray you try & concentrate your thoughts on your work. Your mother would be in such good spirits if she thought you were going to do real well in yr examination. Kiss Jack for me.

Ever your affte father
RANDOLPH S. C.

In fact Lady Randolph had been very unwell for at least two weeks before Lord Randolph wrote this letter. It seems that she was suffering from a form of peritonitis for which at that time surgery was not recommended—the first well-known case for removal of the appendix was ten years later when King Edward VII was the patient. Lord Randolph was all this time in Scotland but an alarming letter from Dr Roose had brought him home to London in the third week of October.

These alarms came just as Winston was finishing his preparation for his second attempt at the Entrance Examination which took place late in November at the time of his eighteenth birthday.

The legend, partly fostered by himself, that Winston was a preternaturally stupid little boy has doubtless encouraged habits of indolence in many generations of other schoolboys, and has no doubt often afforded some solace to their parents. We have seen enough of his work to denounce this legend as false. He was not stupid; indeed he early showed originality of mind. He was obstinate, rebellious and mischievous. No one could make him do or learn anything against his will. Unthinking schoolmasters found it easier to write him off as stupid than to scrutinize and adapt their own methods. Yet, despite his ostensible failure at school, these unhappy years were far from wasted. His parents kept him at a distance and this, combined with his mutinous outlook at school, early compelled him to stand on his own feet and to make his way in the world by his own exertions and by his own methods. He had to fight every inch of his road through life; nothing came easily to him, not even oratory and writing, in which he was later to excel. To achieve success he had to develop that intense power of concentration which, as it grew, was to serve him and his fellow countrymen so well. In later life he was fond of quoting Napoleon's phrase : *L'art de fixer les objets long-temps sans être fatigué.* This priceless gift was perhaps intuitive to Napoleon—but it had to be remorselessly mastered by Winston. Nonetheless history may decide that he ultimately exercised this mental power as abundantly as did Napoleon.

6

SANDHURST

ON ABOUT 20 JANUARY 1893, Winston heard that he had
failed in his 'Further' Examination for Sandhurst for the
second time. On this occasion he came 203rd out of 664
candidates with 6106 marks, compared with 5100 at his
previous attempt.

To Winston Welldon wrote:

Reverend J. E. C. Welldon to Winston

23 January 1893   Harrow

My dear Churchill,

I am very much obliged to you for sending me the telegram. It seems to me to bear out what I have ventured to
say to your father and yourself, *viz* that you would have
passed or would have been on the borderline of passing, if
the standard of marks had remained what it was two years
ago, and that, if you make the same progress in the next six
months as you made in the last your passing is assured.
That is in my opinion not an unsatisfactory result; only,
if you are going up again, do let me beg you to begin work
at once and to carry it on with the greatest energy and
regularity. I wish I had got you here.

Sincerely Yours
J. E. C. WELLDON

But Winston had left Harrow, and it was decided that
he should go to Captain James's establishment.

5 Lexham Gardens
London W.

28 January 1893

My Lord,

I shall be very happy to receive your son and should be pleased to see you at 12.30 on Monday next.

Yours faithfully
WALTER H. JAMES

Before these arrangements could be implemented, however, Winston first had to recover from an accident in which he came near to killing himself in a reckless escapade on January 10, at his aunt Cornelia's place, Canford, at Branksome Dene, near Bournemouth.

Winston later provided a full account in *My Early Life*:

My Aunt, Lady Wimborne, had lent us her comfortable estate at Bournemouth for the winter. Forty or fifty acres of pine forest descended by sandy undulations terminating in cliffs to the smooth beach of the English Channel. It was a small, wild place and through the middle there fell to the sea level a deep cleft called a 'chine'. Across this 'chine' a rustic bridge nearly 50 yards long had been thrown. I was just 18 and on my holidays. My younger brother aged 12, and a cousin aged 14, proposed to chase me. After I had been hunted for twenty minutes and was rather short of breath, I decided to cross the bridge. Arrived at its centre I saw to my consternation that the pursuers had divided their forces. One stood at each end of the bridge; capture seemed certain. But in a flash there came across me a great project. The chine which the bridge spanned was full of young fir trees. Their slender tops reached to the level of the footway. 'Would it not,' I asked myself, 'be possible to leap on to one of them and slip down the pole-like stem, breaking off each tier of branches as one descended until the fall was broken?' I looked at it. I computed it. I meditated. Meanwhile I climbed over the

114

balustrade. My young pursuers stood wonderstruck at either end of the bridge. To plunge or not to plunge, that was the question! In a second I had plunged, throwing out my arms to embrace the summit of the fir tree. The argument was correct; the data were absolutely wrong. It was three days before I regained consciousness and more than three months before I crawled from my bed. The measured fall was 29 feet on to hard ground. But no doubt the branches helped. My mother, summoned by the alarming message of the children, 'He jumped over the bridge and he won't speak to us,' hurried down with energetic air and inopportune brandy. It was an axiom with my parents that in serious accident or illness the highest medical aid should be invoked, regardless of cost. Eminent specialists stood about my bed. Later on when I could understand again, I was shocked and also flattered to hear of the enormous fees they had been paid. My father travelled over at full express from Dublin where he had been spending his Christmas at one of old Lord [Justice] Fitzgibbon's once-celebrated parties. He brought the greatest of London's surgeons with him. I had among other injuries a ruptured kidney. It is to the surgeon's art and to my own pronounced will-to-live that the reader is indebted for this story. But for a year I looked at life round a corner. They made a joke about it in those days at the Carlton Club, 'I hear Randolph's son met with a serious accident,' 'Yes?' 'Playing a game of "Follow my Leader" '—'Well, Randolph is not likely to come to grief in that way!'

In this account Winston, as will emerge, had somewhat exaggerated the length of his convalescence. In fact he was able to go back to work in less than two months. One feels too, from this account, that his decision to jump from the bridge may have been influenced by Macaulay's lines of brave Horatius, which he had memorized at Harrow nearly five years before.

Winston did not arrive at James's until the end of February. Immediately he seems to have come into conflict with authority:

7 March 1893   5 Lexham Gardens

Dear Lord Randolph,

I have issued orders for your son to be kept at work and that in future he is to do the full hours. I had to speak to him the other day about his casual manner. I think the boy means well but he is distinctly inclined to be inattentive and to think too much of his abilities. These are certainly good and if he do as he ought he should pass very well in the summer, but he has been rather too much inclined up to the present to teach his instructors instead of endeavouring to learn from them, and this is not the frame of mind conducive to success. I may give as an instance that he suggested to me that his knowledge of history was such that he did not want any more teaching in it! I think you will agree with me that this is problematical. I have no doubt that between the two of us we can manage him well enough and I am glad to have received your letter of today.

I am sorry that I cannot see him personally as I am confined to my room with a bad cold on my chest but he will be spoken to and I shall let you know how he gets on.

The boy has very many good points in him but what he wants is very firm handling.

Yours very truly
WALTER H. JAMES

My Early Life recorded the methods used at this 'crammer's' establishment:

It was said that no one who was not a congenital idiot could avoid passing thence into the Army. The Firm had made a scientific study of the mentality of the Civil Service Commissioners. They knew with almost Papal infallibility the sort of questions which that sort of person would be bound on the average to ask on any of the selected subjects. They specialised on these questions and on the answering of them. They fired a large number of efficient shot-guns into the brown of the covey, and they claimed a high and steady average of birds. Captain James—if he had known it—was really the ingenious forerunner of the inventors of the artillery barrages of the Great War. He fired from carefully selected positions upon the areas which he knew must be tenanted by large bodies of enemy troops. He had only to fire a given number of shells per acre per hour to get his bag. He did not need to see the enemy soldiers. Drill was all he had to teach his gunners. Thus year by year for at least two decades he held the Blue Ribbon among the Crammers. He was like one of those people who have a sure system for breaking the Bank of Monte Carlo, with the important difference that in a great majority of cases his system produced success. Even the very hardest cases could be handled. No absolute guarantee was given, but there would always be far more than a sporting chance.

Towards the end of June Winston sat for the Sandhurst Entrance Examination for the third time. On this occasion he was successful—but only just. He came 95th out of 389, four places and 18 marks too low to gain an infantry cadetship, but enough for a cavalry cadetship.

Winston received the news of his success just as he was about to leave England for a walking tour in Switzerland with his brother and a tutor, Mr J. D. G. Little, a young master from Eton.

Fortified by what he regarded as a scholastic triumph Winston wrote a somewhat insouciant letter to his father.

Winston to Lord Randolph
(Blenheim Papers)

6 August [1893]   Schweizerhof Hotel
                                                      Lucerne

Dear Papa,

    I was so glad to be able to send you good news on Thursday. I did not expect that the list would be published so soon & was starting off in the train, when Little congratulated me on getting in. I looked in the paper and

117

found this to be true. Several boys I know very well have got in too.

At Dover I sent off a lot of telegrams, and on the boat I received one from Grandmamma telling me I had passed.

We had a very rough crossing & poor Jack was very sick. At Calais we secured an empty first class carriage & travelled very comfortably to Amiens where 5 horrid people got in & stayed with us all night—till we got to Bale. Very uncomfortable it was—8 people in one carriage.

We changed carriages at Bale & came on here in a coupé.

This is a splendid hotel—lifts, electric light, & fireworks (every Saturday). Tomorrow we are going away to Andermatt where our address will be . . . Hotel Bellevue Andermatt. We leave here on the 9th. Lucerne is a lovely place. There are excellent swimming baths, & good food, & magnificent scenery. Yesterday we went up Pilatus, which was very interesting, & came down by the mountain Railway to Alpnack & so home by steamer. I had a telegram from Duchess Lily saying that she was going to look out for a good horse for me when I return. . . Also a letter.

* * * * *

I like Mr Little very much. He is unfortunately very lame, but is getting better slowly.

Miss Welldon is here with her husband a Harrow master named Stephen. She was married 3 days ago & this is the honeymoon. I talk lots of French to the waiters etc. Altogether we are enjoying ourselves immensely & I should be very sorry to come back if I were not going to Sandhurst.

Hoping that you are quite well & that the waters suit you

I remain your ever loving son
WINSTON S. C.

P.S. If you have time to write to us write to Hotel des Couronnes, Brigue.

This letter drew upon him one of the most formidable rebukes of Lord Randolph that survive; a short holograph extract is first reproduced:

9 August 1893   Kissingen

My dear Winston   I am rather surprised at your tone of exultation over your inclusion in the Sandhurst list. There are two ways of winning in an examination one creditable the other the reverse. You have unfortunately chosen the latter method, and appear to be much pleased with you

My dear Winston,

I am rather surprised at your tone of exultation over your inclusion in the Sandhurst list. There are two ways of winning an examination, one creditable the other the reverse. You have unfortunately chosen the latter method, and appear to be much pleased with your success.

The first extremely discreditable feature of your performance was missing the infantry, for in that failure is demonstrated beyond refutation your slovenly happy-go-lucky harum scarum style of work for which you have always been distinguished at your different schools. Never have I received a really good report of your conduct in your work from any master or tutor you had from time to time to do with. Always behind-hand, never advancing in your class, incessant complaints of total want of application, and this character which was constant in yr reports has shown the natural results clearly in your last army examination.

The second discreditable fact in the result of your examination is that you have not perceptibly increased as far as my memory serves me the marks you made in the examination, & perhaps even you have decreased them, in spite of there being less competition in the last than in the former examination. You frequently told me you were sure to obtain 7000 marks. Alas! your estimate of your capacity was, measured arithmetically, some seven hundred marks deficient. You say in your letter there were many candidates who succeeded whom you knew; I must remind you that you had very few below you some seven or eight. You may find some consolation in the fact that you have failed to get into the '60th Rifles' one of the finest regiments in the army. There is also another satisfaction for you that by accomplishing the prodigious effort of getting into the Cavalry, you imposed on me an extra charge of some £200 a year. Not that I shall allow you to remain in the Cavalry. As soon as possible I shall arrange your exchange into an infantry regiment of the line.

Now it is a good thing to put this business vy plainly before you. Do not think I am going to take the trouble of writing to you long letters after every folly & failure you commit & undergo. I shall not write again on these matters & you need not trouble to write any answer to this part of my letter, because I no longer attach the slightest weight to anything you may say about your own acquirements & exploits. Make this position indelibly impressed on your mind, that if your conduct and action at Sandhurst is similar to what it has been in the other establishments in which it has sought vainly to impart to you some education. Then that my responsibility for you is over.

I shall leave you to depend on yourself giving you merely such assistance as may be necessary to permit of a respectable life. Because I am certain that if you cannot prevent yourself from leading the idle useless unprofitable life you have had during your schooldays & later months, you will become a mere social wastrel one of the hundreds of the public school failures, and you will degenerate into a shabby unhappy & futile existence. If that is so you will have to bear all the blame for such misfortunes yourself. Your own conscience will enable you to recall and enumerate all the efforts that have been made to give you the best of chances which you were entitled to by your position & how you have practically neglected them all.

I hope you will be the better for your trip. You must apply to Capt James for advice as to your Sandhurst equipment. Your mother sends her love.

Your affte father
RANDOLPH S. C.

Lord Randolph had less than eighteen months to live. His performances alike in private and public were already causing deep concern to his friends and family. He was in the grip of the progressive mental paralysis from which he was to die. The shadows were closing very quickly around him. On his return to England in the autumn he embarked on another programme of political speeches up and down the country. But it was a pathetic tour : his son recalled how 'the crowds who were drawn by the old glamour of his name departed sorrowful and shuddering at the spectacle of a dying man, and those who loved him were consumed with embarrassment and grief.'

Mr Little, in a letter to Lord Randolph, gives some idea of the effect of Lord Randolph's letter on Winston :

J. D. G. Little to Lord Randolph
(Blenheim Papers)

EXTRACT

19 August [1893]   Hotel de Zermatt
                                   Zermatt

. . . Your letter to Winston arrived while we were at Milan. I had not of course received your letter to myself. When he showed me your letter, we had a long talk and he told me a good deal about his views of men and things. He was a good deal depressed; I pointed out to him that in going to Sandhurst he began, what was practically a new page in his Life; and that such opportunities were a completely new start, occurred at most but once or twice in a lifetime, and ought therefore to be made the most of. Whatever he did at Sandhurst would have a permanent effect on his career in the army, and he ought therefore to make a sustained effort for the next year and a half to do his best, and pass out high. I think he intends to try hard. . . .

Mr Little had been recommended to Lord Randolph by his old Merton contemporary (and opponent at Woodstock) George Brodrick, from whom he received the highest recommendation—'He is a thorough gentleman and anything but a Don.' Both Mr Little and Winston sent detailed accounts of their holiday to Lord and Lady Randolph who were at Kissingen for the cure. Winston did not, however, tell either his tutor or his father of the narrow escape he had from drowning while on the lake near Lausanne. It is related in *My Early Life*. He rowed out with another boy a mile from the shore; they took off their clothes and went swimming. Suddenly a breeze sprang up and it was only with the utmost difficulty that Winston managed to regain the boat and row back for his companion. He had seen Death, he recalled later, 'as near as I believe I have ever seen him. He was swimming in the water, whispering from time to time in the rising wind . . .'

On his arrival in London he found that because a number of other aspirants had failed to take up their cadetships to Sandhurst that year, he had after all been given the opportunity of going into the Infantry.

*   *   *   *   *

The Royal Military College was founded in 1802 and ten years later it was established on its present site near the village of Sandhurst, some thirty miles from London on the main Portsmouth road. About 120 young men were accepted for cadetships every half year, and when Winston was there the course consisted of three terms spread over 16 months. The college was divided into six companies each under the command of an officer-instructor. Winston's E Company, was commanded by Major Oswald James Henry Ball of the Welsh Regiment. The commandant, or Governor as he was then known, had arrived at Sandhurst at the same time as Winston. He was Major-General Cecil James East. Unlike Major Ball, who had the misfortune of never having seen active service, General East had been present at the siege of Sevastopol and had taken part in the fighting in the Indian Mutiny in which he was severely wounded. The cadets themselves received promotion while they were at the college, each company having a quota of under-officers, senior corporals and corporals. They wore a uniform of blue serge, and for full dress, one of scarlet and gold. A number of changes were made at Sandhurst around the time Winston was there. Musketry became a compulsory subject—one in which Winston was to persevere after he had obtained his commission; polo, on the other hand, was soon to be abolished on the grounds of expense. The Visitors who reported on the college in 1893 complained of 'great laxity in collecting the mess bills of the college'; the consequent reforms more than once led Winston into financial embarrassment.

* * * * *

Though his mind by this time was clouded Lord Randolph seemed to show more understanding of Winston's latent interests and ambitions. In *My Early Life* the son was to give a sympathetic account of his father's treatment of him at this time:

> Once I became a gentleman cadet I acquired a new status in my father's eyes. I was entitled when on leave to go about with him, if it was not inconvenient. He was always amused by acrobats, jugglers, and performing animals, and it was with him that I first visited the Empire Theatre. He took me also to important political parties at Lord Rothschild's house at Tring, where most of the leaders and a selection of the rising men of the Conservative Party were often assembled. He began to take me also to stay with his racing friends; and here we had a different company and new topics of conversation which proved equally entertaining. In fact to me he seemed to own the key to everything or almost everything worth having. But if ever I began to show the slightest idea of comradeship, he was immediately offended; and when once I suggested that I might help his private secretary to write some of his letters, he froze me into stone. I know now that this would have been only a passing phase. Had he lived another four or five years, he could not have done without me. But there were no four or five years! Just as friendly relations were ripen-

123

ing into an Entente, and an alliance or at least a military agreement seemed to my mind not beyond the bounds of reasonable behaviour, he vanished for ever.

At this time the financial embarrassments with which

Lord and Lady Randolph were much afflicted combined with difficulties inseparable from 'doubling up' with relations, even in Grosvenor Square with Duchess Fanny, who herself was not very well off, resulted in what one must be inclined to regard as the rather shabby treatment of Mrs Everest. This provoked an honourable and intrepid reaction from Winston. It should, however, in justice to Duchess Fanny and Lord and Lady Randolph, be pointed out that Winston cannot have known of the financial difficulties which explained, if they do not excuse, what seems on the face of it to have been a particularly thoughtless action :

Winston to Lady Randolph

EXTRACT

29 October [1893]   [Sandhurst]

My dear Mamma,

I have felt very uncomfortable since I got here about Everest. I fear that at the time you told me—I was so occupied with Jack & Harrow that I did not think about it seriously. Now however—I have a very uneasy conscience on the subject. It is quite easy, dear Mamma, for you to say that it is not my business or for you to refuse to read what I have got to say—but nevertheless I feel I ought in common decency to write to you at length on the subject.

In the first place if I allowed Everest to be cut adrift without protest in the manner which is proposed I should be extremely ungrateful—besides I should be very sorry not to have her at Grosvenor Square—because she is in my mind associated—more than anything else with *home*.

She is an old woman—who has been your devoted servant for nearly 20 years—she is more fond of Jack and I than of any other people in the world & to be packed off in the way the Duchess suggests would possibly, if not probably break her down altogether.

Look too at the manner in which it would be done. She is sent away—nominally for a holiday as there is no room at Grosvenor Square for her. Then her board wages are refused her—quite an unusual thing. Finally she is to be given her congé by letter—without having properly made up her mind where to go or what to do.

At her age she is invited to find a new place & practically begin over again. Of course I am extremely fond of Everest & it [is] perhaps from this reason that I think such proceedings cruel & rather mean.

I know you have no choice in the matter & that the Duchess has every right to discharge a servant for whom she has 'no further use'. But I do think that you ought *to arrange that she remains at Grosvenor Square—until I go* back to Sandhurst & Jack to school.

In the meantime she will have ample time to make up her mind where to go—to find a place & resign herself to a change.

Then when a *good* place *has been* secured for her she could leave and be given a pension—which would be sufficient to keep her from want—& which should continue during her life.

This is what I should call a fair and generous method of treating her. It is in your power to explain to the Duchess that she *cannot* be sent away until she has got a good place.

She has for 3 months been boarding herself out of her own money and I have no doubt is not at all well off. Dearest Mamma—I know you are angry with me for writing—I am very sorry but I cannot bear to think of Everest not coming back much less being got rid of in such a manner. If you can arrange with the Duchess & persuade her to let Everest stay till after Christmas—I should feel extremely relieved. If you can't, I will write and explain things to Papa, who will I am sure forgive me troubling him. . . .

*　　*　　*　　*　　*

In his second term at Sandhurst Winston was involved in a misadventure which shed much light on the characters of both Winston and his father : he lost his watch. It was a good gold watch which he had been given by his father. One day it was broken and taken to Messrs Dent's, who early in March 1894 informed Winston that the watch required a new balance staff, minute wheel, pinion, second hand and glass, re-adjustment, compensation, a repaired

case and cleaning. The cost would be £3, and a watch was
being forwarded on loan by registered post. As ill luck
would have it Lord Randolph, six weeks later, went into
Mr Dent's to see about his own watch.

Lord Randolph to Winston

21 April 1894   50 Grosvenor Square

Dear Winston,
    I have received your letter of yesterday's date & am glad
to learn that you are getting on well in your work. But I
heard something about you yesterday which annoyed &
vexed me very much. I was at Mr Dent's about my watch,
and he told me of the shameful way in which you had mis-
used the very valuable watch which I gave you. He told
me that you had sent it to him some time ago, having with
the utmost carelessness dropped it on a stone pavement &
broken it badly. The repairs of it cost £3 17s. which you
will have to pay Mr Dent. He then told me he had again
received the watch the other day and that you told him it
had been dropped in the water. He told me that the whole
of the works were horribly rusty & that every bit of the
watch had had to be taken to pieces. I would not believe
you could be such a young stupid. It is clear you are not to
be trusted with a valuable watch & when I get it from Mr
Dent I shall not give it back to you. You had better buy one
of those cheap watches for £2 as those are the only ones
which if you smash are not very costly to replace. Jack has
had the watch I gave him longer than you have had yours;
the only expenses I have paid on his watch was 10/s for
cleaning before he went back to Harrow. But in all qualities
of steadiness taking care of his things & never doing stupid
things Jack is vastly your superior.

Your vy much worried parent
RANDOLPH S. CHURCHILL

Once again Lord Randolph did not confine his angry
words to Winston. He wrote to Lady Randolph in Paris:

. . . I have written a letter to Winston he wont forget . . .
I assure [you] the old Mr Dent was quite concerned at
one of best class of watches being treated in such a

manner. . . . I wound up by telling him that in all qualities of steadiness taking care of thing[s] and of not doing stupid things Jack was vastly his superior. You see I was really angry for I cannot understand anybody not taking the greatest care of a good watch, but also because he had never told me a word about it. However as I said he wont forget my letter for some time & it will be a long time before I give him anything worth having. I wanted you to know this as he may tell you a vy different story. . . .

Winston replied to his father :

Winston to Lord Randolph
(Blenheim Papers)

22 April [1894]   Sandhurst

My dear Father,

I have been very unfortunate about the watch—which I kept safely the whole time I was at James's during our tour in Switzerland—and all last term. But about 6 weeks ago I broke it and within a fortnight of its being mended it is broken again. So really I have had it for over a year without an accident and then come 2 in a fortnight. Yet I have been no less careful of it during that fortnight than during the preceding year.

The first accident was not my fault at all. I had a leather case made for the watch—during the daytime to protect it and I was putting it into it when it was knocked out of my hand by a boy running past.

This time I am more to blame. I placed the watch (last Sunday) in my breast pocket—not having with uniform a waistcoat to put it in—and while walking along the Wish Stream I stooped down to pick up a stick and it fell out of my pocket into the only deep place for miles.

The stream was only about 5 inches deep—but the watch fell into a pool nearly 6 feet deep.

I at once took off my clothes and I dived for it but the bottom was so uneven and the water so cold that I could not stay in longer than 10 minutes and had to give it up.

The next day I had the pool dredged—but without result. On Tuesday therefore I obtained permission from the Governor to do anything I could provided I paid for having it all put straight again.

I then borrowed 23 men from the Infantry Detachment —dug a new course for the stream—obtained the fire engine and pumped the pool dry and so recovered the watch. I tell you all this to show you that I appreciated fully the value of the watch and that I did not treat the accident in a casual way. The labour of the men cost me over £3.

I would rather you had not known about it. I would have paid for its mending and said nothing. But since you know about it—I feel I ought to tell you how it happened in order to show you I really valued the watch and did my best to make sure of it.

I quite realise that I have failed to do so and I am very very sorry that it should have happened. But it is not the case with all my things. Everything else you have ever given me is in as good repair as when you gave it first.

Please don't judge me entirely on the strength of the watch. I am very very sorry about it.

I am sorry to have written you such a long and stupid letter, but I do hope you will take it in some measure as an explanation.

With best love
I remain ever your loving son
WINSTON S. CHURCHILL

Thus early did Winston reveal his resourcefulness, his ability to organize and his talent for command. Lady Randolph at once wrote to soothe Winston :

Lady Randolph to Winston

Sunday [22 April 1894]   Hotel Scribe

Dearest Winston,

I am *so* sorry you have got into trouble over yr watch— Papa wrote to me all about it. I must own you are awfully careless & of course Papa is angry after giving you such a valuable thing. However he wrote very kindly about you so you must not be too unhappy. Meanwhile I'm afraid you

Scenes from Young Winston

SIMON WARD as YOUNG WINSTON
during the Boer War

JACK HAWKINS as Mr. Harrow, Headmaster at Harrow

JOHN MILLS as General Kitchener

Young Winston under Boer fire

Holding off the attack

Fleeing the besieged train

ANNE BANCROFT
as Jenny Jerome Churchill

ROBERT SHAW
as Lord Randolph Churchill

ANNE BANCROFT and ROBERT SHAW
as Lady and Lord Randolph Churchill

**Winston with
Clementine Hozier
(PIPPA STEEL) his
bride-to-be**

**Winston with
Pamela Plowden (JANE SEYMOUR)
his first love**

Charging with the 21st Lancers at the Battle of Omdurman

British armored train under Boer fire

Young Winston escaping from the Boers

Lord Randolph in Parliament

Young Winston and
Jenny mourn the
death of Randolph

Entering politics

will have to go without a watch. Oh! Winny what a harum scarum fellow you are! You really must give up being so childish. I am sending you £2 with my love. I shall scold you well when we meet.

Yr loving
MOTHER

Winston appreciated this letter:

Winston to Lady Randolph

24 April [1894]   Sandhurst

My dearest Mamma,

Thank you so much for your letter—which I have just received. Papa wrote me a long letter about the watch and seems to be very cross. I wrote back at once saying how sorry I was and explaining the whole affair & got a letter by return post—last night. I think that by his letter Papa is somewhat mollified. I hope so indeed. But how on earth could I help it. I had no waistcoat to put the watch in and so have had to wear it in the pocket of my tunic.

Papa writes, he is sending me a Waterbury—which is rather a come down.

I am very sorry it should have happened—as you can well believe—and sorrier still that Papa should have heard of it. But I feel quite clear in my own mind that I am not to blame except for having brought so good a watch back here—where there is everything in the way of its safety.

But Winston was not quite sure whether in fact his father had been 'mollified'. On April 30 he writes to his mother: 'Papa has not written to me for some time and I am uncertain whether he is still angry with me or not'. And on the following day: 'I hope he is not incensed about the watch anymore. I wish you would send me a line on the subject. Also I wd be very grateful if you would draw Papa's attention to the date (May 1) as I am not particularly rich owing to the £3 I had to disburse for my watch.'

30 April [1894]   Sandhurst

My dear Papa,

I got the watch on Saturday morning—for which many thanks. I do hope you are not angry with me anymore about it. On Sunday I stayed with Col Brabazon at Aldershot. He very kindly asked me down and I enjoyed myself very much indeed.

We are going through a course of Musketry which is very interesting and which we all like as it does not begin until half past seven and so we get a little longer in bed. The riding is going on very well and so is work etc.

This morning I had a letter from a man offering to lend me money on note of hand—I took it to Major Ball and he has forwarded it to the Governor—but I am afraid there is no chance of bringing the man to book.

I will write to you again very soon—but for the present have nothing more to say.

Hoping that you will not think any more of the watch and with best love

I remain, ever your loving son
WINSTON S. CHURCHILL

Lord Randolph drew the incident to a close in a calmer tone than he had adopted at the beginning :

Lord Randolph to Winston

1 May 1894   50 Grosvenor Square

Dear Winston,

You need not trouble any more about the watch. It is quite clear that the rough work of Sandhurst is not suitable for a watch made by Dent. I daresay you had a pleasant Sunday with Colonel Brabazon. I am glad to hear the work is going on well, and the riding. I suppose your old volunteer experiences [at Harrow] will make the course of musketry less strange to you. Never attend to moneylenders, put their letters into the waste paper basket. If you would like to come up on the 5th of May I am afraid you won't find me at dinner for I dine at the Royal Academy dinner, but your mother will be here & you might do a play.

Ever your affte father
RANDOLPH S. C.

The affair of the moneylender was treated with great earnestness. The papers were forwarded to the Director of Public Prosecutions with a view to prosecuting the moneylender, one Fred Ellis, for attempting to obtain business from a minor. But after careful enquiries it emerged that the moneylender's letter had not been sent to Winston direct at Sandhurst (where the moneylender must have known he was writing to a minor) but had been forwarded from Blenheim. No action was consequently taken.

Winston had seen Colonel Brabazon the previous month when the latter, 'magnificently dressed', had come over from Aldershot to Camberley to officiate at the Staff College riding examination there. Winston told his father (March 13): 'He has asked me to go and stay at Aldershot the first Saturday we are here after Easter'.

Colonel Brabazon, a 10th Hussar, had just taken command of the 4th Hussars at Aldershot. An impoverished Irish landlord, his military career had on several occasions suffered for lack of funds. Nevertheless, by his dash and gallantry in the field and by the sheer force of his personality off it, he established himself as a man of redoubtable character in the eyes of the War Office and of Society. Lord and Lady Randolph had known him for many years and it seemed therefore natural that Winston should have turned to him for help in his efforts to get into the cavalry.

Winston to Lady Randolph

EXTRACT

11 January [1894]

Hindlip Hall
Near Worcester

My dearest Mamma,
I have written to Colonel Brabazon and have stated my

various arguments in favour of cavalry regiment. I have asked him to say whether or no they are correct—when he writes to you—but in case he should not state this clearly I will put them down for you.

1. Promotions much quicker in Cavalry than in Infantry (60th Rifles slowest regiment in the army).

2. Obtain your commission (3 or 4 months) in Cav much sooner than in Infantry.

3. 4th Hussars are going to India shortly. If I join before 'Augmentation' I should have 6 or 7 subalterns below me in a very short time.

4. Cavalry regiments are always given good stations in India and generally taken great care of by the Government —while Infantry have to take what they can get.

5. If you want to keep a horse you can do it much cheaper in the cavalry than in infantry—government will provide stabling—forage—and labour.

6. Sentimental advantages grouped under heading of
    a. uniform
    b. increased interest of a 'life among horses' etc
    c. advantages of riding over walk
    d. advantages of joining a regiment some of whose officers you know. i.e. 4th Hussars.

The first 5 of these reasons I wrote to Col Brabazon the last I write to you.

There you are—now don't ever say I did not give you any reasons—There are 5 good solid arguments.

On April 26 Brabazon had confirmed in writing his verbal invitation to Winston to spend Saturday to Monday with the 4th Hussars; 'If you can come go and see Captain Julian Byng of the 10th Hussars who is coming over also. You might come over with him'. Winston duly went with the future hero of Vimy Ridge but news of the visit travelled fast and on the Sunday Lady Randolph wrote: 'A bird whispered to me that you did not sleep in yr own bed last night. Write to me all about it. I am not sure if Papa wld approve.' Lady Randolph had divined the ulterior motive behind Winston's visit which Lord Randolph, from his letter, did not seem to have guessed at. Winston did not trouble to hide it from her :

Winston to Lady Randolph

EXTRACT

1 May [1894]   Sandhurst

My dearest Mamma,

I have just got your letter. I should not think that Papa would object to my having stayed with Col Brab at Aldershot. He distinctly wrote to me that he did not want me to come up to London much. I wrote yesterday to him and told him all about it.

I should like to come up on Saturday as I have not been to London once this term—and want to see Jack & yourself. I altogether protest against being perpetually immured down here.

I had great fun at Aldershot—the regiment is awfully smart.—I think they did not always have a good name— but Col Brab did not take long in knocking them into shape. I met Capt Bobby White who asked to be remembered to you.

How I wish I were going into the 4th instead of those old Rifles. It would not cost a penny more & the regiment goes to India in 3 years which is just right for me. I hate the Infantry—in which physical weaknesses will render me nearly useless on service & the only thing I am showing an aptitude for athletically— riding—will be no good to me.

Furthermore of all regiments in the Army the Rifles is slowest for promotion. However it is not much good writing down these cogent arguments—but if I pass high at the end of the term I will tackle Papa on the subject. . . .

To his father, however, he did not confide these hopes.

*   *   *   *   *

Although Winston had after all obtained a place in the infantry list, Lord Randolph was determined to leave nothing to chance; he had sought out the Duke of Cambridge to remind him of a former promise to get Winston into his regiment, the 60th Rifles. The October meeting at

Newmarket provided the ideal opportunity. On 12 October 1893 Lord Randolph reported from the Jockey Club Rooms to both his mother and to Lady Randolph that he had settled the matter and that the Duke had promised to get Winston into the 60th; but Winston, as we have seen, and soon Brabazon himself, had other ideas.

*   *   *   *   *

Winston's increasing independence showed itself in a determination to choose not only his own career but also his own friends, especially those among his relations. The very size of the Marlborough family and the extensive correspondence among them which the scattered nature of their homes entailed lent itself to the building up of formidable legends about individuals, some based on fact or bitter experience, others on mere hearsay or a desire to make mischief. Duchess Lily who had early befriended Winston came under Lord Randolph's gravest suspicion :

Lord Randolph to Frances, Duchess of Marlborough

EXTRACT

28 October 1893

. . . Winston has gone to Eton to spend a day & night with Mr Little. He comes back here on tomorrow. He wanted to go & stay with Dss of Lily but I told him he had seen nothing of his mother & ought to devote himself to her. For some reason or other also I do not care about his being with the Duchess Lily. A dinner or lunch *'ça se passe'* but staying in her house is not vy good for him. You never know what state she may be in. . . .

This would seem to imply that Duchess Lily was bibulous; apart from Lord Randolph's passing remark there is no evidence for this. Sir Shane Leslie, who knew her when he was a young man, has told the author that as far as he knew the suggestion is untrue. Lord Randolph had for some years effectively cut himself off from his brother the 8th Duke. The breach over the Aylesford affair was healed for a brief period following the death of their father in 1883; but almost immediately it was reopened when the new Duke decided to sell the great collection of paintings at

Blenheim. Apart from a few nights' shelter at Blenheim for Winston and Jack when Duchess Fanny asked them to Blenheim to escape the diphtheria in 1888, Lord Randolph's family was completely estranged from the Duke. So that when he died unexpectedly in November 1892 Winston hardly knew his cousin Sunny, who succeeded as 9th Duke a few days before his twenty-first birthday. When it was time to make arrangements for Christmas the following year, it was hoped that Winston and his brother Jack would spend the holiday with their uncle's family, the Leslies at Glaslough in Ireland, and this was indeed arranged by Lady Randolph. But a more attractive proposition presented itself and Winston gladly availed himself of it. Lady Blandford, 'Bertha', the new Duke's mother, now came back to Blenheim and invited him there.

Winston was fascinated by Blenheim:

Winston to Lady Randolph

25 December [1893]   Blenheim

My dear Mamma,

I am enjoying myself here very much—though there is plenty of divine service. Every one is very kind and civil to me & Lady Blandford has really gone out of her way to make me comfortable. I suggested going on Tuesday but she would not hear of it & told me that she expected me to stay until the following Monday. It would be very convenient if I were to go direct from her to Hindlip as it is only an hour and a quarter—by train.

There is no sort of party & I am quite alone with Sunny. He is very good company and we have sat talking till 1.30 every night since I have been here.

I have also had long talks with Lady Blandford or 'Aunt Bertha' as I am getting to call her. She really is most kind. Altogether I am quite content at the prospect of staying a week here & am in no hurry to get back to town.

On my way back from Hindlip I think I shall go—with your permission—and stay with the Dillon's at Ditchley . . . but that can be arranged later.

Hoping you were not bored to death in town—that Papa looked well—and that you had a 'Happy Christmas'

> I remain Ever your loving son
> WINSTON S. CHURCHILL

To his aunt Leonie he wrote on Boxing Day from Blenheim : 'Perhaps you are astonished at the paper. Sunny very kindly asked me down here for the Christmas week. He is such an interesting companion and anything but the idiot I was taught to believe him to be'.

Winston's friendship with his cousin became a firm and lasting one, and it remained constant, despite family quarrels of the past and political differences, over the next forty years.

* * * * *

In July 1894 Lord Randolph's health had started to deteriorate to an alarming extent; the older members of the family knew that he was suffering from a severe mental disease. His speeches both in the country and in the House had become increasingly embarrassing; he often became confused and lost the thread of his argument; his enemies chattered or left the House; his friends absented themselves discreetly or sat in silence in embarrassed grief. Sir Henry Lucy, *Punch*'s Parliamentary correspondent, had described how in April 1894 during a debate in the House Balfour listened to Lord Randolph 'bowed down with physical and mental suffering'. Lord Rosebery was to write in his sensitive memoir of Lord Randolph : 'There was no curtain, no retirement, he died by inches in public'.

The doctors prescribed rest but this Lord Randolph would not undertake. He seemed quite oblivious to the deterioration of his powers or the anguish suffered by his friends and family. It was decided that Lady Randolph should take him on a world tour as the likeliest chance of effecting a cure, or at least arresting the progress of the disease. Some members of the family were concerned at the idea of Lady Randolph accompanying him since, as Marjoribanks wrote to Lord Rosebery, she 'always grates on his nerves'. According to Lord Randolph in a letter to his mother quoted in Winston's Life, the doctors at first verbally agreed to a journey round the world on condition he gave up political life for a year; almost at the last

minute the doctors became alarmed at the idea of so prolonged an absence from their care :

Drs Thomas Buzzard & Robson Roose to Lady Randolph

25 June 1894   74 Grosvenor Gardens W.
Private

Dear Lady Randolph Churchill,
    As you are aware, it is against our advice that Lord
Randolph is starting for the United States, and you have
doubtless seen the letter which we sent to his Lordship.
Our wish was that previous to his attempting a lengthened
journey he should go with a Medical man to some place
near at hand by way of experiment as to the effect of
change upon him. In these circumstances it appears to us
advisable to repeat in writing, what we have already expressed by word of mouth, that we cannot help feeling a
good deal of anxiety in regard to the future, and would
earnestly counsel your Ladyship to insist upon an immediate return to England in case Lord Randolph should shew
any fresh symptom pointing possibly to disturbance of the
Mental faculties.
    As it is necessary that Dr Keith, as well as your Lady-
ship, should be thoroughly aware of our views, we are sending him a duplicate of this letter. We have arranged to hear
from him once a week by letter sent to Dr Roose for our
joint perusal.

                         Believe us to be Yours very truly
                            THOMAS BUZZARD
                            ROBSON ROOSE

    Lord and Lady Randolph sailed for the United States on
27 June 1894 in the S.S. *Majestic*. Winston and Jack came
up to London to see their parents off. Rosebery, now Prime
Minister, was among those who also came to the station.
After a short stay at Bar Harbour in Maine Lord and Lady
Randolph went by train across Canada, breaking their
journey at Banff in the Rocky Mountains. They visited
Vancouver and San Francisco, crossed the Pacific to Japan
and then after another long sea voyage across the Indian
Ocean arrived in Madras five months after they had left
England. It had been intended to make a considerable
journey through India but the deterioration in Lord Ran-

dolph's health was now so rapid, and his condition often so violent, that on the basis of Keith's reports to Buzzard and Roose in London they recommended his immediate return.

While his parents were going round the world Winston wrote them more than thirty letters. To begin with he did not understand the gravity of his father's illness since there was a family conspiracy to keep bad news from Duchess Fanny and the children. But during October Winston began by degrees to learn a great deal more about his father's illness.

Winston to Lady Randolph

EXTRACTS

2 November [1894]   50 Grosvenor Square

. . . I persuaded Dr Roose to tell exactly how Papa was— as I thought it was only right that I should know exactly how he was progressing. You see I only hear through grandmamma Jerome who does not take a very sanguine view of things—or through the Duchess who is at one extreme one minute and at the other the next. So I asked Dr Roose and he told me everything and showed me the medical reports. I have told no one—and I beg you above all things not to write to Roose on the subject of his having told me as he told it me in confidence. I need not tell you how anxious I am. I had never realised how ill Papa had been and had never until now believed that there was anything serious the matter. I do trust & hope as sincerely as human beings can that the relapse Keith spoke of in his last report was only temporary and that the improvement of the few months has been maintained. Do, my darling mamma when you write let me know *exactly* what you think. . . .

. . . Now about yourself, Darling Mummy I do hope that you are keeping well and that the fatigues of travelling as well as the anxiety you must feel about Papa—are not telling on you. I can't tell you how I long to see you again and how I look forward to your return. Do what you can with Papa to induce him to allow me to come out and join you. . . .

8 November [1894]   Sandhurst

My dearest darling Mamma,

I got yesterday a report of Papa from Yokohama. Dr
Roose was good enough to let me see it. It describes his
having been ill with numbness in the hand—I have no
doubt you remember the occasion. I am very very sorry to
hear that so little improvement has been made, and that
apparently there is not much chance of improvement. My
darling Mummy—you must not be cross with me for having
persuaded Roose to keep me informed as I shall never tell
anyone and it is only right I should know. Above all things
you must not write to him and scold him—as I promised I
would not tell anyone but have made an exception in your
case.

I hope and trust as sincerely as it is possible there may
still be time for some improvement & some really favourable signs. Do please write and tell me all about him—quite
unreservedly. You know you told *me* to write to *you* on
every subject freely.

> With best love my darling Mummy,
> Ever your loving son
> WINSTON

On November 24 Winston went to Dr Roose's and was
shown a telegram just received from Madras that stated
that Lord Randolph's condition had become very much
worse and that it had been decided to cut short the tour
and to return to England immediately. Lord and Lady
Randolph reached London on December 24. Despite a few
misleading symptoms of recovery there was now no hope
that he could live and the family awaited his death with
miserable resignation. 'For a month,' Winston wrote in the
Life of his father, 'at his mother's house, he lingered piti-
fully, until very early in the morning of 24 January 1895
the numbing fingers of paralysis laid that weary brain to
rest.' Seventy years to the day Winston himself was to die.
On January 28 Lord Randolph was buried in Bladon
churchyard, and a memorial service was held for him in
Westminster Abbey.

Winston was just twenty at the time of his father's death

and must henceforward be regarded as a man and no longer a boy. Despite his lack of means he plainly felt himself responsible for the small family—there was only his mother and Jack. Both his grandfathers, the Duke and Leonard Jerome, had been dead for some time. His grandmother Jerome was to die within a few months; so too was Everest. The old Duchess died four years later. These three Churchills were to be alone in the world. Lady Randolph still had her private income which she quickly dissipated or mortgaged; and their fortunes were to be increasingly dependent on the impecunious gentleman cadet who was shortly to receive the Queen's Commission in the 4th Hussars with pay of £120 per annum. Within the confinements of his slender means and the limitations of the career to which he was committed—the only one for which he had any training—he was his own master. He had a stout heart, an audacious spirit, colossal ambition, a late-maturing but massive brain from which elements of genius cannot be excluded, a sharp sword; and he was soon to fashion himself a valuable and rewarding pen, which was in the next few years, combined with his thirst for adventure, to liberate him from the thraldom of penury and open all doors during the seventy years that lay ahead.

'It is said', Winston was to write nearly forty years later in his Life of Marlborough, 'that famous men are usually the product of an unhappy childhood. The stern compression of circumstances, the twinges of adversity, the spur of slights and taunts in early years, are needed to evoke that ruthless fixity of purpose and tenacious mother-wit without which great actions are seldom accomplished.' And in 1898 he wrote of the Mahdi : 'Solitary trees, if they grow at all, grow strong; and a boy deprived of a father's care often develops, if he escapes the perils of youth, an independence and vigour of thought which may restore in after life the heavy loss of early days.'

There was now no one to help him—or stand in his way; for if Lord Randolph had lived, even in better health, he would have been an obstacle to Winston's career and prospects which were soon to burgeon. He was free to leave the nest and soar through many hazards to the empyrean.

7

THE FOURTH HUSSARS

In *My Early Life* Churchill, as we now shall call him, relates how Lord Randolph, in one of his last remarks, had said 'Have you got your horses?' Earlier, however, while Lord Randolph was still on his voyage round the world, he had told his son to put the idea of joining the cavalry 'out of your head altogether, *at any rate during my lifetime*'. And Lord Randolph had warned : 'The Army is the finest profession in the world if you work at it and the worst if you loaf at it'. Certainly Churchill seems to have worked hard for his final examinations at Sandhurst. Having entered 92nd in a list of 102, he passed out 20th in a class of 130.

Before his death Lord Randolph had come to accept the idea that his son should go into the cavalry and not into the infantry; into the 4th Hussars and not into the 60th Rifles to which the Duke of Cambridge, the Queen's first cousin and for nearly forty years Commander-in-Chief of the British Army, had nominated him more than five years before.

Churchill wasted little time. Within a week of Lord Randolph's funeral at Bladon he determined to take the necessary action to start his own career. At his behest his mother telegraphed to Colonel Brabazon who promptly replied on 2 February 1895 suggesting that she should at once get in touch with the Duke of Cambridge. Colonel Brabazon told Lady Randolph to write to the Duke that Lord Randolph had often said that if his son were to go into the cavalry he should like him to join under Brabazon.

Lady Randolph wrote to the Duke of Cambridge who was at the Hotel Prince de Galles at Cannes on the Riviera. He very promptly replied on February 6 that he would write immediately to the Military Secretary at the War Office and that if the transfer from the list for the 60th Rifles to that for the 4th Hussars could be arranged it would be carried out. 'The 4th Hussars is a very good

Cavalry Regiment, & Colonel Brabazon an excellent Commanding Officer so I think your selection is in that respect a very good one. I am delighted to hear that your son has passed so well out of Sandhurst, a proof that he has made good use of his stay at the College'.

Twelve days after the Duke's letter Churchill reported to the 4th Hussars at Aldershot, and on February 20 he received his Commission. It was signed by H. Campbell-Bannerman, then Secretary of State for War, from whom he was less than eleven years later to receive his first Ministerial appointment as Under-Secretary for the Colonies.

His regular letters to his mother and to his younger brother Jack at Harrow continue to afford a lively and almost complete account of his early months in the 4th Hussars. At first we learn that 'the riding school is fearfully severe and I suffer terribly from stiffness—but what with hot baths and *massage* I hope soon to be better. At present I can hardly walk. I have however been moved up in the 2nd Class recruits which is extremely good. These horses are very different to the Sandhurst screws. Rather too broad I think for me—and I am rather worried about my old strain [hernia]. Sundry queer pains having manifested themselves, which may or may not be the outcome of the rest of the stiffness.'

In a letter to his brother he gives an outline of his daily routine.

WSC to Jack

EXTRACT

21 February [1895]   Aldershot

7.30	Called
7.45	Breakfast in bed
	Papers, Letters, etc
8.45	Riding School—2 hours
10.45	Hot bath and massage
11.30	Carbine exercises—privately with a Sergeant to catch up a higher class
12	Noon 'Stables'. Lasts 1 hour. I have charge of 1 squadron, 30 men and have to see the horses groomed—watered—fed & the men's rooms clean etc

| 1 o'clock | Lunch is ready. It does not matter being late |
| 2.15 | Drill. $1\frac{1}{2}$ hours nominally—but as I can't walk I get off at present after a half an hour—which is mostly spent in drilling the men myself. After which for the present—hot baths—medical rubber—Elliman's and doctor—until Mess at 8 —Bezique—3d points. Bed. |

With his lack-lustre school days behind him and an unpromising future ahead Churchill plainly aspired to mount and excel in his new profession. The time-table he sent to Jack shows how he sought to gain promotion by extra practice in the mastery of the carbine. Within a week of arriving at Aldershot he was moved up into a higher riding class. 'And should all go well,' he reported to his mother, 'I shall be dismissed riding school in three months instead of the normal twelve.' At the same time he was allowed out with the Regiment on a route march. 'No one has ever been allowed out before until they have been three to four months in the riding school, so I established a precedent.' His only complaint was about Drill, 'which as usual I loathe and abominate'.

In the evenings he played either bezique for 3d points— 'which is a shocking descent from the shillings at Deepdene' (Duchess Lily's new home near Dorking)—or whist—'a most uninteresting game and one at which I have but little luck'. Rarely, even in later life, was Churchill apt to take an objective view of affairs. A game at which he did not prevail was naturally a bore. He was already developing that egocentricity which was to become such a predominant characteristic, and to which must be attributed alike his blunders and his triumphant successes.

* * * * *

He rode, if anything, rather better than the other young officers of his rank. He early indulged in steeplechasing, and, as soon as he could organise credit on his precarious background, in polo as well. His steeplechasing involved him in an accident early in March. 'The animal refused and swerved', he told his mother. 'I tried to cram him in and he took the wings. Very nearly did he break my leg, but as it is I am only bruised and very stiff.' He was in bed for three days.

* * * * *

Winston's love for Mrs Everest was now to be shown to advantage. Despite his earlier letter to his mother Mrs Everest does not seem to have been treated very well. She kept writing very complaining, endearing letters to Winston and Jack who were obviously her sole interest in the world. She had spent much of the year 1894 with her former employer the Venerable Thompson Phillips, Archdeacon of Barrow-in-Furness; but during the autumn she broke her arm. 'I am always to be a cripple,' she wrote to Jack in December, 'unless I have it seen to.'

On January 31 she wrote to Jack about Lord Randolph's memorial service in Westminster Abbey. She told him that Mr Welldon looked at her rather hard and she thought that he recognized her. She was of course too modest to approach him.

Early in 1895 she went to stay with her sister Mrs Emma Richmond and her family in Crouch Hill, Islington. Churchill did not forget his old nurse :

Mrs Everest to WSC

1 April 1895

15 Crouch Hill
London N.

April 1st 195

My darling Precious Boys
th . s I have just rec'd
2 . 10 from Cox & Co.
Charing Cross on your
Account . I thank you very
Much indeed dearest it is

My darling Precious Boy,

I have just recd £2. 10s from Cox & Co Charing
Cross on your account. I thank you very much indeed
dearest it is awfully kind & thoughtful of you. My dear
dear Boy you are one of ten thousand but I am afraid
you will find your income not any too much for your
expenses dear. It really is too good & kind of you I don't
know how to thank you enough. I am afraid Her Ladyship will think me a terrible imposter. I have written to
the London & Westminster Bank today to give them my
address. I don't know whether they will forward me the
usual remittance that your poor dear Papa arranged for
me. I had a letter from Jackie this morning he tells me
Grandmamma Jerome is very ill indeed in a critical condition. Her Ladyship is at Tunbridge Wells & Mrs Leslie
too. They are both with her, poor Mama she has had a
lot of troubles lately. Jackie will have dull holidays again
I'm afraid. How are you darling I hope you are keeping
well. I should so like to know if you are well. Did you get
my letter I wrote you last week. I am longing to see you
in your uniform. Do let me know when you are in
London. I am quite well & my Arm improving slowly. I
can put my hand on the top of my head now & I can use
my knife & cut bread & butter. The Duchess has let 50
Gr Square & goes away on the 11th. Where are you going
to make your home in your holidays? I hope you will
take care of yourself my darling. I hear of your exploits
at steeple chasing. I do so dread to hear of it. Remember
Count Kinsky broke his nose once at that. It is a dangerous pastime but I suppose you are expected to do it. Only
don't be too venturesome. Goodbye darling with much
love to you.   I remain ever your old
                                                    W O O M

Mrs Jerome died at Tunbridge Wells on the day after
Mrs Everest had written this letter. In May Mrs Everest
went to stay at Ventnor with her relations the Balaams
and reported that she felt better. On June 4 she wrote to
Jack that she was still at Ventnor but was 'fit for work'. She
asked when Lady Randolph would get her new house—she
obviously wanted to work for her again. Lady Randolph
was in Paris at this time. But in July Mrs Everest fell ill
again and died within a few days.

3 July [1895]   Aldershot

My dearest Mamma,

I have just got back from London as I telegraphed to
you—poor old Everest died early this morning from
peritonitis. They only wired to me on Monday evening—to
say her condition was critical. That was the first intimation
I had of her illness. I started off and got Keith—who was
too kind. He thought then that she might pull through—
but it was problematical. Instead of rallying however, she
only sank into a stupor which gave place to death at 2.15
this morning.

Everything that could be done—was done. I engaged a
nurse, but she only arrived for the end. It was very sad &
her death was shocking to see—but I do not think she
suffered much pain.

She was delighted to see me on Monday and I think my
coming made her die happy. I went down to Harrow to
tell Jack—early this morning—as I did not want to telegraph the news. He was awfully shocked but tried not to
show it.

I made the necessary arrangements for the funeral which
takes place on Friday. I ordered a wreath for you from
Mackay & I thought you would like to send one.

Please send a wire to Welldon to ask him to let Jack come
up for the funeral—as he is very anxious to do so.

Well my dearest Mummy I am very tired as I have been
knocking about for two nights & have done all my duty
here at the same time. I feel very low—and find that I
never realised how much poor old Woom was to me. I don't
know what I should do without you.

> With best love Ever your loving son
> WINSTON S. CHURCHILL

WSC to Lady Randolph
EXTRACT

6 July 1895   Aldershot

My dear Mamma,

I went yesterday to poor Everest's funeral & Welldon let
Jack come up too. All her relations were there—a good
many of whom had travelled from Ventnor overnight—and

I was quite surprised to find how many friends she had made in her quiet and simple life. The coffin was covered with wreaths & everything was as it should be. I felt very despondent and sad—the third funeral I have been to within five months! [*The other two were Lord Randolph's and Mrs. Jerome's.*] It is indeed another link with the past gone—& I look back with regret to the old days at Connaught Place when fortune still smiled. . . .

Lady Randolph was evidently not present. But the Archdeacon, with a 'long memory for faithful service', travelled all the way down from Cumberland to be at the graveside. Winston paid for a headstone to be erected on Mrs Everest's grave at the City of London Cemetery in Manor Park with the following simple inscription :

Erected in Memory
of
Elizabeth Anne Everest
who died 3rd July 1895
Aged 62
by
Winston Spencer Churchill
Jack Spencer Churchill

For many years afterwards he paid an annual sum to the local florist for the upkeep of the grave.

Churchill was later to write in *My Early Life* a moving account of Mrs Everest's death. A middle-aged politician battling away in the wilderness against the entrenched debilitating forces of MacDonald, Baldwin and Neville Chamberlain might well have been suspected of seeking popular support by evincing a fabricated solicitude for his old nurse. The action he took on Everest's death and the two letters he wrote to his mother at the time show that he was a proud and generous young man ready to accept family responsibilities for which his mother was unsuited and his brother Jack too young.

*　*　*　*　*

Churchill was often plagued and sometimes tormented by money matters. He wrote in *My Early Life* about his mother that when he was a small boy she seemed to him a fairy princess : a radiant being possessed of limitless riches and power. He had not then discovered that Lord and Lady Randolph had practically run through all the money they had; and quite soon, as we shall see, his own small patrimony was to be summoned in aid of his mother's extravagances.

*   *   *   *   *

We already know how ardently Churchill had from a very young age followed his father's political career. His father's resignation and the understandable obstinacy of Lord Salisbury to recall Lord Randolph into his Government encouraged his interest in politics; his father's tragic death now quickened that interest, as his letters to his mother increasingly reveal.

He writes to his mother on March 2 of the local government elections in London:

WSC to Lady Randolph

EXTRACT

2 March 1895   Metropole
                                      Brighton

. . . The County Council—at least the Progressive Party— have received a dreadful blow—which will probably have much more widespread results than is generally imagined— at least so I think. Though they will still keep a majority— it will not be large enough to warrant a continuation of their arrogant—grasping and intolerable policy. It is also another blow to the Government who have identified them- selves with the Progressives entirely. . . .

And again on the same day about the Primrose League Habitation in Paddington named after his father :

. . . Fardell tells me that the R.C. [Randolph Churchill] Habitation is languishing and in a most effete condition. I sincerely hope that you will not withdraw from the office you hold in it—for it is an institution which assists to com- memorate Papa's name—as well as helping on work which he began. . . .

And when in the summer of 1895 Lord Salisbury and the Conservatives were returned to power in the General Election he wrote :

WSC to Lady Randolph

EXTRACT

3 August [1895]   Aldershot

. . . The radical papers go on piling up figures to show that 'the verdict of the country' is only a question of chance— and never indicates any real feeling—without for one moment reflecting that this argument knocks the backbone out of their agitation against the Peers. A more disappointed & broken down party never was seen.

Meanwhile the Unionists come in with very nearly every able man in both houses in their cabinet—with the House of Commons at their feet—& the Lords at their back— supported by all sections of the nation—unfettered by promises or hampered by pledges. No party has ever had such a chance—it remains to be seen what use they will make of it.

To my mind they are *too* strong—Too brilliant altogether. They are just the sort of Government to split on the question of Protection. Like a huge ship with powerful engines they will require careful steering—because any collision means destruction. . . .

This was precocious prescience in a young man of twenty. Nearly eight years were to pass before Joseph Chamberlain, having already destroyed the Liberal Party over Home Rule, was to destroy the Tory Party on the tariff issue. It may have been a lucky guess on Churchill's part, but it shows that he was already beginning to think things out for himself rather than to accept the cant thought of the hour. This tendency was to grow throughout his life and was to bring him frequently into collision with large organized sections of unthinking and wrongheaded opinion.

We can already see that before he was twenty-one he was ardent to emulate and vindicate his father and to carve a career for himself. However, circumscribed as he was, he had to wait another four or five years before he could undertake the battle of politics. Meanwhile he was educating himself and preparing himself for that battle in which he already knew he must engage as soon as he could escape from the poverty of his circumstances and the discipline of the Army.

While the summer at Aldershot dragged on, Churchill's agile mind became increasingly restless. To his mother, who was travelling in France and Switzerland, he wrote :

WSC to Lady Randolph

EXTRACT

24 August 1895   Aldershot

. . . We have just reached the Saturday of a very hard week—on no day of which have I been in the saddle less than 8 to 9 hours and on no day of which have I omitted to play polo. Next week will be the same only more so—so my time is well employed. . . .

I find I am getting into a state of mental stagnation—when even letter writing becomes an effort & when any reading but that of monthly magazines is impossible. This is of course quite in accordance with the spirit of the army. It is indeed the result of mental forces called into being by discipline and routine. It is a state of mind into which all or nearly all who soldier—fall.

From this 'slough of Despond' I try to raise myself by reading & re-reading Papa's speeches—many of which I almost know by heart—but I really cannot find the energy to read any other serious work.

I think really that when I am quartered in London I shall go and study one or two hours a week with one of James's men—a most capable fellow—either Economics or Modern History. If you know what I mean, I need some one to point out some specific subject to stimulate & to direct my reading in that subject. The desultory reading I have so far indulged in has only resulted in a jumble of disconnected & ill assorted facts. . . .

8

NEW YORK AND CUBA

THAT SUMMER the 4th Hussars were withdrawn from the Cavalry Brigade at Aldershot. They marched to Hounslow to make leisurely preparations for their departure the following year for nine years' service in India. In those peaceful days with scarcely a shot being fired anywhere in the world, officers, if they could afford it, were allowed five months' leave each year, including one uninterrupted spell of ten weeks. Cavalry subalterns were encouraged to spend the winter fox-hunting. Churchill, who had invested perhaps more than all his money in polo ponies, began to look around for some less expensive and more exciting adventure. Such things were hard to come by, particularly in the military sphere. By the beginning of October, however, he had made up his mind and formulated a plan.

WSC to Lady Randolph

4 October [1895]   Hounslow

My dearest Mamma,

I daresay you will find the content of this letter somewhat startling. The fact is that I have decided to go with a great friend of mine, one of the subalterns in the regiment, to America and the W. Indies. I propose to start from here between Oct 28 & November 2—according as the boats fit. We shall go to New York & after a stay there move in a steamer to the W. Indies—to Havana where all the Government troops are collecting to go up country and suppress the revolt that is still simmering on; after that back by Jamaica and Hayti to New York & so home. The cost of the Ticket is £37 a head return—which would be less than a couple of months [hunting] at Leighton Buzzard by a long way. I do not think the whole thing should cost £90 —which would be within by a good margin what I can afford to spend in 2 months. A voyage to those delightful islands at the season of the year when their climate is at its best will be very pleasant to me—who has never been on sea more than a few hours at a time. And how much more safe than a cruise among the fences of the Vale of Aylesbury.

I come home the 24th and hope to see you for a couple of days before we sail.

Now I hope you won't mind my going my dear Mamma —as it will do me good to travel a bit and with a delightful companion who is one of the senior subalterns and acting adjutant of the regiment & very steady.

Please send me a line.

Your ever loving son
WINSTON

Churchill had already brought his friend and fellow-subaltern, Reggie Barnes, into the plan and had persuaded him to accompany him. They had both received permission from the Commanding Officer, Colonel Brabazon, to proceed 'to the seat of war'—an insurrection which the Spanish authorities were trying to put down in Cuba. Even before he had received his mother's somewhat grudging assent to the project Churchill was already laying his plans with his customary thoroughness and on his lifelong basis of 'doing business with the people at the top'. He had written to his father's old Fourth Party friend, Sir Henry Drummond Wolff, who at this time was her Majesty's Ambassador in Madrid. He received the following reply :

Sir H. Drummond Wolff to WSC

8 October 1895   San Sebastian

My dear Winston,

After receiving yesterday your letter I saw the Minister for Foreign Affairs (The Duke of Tetuan) & spoke to him about your wish to go to Cuba.

He said he would get you a letter from the Minister of War & give you one himself to Marshal Martinez Campos who is personally his great friend but it must depend on the Marshal what he lets you and Mr Barnes do as everything is in his hands. I fear I cannot obtain any thing more but should think these letters would be enough.

How is your mother & what is Jack about?

Pray give them my love.

Yours affecte

H. DRUMMOND WOLFF

Pray write at once if these letters reach you as I am leaving this [address] before long.

It seems as if Brabazon became a little worried that there might be trouble with the War Office; Churchill was advised to consult them. He naturally applied directly to the Commander-in-Chief, Lord Wolseley (formerly Sir Garnet Wolseley), who had recently succeeded the Duke of Cambridge at the Horse Guards, the office of the military headquarters of the whole British Army, the political direction being maintained nearby in the War Office.

Lord Wolseley, like Colonel Brabazon, felt somewhat embarrassed. 'He said he quite approved', Churchill wrote to his mother on October 19, 'but rather hinted that it would have been better to go without asking leave at all.' The fact was that the popular press in England was very much on the side of the Cuban insurgents and the military authorities saw that it would be very undesirable if the expedition of the two young subalterns to the Spanish forces were to be interpreted as anything like an official mission. Nonetheless the Commander-in-Chief, thinking perhaps that he might make the best of it, sent Churchill and Barnes to see General E. F. Chapman, the Director of Military Intelligence. General Chapman furnished them with maps and background information. Moreover, Churchill wrote to Lady Randolph on October 21, 'we are also requested to collect information and statistics on various points and particularly as to the effect of the new bullet—its penetration and striking power. This,' Churchill concluded, 'invests our mission with almost an official character & cannot fail to help one in the future'.

At the same time Churchill arranged with the *Daily Graphic,* for whom his father had written from South Africa in 1891, that he should send occasional letters from the front. For this, his first journalistic venture, Churchill was to be paid five guineas a letter. So all was now 'Sir Garnet', to use a popular phrase current at the time : it was the equivalent of the naval phrase 'ship-shape'. 'Sir Garnet' arose from the widespread admiration for Sir Garnet Wolseley who was always sent to any part of the Empire which was in trouble.

Barnes and Churchill sailed from Liverpool in the Cunard Royal Mail Steamship *Etruria*.

In New York they stayed at the very comfortable apartment of Mr Bourke Cockran at 763 Fifth Avenue. Cockran, who was then forty-one, was a distinguished lawyer prominent in New York Democratic politics. He had been a member of Congress since 1891 and was coming to the end of his second term. He had aroused considerable controversy by opposing Cleveland for the Democratic nomination in 1892 and in the following year he was to campaign for the Republican nominee, McKinley. Years later in *Thoughts and Adventures* Churchill wrote of Cockran : 'I must record the strong impression which this remarkable man made upon my untutored mind. I have never seen his like, or in some respects his equal. With his enormous head, gleaming eyes and flexible countenance, he looked uncommonly like the portraits of Charles James Fox. It was not my fortune to hear any of his orations, but his conversation, in point, in pith, in rotundity, in antithesis, and in comprehension, exceeded anything I have ever heard'.

'Every body is very civil,' wrote Churchill to his mother, 'and we have engagements for every meal for the next few days about three deep. It is very pleasant staying here as the rooms are beautifully furnished and fitted with every convenience & also as Mr Cockran is one of the most charming hosts and interesting men I have ever met.'

Churchill's mind might with reasonable excuse have been in something of a whirl. 'I feel', he wrote to his aunt Leonie on November 12, 'that I should like to think over and digest what I have seen for a few weeks before forming an opinion on it.' This letter to Mrs Leslie, as do other contemporary letters to his mother and his brother, reveals that he was already acquiring an eye for detail, the power to reflect and the ability to relate it all together as a clear, concise impression:

EXTRACT

12 November 1895   763 Fifth Avenue

. . . So far I think the means of communication in New
York have struck me the most. The comfort and convenience of elevated railways—tramways—cable cars & ferries,
harmoniously fitted into a perfect system accessible alike to
the richest and the poorest—is extraordinary. And when
one reflects that such benefits have been secured to the
people not by confiscation of the property of the rich or by
arbitrary taxation but simply by business enterprise—out of
which the promoters themselves have made colossal fortunes, one cannot fail to be impressed with the excellence
of the active system.

But New York is full of contradictions and contrasts. I
paid my fare across Brooklyn Bridge with a paper dollar. I
should think the most disreputable 'coin' the world has
ever seen [*He was used to golden sovereigns and half-
sovereigns*]. I wondered how to reconcile the magnificent
system of communication with the abominable currency for
a considerable time and at length I have found what may
be a solution. The communication of New York is due to
private enterprise while the state is responsible for the currency : : and hence I come to the conclusion that the first
class men of America are in the counting house and the less
brilliant ones in the government. . . .

One evening they went over the ironclad cruiser *New
York*. 'I was much struck by the sailors : their intelligence,
their good looks and civility and their generally business-
like appearance. These interested me more than [the]
ship itself, for while any nation can build a battleship
—it is the monopoly of the Anglo-Saxon race to breed good
seamen'.

Then they went to the Military Academy at West Point.
'I am sure,' he wrote to his brother, 'you will be horrified
by some of the Regulations of the Military Academy. The
cadets enter from 19–22 & stay 4 years. This means that
they are most of them 24 years of age. They are not

allowed to smoke or have any money in their possession nor are they given any leave except 2 months after the first two years. In fact they have far less liberty than any *private* school boys in our country. I think such a state of things is positively disgraceful and young men of 24 or 25 who would resign their personal liberty to such an extent can never make good citizens or fine soldiers. A child who rebels against that sort of control should be whipped—so should a man who does not rebel.'

'Altogether my dear Aunt Leonie', wrote Churchill, 'my mind is full of irreconcilable & conflicting facts. The comfort of their cars & the disgraceful currency—the hospitality of American Society and the vulgarity of their Press—present to me a problem of great complexity'.

WSC to Jack

EXTRACT

15 November [1895]   763 Fifth Avenue

. . . The essence of American journalism is vulgarity divested of truth. Their best papers write for a class of snotty housemaids and footmen & even the nicest people here have so much vitiated their taste as to appreciate the style.

Picture to yourself the American people as a great lusty youth—who treads on all your sensibilities, perpetrates every possible horror of ill manners—whom neither age nor just tradition inspire with reverence—but who moves about his affairs with a good hearted freshness which may well be the envy of older nations of the earth. Of course there are here charming people who are just as refined and cultured as the best in any country in the world—but I believe my impressions of the nation are broadly speaking correct. . . .

What had originally been planned as a three-day visit to New York, possibly to be reduced to a day and a half, was expanded into a full week. Lady Randolph's dictum that all men found New York very dull was certainly belied in her son's case. After travelling by train to Key West in Florida in thirty-six hours (about the same time as it takes today) Churchill and Barnes embarked on board the Steamer *Olivette* and arrived in Havana Harbour on November 20—ten days before Churchill's twenty-first birthday.

Cuba was discovered by Christopher Columbus in 1492 : his tomb, though not his remains, is still in the cathedral in Havana. In 1511 the Spaniards began the conquest of the island which they ruled until 1762 when Havana was captured by the British, who opened the port to commerce and the slave trade; it was returned to Spain the next year in exchange for the Floridas. Cuba became, after the break-up of the Spanish Empire, the richest of Spain's colonial possessions, but throughout the nineteenth century the island was to be the scene of insurrection against Spanish rule. In 1868 there began a native rebellion which was to simmer for ten years. Afterwards the Captain General, Marshal Martinez Campos, pursued a conciliatory and humane policy (slavery was formally abolished in 1880 and ended in practice in 1886) but the rapid economic decline of the country which followed a disastrous fall in sugar prices in 1893–4 once more ripened the native population —creoles as well as negroes—for revolt. Early in 1895 the rebel leaders of the ten years' war, Maximo Gomez and Jose Marti, returned from exile in America and gave leadership to a new insurrection in the island.

From Spain Marshal Martinez Campos was recalled to command a large expeditionary force to Cuba, and he set out on 2 April 1895 at the head of 200 picked officers and 7,000 men accompanied by General Valdez, director of the Military School at Madrid, whom he had selected to be his Chief-of-Staff.

Martinez Campos announced at the outset that his plan was to occupy the principal towns in Cuba and thus confine the insurrection to isolated areas, whilst at the same time embarking on a new series of internal reforms. Unfortunately the isolated outbreaks severely taxed the Marshal's resources : more and more men, money and *matériel* were poured into the island from Spain, yet the strength of the rebels seemed only to increase. The longer drawn-out the war became the more sympathy and support was gained by the rebels. In the United States the Government as well as public opinion openly espoused their cause.

'Tomorrow we start "for the front" ', Churchill wrote to his mother on November 20 from the Gran Hotel Inglaterra, Havana, 'or rather to Santa Clara where the Headquarters Staff are. We go by rail via Matanzas and Cienfuegos. The journey takes twelve hours as the trains move very slowly on account of the rebels damaging the line and trying to wreck the locomotives. I believe they also fire at the train and throw dynamite cartridges—but the vigilance of the patrols and also the fact that 40 or 50 riflemen go with each train have reduced risks considerably—and the General recommended the route.'

CUBA: AREA OF OPERATIONS

Unfortunately, or perhaps fortunately for Churchill, the General's recommendation did not by itself carry any guarantee of safe conduct. Long before he got 'to the front' Churchill had some exciting news for his first despatch to the *Daily Graphic* :

As far as Colon the journey is safe, but thenceforward the country is much disturbed . . . At Santa Domingo a pilot engine and an armoured car are added to the train, as the rebels often indulge in target practice—from a respectful distance. In the car rides the escort, the passengers being permitted the privilege of using the

158

ordinary compartment. When we reached this place the line thence to Santa Clara had just been cut, and the traffic had to go round by Cruces, thus causing a great delay. On arrival there it was announced that the train which preceded ours, and in which was General Valdes, had been thrown off the line a few miles beyond Santa Domingo, and that fifteen of its occupants had been severely injured. This had been effected by weakening the supports of a small culvert. The general fortunately escaped uninjured, and at once started up country. Marshal Campos, to whose headquarters we went, received us very kindly, and readily gave us the necessary passes and letters. Unfortunately, we found that the column of General Valdes was already twenty miles away, through a country infested by the enemy, and it would therefore be necessary to go to Cienfuegos, thence by steamer to Tuna, and from there on to Sancti Spiritu. Though this route forms two sides of a triangle, it is— Euclid notwithstanding—shorter than the other, and we shall catch the column there.

When Barnes and Churchill got to Tuna, however, they found that the daily train to Sancti Spiritus had already left—they missed it by half an hour—and shortly afterwards news came that the insurgents had thrown a bomb at the train.

They then exploded some dynamite successfully, and broke down a small bridge. As soon as the train arrived at the obstruction it was fired upon, and when its occupants had had enough they returned to Tuna to wait until the line was repaired. We were in the same position, and had to spend the day in the local hotel—an establishment more homely than pretentious.

But the next morning they were able to go to Sancti Spiritus—'a forsaken place, and in a most unhealthy state. Smallpox and yellow fever are rife.' They beat General Valdez and his column by a short head and on the following day set out with them on a march to the village of Iguara, blockaded by the insurgents with the object of protecting a supply convoy.

On November 29 news came that a band of 4000 insurgents under Maximo Gomez was encamped a few miles to the east of Iguara and at 5 a.m. on November 30 General Valdez set out from Arroyo Blanco, in pursuit of the insurgents.

There was a low mist as we moved off in the early morning, and all of a sudden the rear of the column was involved in firing. In those days when people got quite close together in order to fight, and used—partly, at any rate—large-bore rifles to fight with, loud bangs were heard and smoke puffs or even flashes could be seen. The firing seemed about a furlong away and sounded very noisy and startling. As, however, no bullets seemed to come near me, I was easily reassured. I felt like the optimist 'who did not mind what happened, so long as it did not happen to him.'

It was Churchill's twenty-first birthday and on that day, he recalls in *My Early Life*, 'for the first time I heard shots fired in anger and heard bullets strike flesh or whistle through the air.'

From that time onwards the column was in contact with the insurgents almost continually for the next three days.

On the night of 1st December a bullet came through the hut in which Churchill and Barnes were sleeping and another wounded an orderly just outside. The following day came the attack by General Valdez in what was to become known as the battle of La Reforma. 'We advanced right across open ground under a very heavy fire', he wrote to his mother when he got back to his hotel in Havana on December 6.

The General, a very brave man—in a white and gold uniform on a grey horse—drew a great deal of fire on to us and I heard enough bullets whistle and hum past to satisfy me for some time to come. He rode right up to within 500 yards of the enemy and there we waited till the fire of the Spanish infantry drove them from their position. We had great luck in not losing more than we did—but as a rule the rebels shot very high. We stayed by the General all the time and so were in the most dangerous place in the field. The General recommended us for the Red Cross—a Spanish Decoration given to

Officers—and coming in the train yesterday, by chance I found Marshal Campos and his staff, who told me that it would be sent us in due course.

Though he was not subsequently to be allowed to wear the Spanish decoration, the Red Cross was to be a heavy one to bear in the ensuing weeks. The popular and provincial press both in England and in New York made scathing comments when they heard that Churchill had been with the government forces. 'Sensible people', wrote the *Newcastle Leader* on December 7, 'will wonder what motive could possibly impel a British officer to mix himself up in a dispute with the merits of which he had absolutely nothing to do. Mr Churchill was supposed to have gone to the West Indies for a holiday, he having obtained leave of absence from his regimental duties at the beginning of October for that purpose. Spending a holiday in fighting other people's battles is rather an extraordinary proceeding even for a Churchill.'

As soon as he returned to Tampa Churchill denied that he had fought against the Cubans. 'I have not even fired a revolver. I am a member of General Valdez's staff by courtesy only, and am decorated with the Red Cross only by courtesy.' In New York he gave interviews to the press who received his views with a mixture of grudging respect and tolerant amusement. 'One conspicuous feature of this war', he told them, 'is the fact that so few men are killed. There can be no question as to the immense amount of ammunition expended on both sides, but the surprising truth remains that ridiculous little execution is done. It has always been said, you know, that it takes 200 bullets to kill a soldier, but as applied to the Cuban war 200,000 shots would be closer to the mark.'

Churchill formed clear and decided views about what he had seen in Cuba. But these did not help him to come down on one side or the other. He had a natural sympathy for people trying to shake off an oppressor, a natural distaste for the high-handed and often stupid actions of the colonial administrators. He saw, moreover, that 'the demand for independence is national and unanimous'. In his very first despatch he had written : 'The insurgents gain adherence continually. There is no doubt that they possess the sympathy of the entire population'.

On the other hand he was frankly contemptuous of the ill-organized, ineffective, destructive and often cruel manner in which the rebels conducted their campaign. 'They neither fight bravely nor do they use their weapons effectively', he later wrote in the *Saturday Review* on 7 March 1896. 'They cannot win a single battle or hold a single town. Their army, consisting to a large extent of coloured men, is an undisciplined rabble'. What he saw of the rebel forces and of the havoc wreaked by them on the economy and administration of the country did not inspire in Churchill any confidence that the insurgents would provide a better alternative for Cuba than the Spanish colonial power. 'The rebel victory offers little good either to the world in general or to Cuba in particular', he wrote on 15 February 1896 in the *Saturday Review*. 'Though the Spanish administration is bad a Cuban Government would be worse, equally corrupt, more capricious, and far less stable. Under such a Government revolutions would be periodic, property insecure, equity unknown.'

Sending his friend Bourke Cockran a copy of this article Churchill wrote :

WSC to W. Bourke Cockran
(*Cockran Papers*)

EXTRACT

29 February [1896]   Bachelors' Club W.

. . .I hope the United States will not force Spain to give up Cuba—unless you are prepared to accept responsibility for the results of such action. If the States care to take Cuba—though this would be very hard on Spain—it would be the best and most expedient course for both the island and the world in general. But I hold it a monstrous thing if you are going to merely procure the establishment of another South American Republic—which however degraded and irresponsible is to be backed in its action by the American people—without their maintaining any sort of control over its behaviour.

I do hope that you will not be in agreement with those wild, and I must say, most irresponsible people who talk of Spain as 'beyond the pale' etc etc. Do write and tell me what you do think. . . .

No doubt Churchill felt the delicacy of the situation of overly criticizing the Spaniards who were his hosts and who necessarily were responsible for his food, his shelter and his safety. Moreover he had been under fire with the Spaniards on his twenty-first birthday. Roughing it and encountering some danger with people who are your hosts inevitably breeds a comradeship which makes completely objective reporting impossible. Just over forty years later he sought to restrain his son from going to the Spanish civil war to report it for the *Daily Mail*. He pointed out how difficult it would be to write objectively about a war (quite apart from the difficulties of censorship) when you were on one side of the lines. He further told his son that he must on no account later go to the other side; in that case he would be suspected by both sides of being a spy. This latter advice was heeded. In retrospect—though it was frustrating at the time—it was a good thing that General Franco's public relations officers only allowed the author once to come under fire about two miles outside Madrid.

A year later, writing to his mother from India on 7 January 1897, Churchill expresses his second thoughts about the articles he had written on his return from Cuba:

> I reproach myself somewhat for having written a little uncandidly and for having perhaps done injustice to the insurgents. I rather tried to make out, and in some measure succeeded in making out, a case for Spain. It was politic and did not expose me to the charge of being ungrateful to my hosts, but I am not quite clear whether it was right.
>
>> This above all—to thine [own] self be true
>> And it must follow as the night the day
>> Thou canst not then be false to any man.
>
> I am aware that what I wrote did not shake thrones or upheave empires—but the importance of principles do not depend on the importance of what involves them.

It was not, however, just courtesy to his hosts that coloured Churchill's views when he returned to England after his expedition to Cuba. He foresaw that in the event of a rebel victory the predominant share in government that was likely to be demanded by the negro element among the insurgents, led by Antonio Maceo, would create renewed and even more bitter conflict of a racial kind and thus reduce 'the richest island in the world', 'the pearl of the Antilles', to ruin. This was the reason that led Churchill to view the rebel cause with less enthusiasm than was popular in large sections of the English Press, and among such of his contemporaries as Hubert Howard, who was reporting for *The Times,* but on the rebel side (and who incidentally was one of the war correspondents later to be killed at Omdurman).

This, too, was the reasoning that led him to look askance at the American Government's recognition of the rebel forces in March 1896. But when America actually intervened and went to war with Spain in 1898 there was no doubt where his sympathy lay. Consistent with the views he had expressed more than two years earlier he now saw the opportunity for firm and stable government in an island which was rich in resources but which had been impoverished and debilitated by mis-government and insurrection. 'America can give the Cubans peace', he told the *Morning Post* in an interview on 15 July 1898, 'and perhaps prosperity will then return. American annexation is what we must all urge, but possibly we shall not have to urge very long'.

The myth has grown up that Churchill was in Cuba during the Spanish-American war, and that he had taken the side of the Spaniards against the Americans. Churchill took every possible step to dispel the myth but it kept recurring, notably at the outbreak of war in 1939 when an American Congressman implied that Churchill had actually been an enemy of the United States in the Spanish-American war.

* * * * *

On his return from Cuba there was still another nine months before Churchill was due to embark for India. Since they were going off for eight or nine years ample embarkation leave was provided in addition to normal winter leave, which he had used to such advantage.

He was longing to express himself : his new-found friendship with Bourke Cockran provided him with an opportunity to do so. Writing to him from Duchess Lily's house,

164

Deepdene, on 12 April 1896, Churchill declared: 'The duty of governments is to be first of all practical. I am for makeshifts and expediency. I would like to make the people who live on this world at the same time as I do better fed and happier generally. If incidentally I benefit posterity— so much the better—but I would not sacrifice my own generation to a principle however high or a truth however great'. He went on to criticize a speech which Cockran had made, and which he had sent to Churchill, on the debilitating effect of English rule on Ireland and on Irish industry in particular. Churchill wrote:

Six years of firm, generous, government in Ireland will create a material prosperity which will counteract the efforts which able and brilliant men—like yourself—make to keep the country up to the proper standard of indignation. Not for twenty years could a Home Rule bill pass the English people—so sick and tired are they of the subject—and by that time the necessity for one will have passed away. Home Rule may not be dead but only sleeping—but it will awake like Rip Van Winkle to a world of new ideas. The problems & the burning questions of today will be solved and Home Rule for Ireland as likely as not will be merged in a wider measure of Imperial Federation.

In his reply from New York dated April 27, Cockran begged Churchill to take up a study of sociology and political economy:

With your remarkable talent for lucid and attractive expression you would be able to make great use of information to be acquired by study of these branches. Indeed, I firmly believe you would take a commanding position in public life at the first opportunity which arose, and I have always felt that true capacity either makes or finds its opportunity. . . . I was so profoundly impressed with the vigor of your language and the breadth of your views as I read your criticisms of my speech that I conceived a very high opinion of your future career.

Churchill at this time was twenty-one. He must already have been able, on occasions, to indicate the genius that was to flower in the next half-century. Bourke Cockran must certainly have been a man of profound discernment and judgement of character. As far as we know, he was the first man or woman Churchill met on level terms who really saw his point and his potentialities. At this time Churchill had few friends among his contemporaries and almost none among his elders; his correspondence with Cockran was the first that he entered into with a mature man. Cockran in some ways fulfilled a role that Lord Randolph should have filled if he had survived. As we shall see Churchill was to continue this political correspondence throughout his early manhood and what he wrote to Cockran affords many revealing insights into the development of his mind.

The vivid impression which Cockran made on Churchill's young mind informed and pervaded his subsequent thought and oratory. In what history may decide was one of the most important speeches he ever made—at Fulton, Missouri, under the chairmanship of President Truman on 5 March 1946—he said : 'I have often used words which I learned fifty years ago from a great Irish-American orator, a friend of mine, Mr Bourke Cockran. "There is enough for all. The earth is a generous mother : she will provide in plentiful abundance food for all her children, if they will but cultivate her soil in justice and in peace".'

*　*　*　*　*

Meanwhile Churchill took advantage of his family connections and of the lively interest and good-will which his name aroused—to make the acquaintance of many of Lord Randolph's friends and associates. All doors were open to him. 'What's Randolph's boy like?' people were inclined to ask. Churchill wondered what his father's friends were like. He had not met many of them in his father's lifetime. He took advantage of the opportunities now presented. His mother and Duchess Lily and her new husband, Lord William Beresford, were also most helpful. Lord William was the third son of the 4th Marquess of Waterford, and he had won the Victoria Cross in the Zulu War. He had recently returned to England after sixteen years as ADC and Military Secretary to four successive Viceroys of India.

On account of his father's reputation and his mother's influence he was often asked to visit the famous 'Natty' Rothschild at Tring. Lord Randolph had taken him there two years before. 'Natty' Rothschild was a tremendous and unique figure in English society. It was only in 1858 that the Bill had been carried removing the civil disabilities of the Jews. The English have long been a stuffy and insular race; they tend to resent the intrusion of foreigners in their midst. But the aristocracy were always prepared to accept and assimilate into their ranks foreigners of outstanding quality, particularly if they had a lot of money and proved serviceable to the country.

Thus the Huguenots, who came out of France at the time of the revocation of the Edict of Nantes, found a comfortable haven in East Anglia and revived and fortified the wool trade : self-made men were made knights, baronets and peers (Pitt once said 'Any man who has £10,000 a year deserves to be a baronet') : Mr Disraeli became the darling of the Tory party: and Nathaniel Rothschild in 1885 at the early age of forty-four became the first Jewish peer. The British nation was not extinguished because the aristocracy welcomed not only self-made Englishmen but also Jews and foreigners into their society.

Churchill was not wasting his time in London, prior to his departure for India. At 'several' social functions he had the opportunity of meeting, among others, the former Home Secretary and future Prime Minister (Asquith); the Leader of the House, First Lord of the Treasury and another future Prime Minister (Balfour); the Colonial Secretary (Chamberlain); the Commander-in-Chief of the British Army (Wolseley); the President of the Local Government Board (Chaplin), the Chancellor of the Duchy of Lancaster (James); the President of the Probate Division and Judge Advocate General (Jeune); and the Lord President of the Council (Devonshire).

Churchill took pains to cultivate the important people he met : he was learning from them about the facts of life and how things were done. He was to make the fullest use of the contacts and friendships which he acquired.

* * * * *

Churchill enjoyed these social amenities, but as he many years later said, in an entirely different context, he thought they should be used 'as a springboard, not as a sofa'. He was for action; and half his interest in meeting all these fascinating and important people was to use them as a personal springboard. The time for his departure for India was approaching : the nearer it came, the less he liked the prospect. For a few brief years he had escaped from nine years of servitude at his private and public schools. Was he now to be imprisoned for another nine years, away from England, the centre of political action?

Whilst still in England he had sought by every means to find adventure elsewhere. When the island of Crete entered one of its periodical phases of conflict and disorder Churchill offered his services as Special Correspondent to the *Daily Chronicle*. This offer was politely declined, though it was suggested that if Churchill were to go of his own accord the paper would be happy to receive his reports.

Then he heard that the Sirdar, General Sir Herbert Kitchener, was organizing another expedition up the Nile. Churchill asked Captain Philip Green, who had married his god-mother, Lady Camden, two and a half years after the death of her first husband, to try to get him out to the Sudan, if possible as a galloper to Kitchener. Green wrote to such varied people as Pandeli Ralli, a former Liberal MP and a notable member of Anglo-Greek society in London, and the Duke of Montrose. Once again, Churchill's offers were declined.

As the day of embarkation drew nearer, Churchill grew more hot-tempered and impatient.

WSC to Lady Randolph

EXTRACT

4 August 1896   Hounslow

. . . I daresay you have read in the papers that the 9th Lancers are to go to Durban on the 25th inst. If they are to be sent straight to Rhodesia they will have to take two or three extra subaltern officers—who will be attached from cavalry regiments. I have applied to their colonel to take me should such a contingency arise—and Bill Beresford has wired to him on my behalf. Consequently it is within the bounds of possibility that I may get out after all—and in the best way too—with an English cavalry regt. This we will talk over on Friday—but my dear Mamma you cannot think how I would like to sail in a few days to scenes of adventure and excitement—to places where I could gain experience and derive advantage—rather than to the tedious land of India—where I shall be equally out of the pleasures of peace and the chances of war.

The future is to me utterly unattractive. I look upon going to India with this unfortunate regiment—(which I now feel so attached to that I cannot leave it for another)—as useless and unprofitable exile.

It is useless to preach the gospel of patience to me. Others as young are making the running now and what chance have I of ever catching up. I put it down here—definitely on paper—that you really ought to leave no stone unturned to help me at such a period. Years may pass before such chances occur again. It is a little thing for you to ask and a smaller thing for those in authority to grant—but it means so much to me.

Three months leave is what I want & you could get it for me. If I can't get this—perhaps I may be able to go with the 9th [Lancers]—but that might only end in police duty in Natal.

You can't realise how furiously intolerable this life is to me when so much is going on a month away from here. . . .

No answer from Lady Randolph survives. All was settled : all was ordained. He sailed from Southampton for India in S.S. *Britannia* with the 4th Hussars on 11 September 1896.

9

INDIA

MANY YOUNG MEN, at the age of twenty-one, with few attachments at home, would have thought it a high adventure to sail for India and to be stationed there for eight or nine years. Churchill had mixed feelings. He was enraptured by any form of adventure—he had had some of a limited character in Cuba; but he doubted if there would be much opportunity in India. In any case he had already determined that his life should be one of politics. But how to escape from the Army? How to pay his debts? How to achieve an income that would permit his entry into the House of Commons? (Members were not paid until 1911, and then only £400 a year.) These were the ugly and at the time unanswerable questions which were in his mind when he sailed for India.

In those days it was difficult for a young gentleman of good but impecunious family to find a way of earning a living. Trade, commerce and the Stock Exchange were still frowned on in many quarters as unfitting for a gentleman; and these institutions did not much solicit the services of young gentlemen, however gifted. If a young man was not clever enough to go to the Bar, or had not enough influence to get himself into a firm of merchant bankers, he had scarcely any other alternative but to go into the Church, the Army or the Navy, all ill-rewarded professions. Though Churchill was now of age he had inherited no estate. He was, after all, the son of a younger son, and his mother, Jennie, was busy dissipating the remains of a considerable fortune which her father Leonard Jerome had settled upon her. He sailed to India with little more prospects than did Clive; but he did not, like Clive, try to kill himself.

Colonel Brabazon did not sail with the regiment to India; he had relinquished command of the 4th Hussars during the summer and handed over to Colonel William Alexander Ramsay. Colonel Ramsay was, in contrast to his predecessor, a quiet unspectacular officer who suffered from

Kabul
Jellalabad
Malakand
Nowshera
Rawalpindi
Peshawar
Kohat
Tirah
Kandahar
Quetta
Mian Mir
Simla
Umballa
Meerut
DELHI
Muthra
Agra
Jodhpur
Itarsi
CALCUTTA
BOMBAY
Poona
Secunderabad
Hyderabad
Raichur
Bangalore
MADRAS
Ootacamund
N
Miles
0   100   200   300   400   500
CEYLON

INDIA

the misfortune of never having seen action in nearly thirty years of service. Churchill's especial friends on the long voyage out were his old travelling companion Reggie Barnes, who had been confirmed as Adjutant in May; Hugo Baring, a son of Lord Revelstoke; Ian Hogg, and, among the senior officers, Major Ronald Kincaid-Smith who was the following year to become second-in-command.

Churchill found agreeable diversion in a kind of 'moot' which was held among the officers towards the end of the voyage and in which he participated. In a letter from the Indian Ocean of 30 September 1896, he told his mother:

> Last night we had rather an amusing 'Breach of Promise' case in which I was counsel for the defence. To my relief I showed myself able to speak without notes or preparation for twenty minutes and as I succeeded in keeping the audience in constant laughter—my harangue was a success. My impediment did not seem to interfere with my articulation at all and of all who spoke I was the best heard. In the army I came like a Duckling among chickens—I don't know whether I or they were most astonished to find I could swim.

All his life Churchill suffered from an impediment in his speech. It is hard to define exactly what it was; some thought it was a stammer: some a lisp. Certainly, like his father before him, he always had a difficulty in pronouncing the letter 's'. He was extremely conscious of this himself from an early age and sought to correct it. Before he left for India he had consulted Sir Felix Semon, a throat specialist, a friend of the family and of the Court. Semon told Churchill (fee four guineas) that there was no organic defect, and that 'with practice and perseverance' he would be cured of his disability. We also have the evidence of Mrs Muriel Warde, formerly Miss Muriel Wilson, who has told the author of how when she was a young girl at Tranby Croft, Churchill used to walk her up and down the long drive rehearsing such phrases as, 'The Spanish ships I cannot see for they are not in sight'. This was designed to cure him of his trouble in pronouncing the sibilant 's'.

Though a lucky man in many ways, Churchill appears to have been unlucky in minor adventures. There had been the pneumonia at Brighton, the misadventures at Harrow, the tumble-down at Branksome Dene, Bournemouth, his fall at steeplechasing at Aldershot. Now, on his arrival at Bombay, he was to experience, through his enthusiasm, a misadventure the effects of which travelled with him for the rest of his life. Eager to go ashore, he tells us in *My Early Life*, he and some of his friends had summoned one of the many tiny boats hovering around the *Britannia* to take them ashore before the rest of the party. After about a quarter of an hour they reached the quays and the Sassoon Dock and 'we came alongside of a great stone wall with dripping steps and iron rings for hand-holds. The boat rose and fell four or five feet with the surges. I put out my hand and grasped at a ring; but before I could get my feet on the steps the boat swung away, giving my right shoulder a sharp and peculiar wrench. I scrambled up all right, made a few remarks of a general character, mostly beginning with the earlier letters of the alphabet, hugged my shoulder and soon thought no more about it.' He had in fact dislocated his shoulder and for the rest of his life this was to plague him. He had to play polo with the upper part of his arm strapped against his body. Once, he related later, his shoulder very nearly went out through a too expansive gesture in the House of Commons. But he always, as will be seen, liked to attribute his survival two years later of the charge of the Lancers at the Battle of Omdurman to the fact that he was unable to use a sword and instead had to defend himself with the more lethal Mauser pistol.

From Bombay the regiment travelled by train to Bangalore, breaking the journey at Poona. Bangalore was a military cantonment in the Madras Presidency. Despite the rigours of the climate even impecunious subalterns like Churchill seem to have been able to live in considerable comfort and with some degree of elegance :

WSC to Lady Randolph

EXTRACT

14 October [1896]   Bangalore

. . . The climate is very good. The sun even at midday is temperate and the mornings and evenings are fresh and

173

cool. Hugo, Barnes and I are safely installed in a magnificent pink and white stucco palace in the middle of a large and beautiful garden. I will send you a photograph of the bungalow as soon as we are thoroughly settled. For servants we each have a 'Butler' whose duties are to wait at table—to manage the household and to supervise the stables : A First Dressing Boy or valet who is assisted by a second DB : and a sais [syce] to every horse or pony. Besides this we share the services of 2 gardeners—3 Bhistis or water carriers—4 Dhobies or washermen & 1 watchman. Such is our menage. . . .

Churchill took advantage of his comfortable bungalow and his leisure hours at Bangalore to resume the hobby which he had not pursued since his holidays at Banstead when he was still a Harrow school-boy : collecting butterflies. At Bangalore he found his garden full of Purple Emperors, White Admirals, Swallow Tails and many beautiful and rare species. 'I shall be able to make a fine collection with very little trouble and much amusement', he told his brother Jack. He sent to England for his implements, nets, collecting boxes, setting boards, pins and a killing tin. But even before they arrived, he had begun amassing a fine collection—so much so that Hugo Baring and Reggie Barnes, with whom he shared his bungalow, complained that the place was 'degenerating into a taxidermist's shop'. His rekindled enthusiasm had an unhappy interruption. On 2 December 1896 Churchill wrote to Jack :

My butterfly collection, which included upwards of 65 different sorts, has been destroyed by the malevolence of a rat who crawled into the cabinet and devoured all the specimens. I have however, caught the brute and had him killed by 'Winston' the terrier, and have begun again perseveringly.

An entirely new interest was provided by gardening—or more precisely, the growing of roses. The bungalow's previous occupier had left a magnificent collection of standard roses in the garden : 'We have now over 50 different kinds of roses', he wrote to his mother on 7 January 1897, 'La France, Gloire de Dijon, Marechal Niel and the rest of them—and all the rest we planted on arrival have come up into bright coloured flowers. I take the greatest interest in their growth. In a year or so it will indeed be beautiful.'

At this time he met the first great love of his life, Miss Pamela Plowden. She was seven months older than he and was still alive at his death.

Pamela Plowden's father, Mr Trevor John Chichele Chichele-Plowden, who was in the Indian Civil Service, was at this time Resident at Hyderabad. It appears that Miss Plowden was known to Lady Randolph but when she came on a visit to Bangalore Churchill had to report to his mother (26 October 1896): 'Alas—I never met her in England so forbore to call'. But the following week, when he went to Secunderabad, just ten miles from Hyderabad, for a polo tournament, Churchill did not let a second opportunity slip. He was smitten with instantaneous love the first time he met Pamela Plowden:

I was introduced yesterday to Miss Pamela Plowden—who lives here. I must say that she is the most beautiful girl I have ever seen—'Bar none' as the Duchess Lily says. We are going to try and do the City of Hyderabad together—on an elephant. You dare not walk or the natives spit at Europeans—which provokes retaliation leading to riots.

The ride through the city of Hyderabad on an elephant with Miss Plowden was sucessfully accomplished. 'She is', wrote Churchill to his mother, on 12 November 1896, 'very beautiful and clever'. He dined with the Plowdens at Hyderabad and not unnaturally enjoyed himself. 'A civilised dinner with ladies present is delightful in this country after nearly three months of messes and barbarism.'

He had little time for the traditional niceties, if such they could be called, of Anglo-Indian society. In his very first letter (4 October 1896) from the mainland he relates how he 'saw a lot of horrid Anglo-Indian women at the races. Nasty vulgar creatures all looking as though they thought themselves great beauties. I fear me they are a sorry lot'. 'Nice people in India are few and far between', he wrote to his mother on 12 November 1896. 'They are like oases in the desert.'

And he summed up his first eight months at Bangalore:

EXTRACT

14 April [1897]   Bangalore

information & knowledge - been utterly barren.
I have met no one who cared to tell me
anything about the problems of the hour &
if I stay here twenty years as do
soldiers I see no prospect of my acquiring
any knowledge worth knowing of
Indian affairs.

Poked away in a garrison
town - which resembles a 3rd rate watering
place, out of season without the sea, with

. . . The 8 months I have been in this country have as
regards Indian information & knowledge, been utterly
barren. I have met no one who cared to tell me anything
about the problems of the hour & if I stay here twenty
years as a soldier I see no prospect of my acquiring any
knowledge worth knowing of Indian affairs.

Poked away in a garrison town which resembles a 3rd
rate watering place, out of season & without the sea, with
lots of routine work and a hot and trying sun—without
society or good sport—half my friends on leave and the
other half ill—my life here would be intolerable were it
not for the consolations of literature. The only valuable
knowledge I take away from India (soldiering apart)
could have been gathered equally well in Cumberland
Place. Notwithstanding all this I have not been unhappy,
though occasionally very bored, and I contemplate without repugnance returning to my books, my butterflies &
my roses. But I must have some holidays & you will be
harsher than the Carthaginians if you refuse me them.

I am alone now in the Bungalow Barnes having gone to Ootacamund a hill station for his leave & Hugo [Baring] to Simla to take up his appointment on the Viceroy's staff—so that things are very dull. Only Kincaid & I really are left with a few subalterns who have joined since we came to India & who are for conversational purposes—useless—and a rather nice fellow (Agnew) gazetted to us as Major from the 7th Hussars, whose experiences in Matabeleland are entertaining. Indeed my chief amusement is to stimulate a discussion between Kincaid-Smith who is a wild filibuster & worships the Raiders & Agnew who has all the Imperial soldier's prejudices against colonials and looks on Jameson, Sir John [Willoughby] the whites etc as scoundrels of the deepest dye. It will be terrible when this topic is worn threadbare. With care and judicious treatment it may however be made to last until the 8th of May.

I have lived the life of a recluse out here. The vulgar Anglo-Indians have commented on my not 'calling' as is the absurd custom of the country. Outside the regiment I know perhaps three people who are agreeable and I have no ambitions to extend my acquaintance. The consequence is that at such a time as this—when ⅔rds of the regt are on leave or ill, I am somewhat thrown on my own resources. Fortunately these are not slender. But I must take a holiday. . . .

Churchill's letters show that he thought he was in a prison—he had no one to write to except his mother who was occupied with other matters and his brother Jack— more than five years younger than he was—only just leaving Harrow. From the time that he arrived in India he plainly had only two desires : one to read and learn about politics; the other to get out of the Army as soon as he could. Meanwhile, since he had no money he had the idea of going to any little wars that he could find. His industry in this matter was astonishing. First he reminded his mother that he was not at all disheartened by the rebuffs his offers of service had met with before his departure for India. 'I suppose', he wrote to her, 18 November 1896, 'you have noticed how de Moleyns has got on in S. Africa. The Distinguished Service Order and the command of the New

Matabeleland Police have been his reward for a few months of enjoyable & active life. Compare that with the reward of those who conscientiously perform the routine duties you are always advocating as the road to success.'

Once again, he was determined to go to Egypt to join Kitchener's advance up the Nile. *'Please do your best'*, he wrote to his mother the following week. 'I should not have forgiven myself if an expedition started next year and I felt it was my own fault I was not there.'

Elections were never very far from his mind as he scanned *The Times*. There was a by-election in November at East Bradford—a constituency in which his father had been much admired and with which Churchill felt he had a strong link. When he heard the result and saw that the Conservative had won, he wrote : 'What a pity I was not home.' Noticing that it was Captain Ronald Greville, formerly of the Life Guards, who won the seat, he added with a touch of bitterness : 'I see a soldier got in.'

The success of others while he was tied down in Bangalore was naturally galling. In Calcutta he met Lord Fincastle who was ADC to the Viceroy and whom he was to encounter several times in the future. 'He got three medals out of Egypt and saw hardly any fighting.'

Sir Herbert Kitchener, writing from the Headquarters of the Frontier Force at Dongola on 30 December 1896 to Lady Randolph, eventually agreed to have her son's name put down on the list for special service with the Egyptian Army though there were no vacancies at that time in the cavalry. Churchill, who had become very disappointed at the lack of progress he was making in that direction, was delighted. He wrote to his mother on 18 February 1897 : 'You will see that if I go to Egypt & if things turn out well, it might be almost worth my while to stick to soldiering. At any rate I am certain of this that unless a good opportunity presents itself of my obtaining a seat in the House of Commons, I *should* continue in the army for two years more. Those two years could not be better spent than on active service. The question is "where"? Egypt seems the only hope & therefore I beg you leave no stone unturned in your endeavour to obtain a vacancy for me.'

Whether or not this 'came off' he was determined not to pass a dull unhealthy summer languishing in Bangalore.

Rather than do that he was prepared to spend such small funds as remained to him on taking passage to England for his three months' leave. He had a half-formed idea that he might stop off in Cairo 'to pay my respects to the Sirdar' and perhaps be taken on on the spot. Perhaps also he might be able to animate his mother's friends in London to better effect if he were actually there to do it. His mother was against it:

Lady Randolph to WSC

EXTRACT

26 February 1897   35A Gt Cumberland Place

. . . It is absolutely out of the question, not only on account of money, but for the sake of yr reputation. They will say & with some reason that you can't stick to anything. You have only been out 6 months & it is on the cards that you may be called to Egypt. There is plenty for you to do in India. I confess that I am quite disheartened about you. You seem to have no real purpose in life & won't realize at the age of 22 that for a man life means work, & hard work if you mean to succeed. Many men at yr age have to work for a living & support their mother. It is useless my saying more—we have been over this ground before—it is not a pleasant one. . . .

'I set great store on going to Egypt if they go on this year', Churchill replied to his mother. 'I long for excitement of some sort and the prospect of joining an English expedition attracts me immensely. I do hope you will not relax your efforts.'

*   *   *   *   *

Throughout his military career Churchill remained a keen follower of public affairs and an avid reader of the newspapers. At first he confined his comments to military matters; while yet on board ship he deplored the iniquity of officers going to India having to declare articles on which duty must be paid. 'Even my regimental saddle is liable to this excise. It seems to me a disgraceful thing to tax public servants going to India by order of the Government in this extraordinary manner and I cannot see that the Indian Government can be constitutionally right in imposing taxes on Europeans who do not have a vote in such taxes. It is contrary to the fundamental principle of government—no taxation without Representation. But to impose such a tax on a saddle used *only* in military employment is so monstrous an act of injustice that you will find it hard to credit it. I expect I shall find many more instances of the same detestable fruit of bureaucracy.'

When Lord Lansdowne advocated an increase in the size of the army Churchill wrote scathingly on 8 December 1896 of his 'stupid speech':

WSC to Lady Randolph

EXTRACT

8 December [1896]   Bangalore

... I cannot help thinking that he is not as great a man as is customary to suppose. I hoped no one would be so foolish as to advocate the expenditure of more money on the army. It is a shocking thing that we should be compelled to have a 'hundred million budget' every year and you may be sure that the strain of taxation is not without its effect on the prosperity and happiness of the nation. I believe that it is necessary for us to have an unequalled navy : A fleet strong enough to render us superior to a combination of any two powers & with an ample margin for accidents. I would support taxation to almost any extent necessary to attain this end. With such a fleet an army does not become a necessity for defence. For offence an army corps or perhaps two would adequately carry out such enterprises in foreign countries—out of Europe—as might be expedient. The only other duty of the British army is to provide a training ground for our army of occupation here. The increase of the Anglo-Indian forces is a question which I do not consider above. It is one which Lord Lansdowne did not allude to either. They consider the garrison adequate. Where then is the necessity of an increase to the army? If money is to be spent & taxes imposed—let it at best be employed in making us supreme at sea. Given the unquestioned command of the sea—there is no part of our Empire which our present army could not protect—and without such command there is no part which two such armies could not maintain. (India is of course the exception—but that is a matter for the Indian Government). For a man like Lansdowne to voice a petty jealousy & I believe to a great extent an imaginary jealousy—between army and navy—is most proper and unwise. . . .

We shall see how six years later, when he had at last entered the House of Commons, he was to oppose, in a series of highly successful speeches, Mr Brodrick's proposal of three Army Corps. The arguments which he had already propounded to his mother at this time were to mature and fructify.

When it was decided that the Guards were to serve abroad he wrote on 7 January 1897 : 'Formerly of course "the Guards" were officered by the nicest fellows in the army & they were a *corps d'elite*. This is now all changed and I would infinitely prefer any Highland regiment or any Rifle Regiment to the Grenadiers, Coldstreams or Scots Guards, either to serve in or with. The army now stands on a democratic basis and "the Guards" have been sacrificed to the spirit of the age. The name however is not wholly divested of its former splendours and "Eton & the Guards" may still afford solid advantages to the wealthy aspirant for position.' And again some weeks later :

WSC to Lady Randolph

EXTRACT

2 March 1897   Bangalore

. . . As to the Guards : I think the War Office have as usual been guilty of meddling & muddling. As usual they have been stupid and tactless. They have proposed a very unpopular change & they have shown no good reason for that change. The Government, also as usual, have had no hesitation in supporting a measure which would seem much better suited to a radical than to a Tory programme.

Two more years will see this government ripe for a fall. A General Election now would probably bring the Radicals in. Certainly if they dropped Home Rule the country would vote for them. The swing of the pendulum has been accelerated by Ld Salisbury's obstinate boorishness, by Balfour's pusilanimous vacillations, by Lansdowne's ridiculous 'reforms' & by Curzon's conceit. In two years more they will not command a majority in the country. When that state of things arises any accident might wreck them in the Houses. At least that is how it seems to me—though perhaps I look through bilious-coloured glasses. . . .

Churchill was beginning to express strong views on political matters. Already in November 1896 he had treated his mother to a lengthy and carefully thought out dissertation on the political situation at home. When Lord Rosebery resigned the leadership of the Liberal Party and explained his reasons for doing so in a speech at Edinburgh on October 9, he wrote to his mother :

WSC to Lady Randolph

EXTRACT

4 November [1896]   Trimulgherry
                                                                        Deccan

. . . A more statesmanlike & impressive utterance is hard to imagine. He is a great man—and one of these days he will again lead a great party. The only two great men now on the political stage will be drawn irresistibly together. Their political reins already coincide and Ld Rosebery and Joe Chamberlain would be worthy leaders of the Tory Democracy. Such a combination is very distant now—but a fresh deal would bring it into the foreground. Since the question of Home Rule has disappeared from English Politics, the Liberal Unionists have lost their status entirely, and it is only the folly of the Radical party in pretending to cling to the ghost of separation which gives the L.U. an excuse to remain in a Tory government. When the Liberals have the courage to throw over their separatist principles, the L.U. are logically bound to return [to the Liberal Party].

The result of so tremendous a juggle would be infallibly —to bring the two popular leaders & finest orators to the front. Divided they would be curbed by the solid remnant of the Conservative party—peers, property, publicans, parsons & turnips. Convergent interests would produce solidarity of action and their similar opinions would interpose no obstacle. Rosebery is only an advanced Tory—Chamberlain a prudent Radical. They would combine, and the fossils & the Fenians—the extremes of either party—would be left in the cold. So much for the Cabinets of the future.

This is my final selection—and though it is unwise to prophesy till afterwards—you would do well to 'expect the event' which is Gibbon for 'await the result'. . . .

In February 1897 Britain, somewhat reluctantly, joined the five Powers in blockading the island of Crete and seeking to prevent Greece from sending reinforcements and supplies to the small Greek expeditionary force 'protecting the Christians against the Turks'. Lord Salisbury's action was part of his policy in trying to maintain the Concert of Europe, but Churchill wrote to his mother in his most indignant vein:

WSC to Lady Randolph

25 February 1897   Bangalore

. . . What an atrocious crime the Government have committed in Crete! That British warships should lead the way in protecting the blood bespattered Turkish soldiery from the struggles of their victims is horrible to contemplate. When Warren Hastings hired out a British Brigade to a native ruler in order that the ruler might destroy the Rohillas—he at least obtained in return for his infamous action substantial remuneration. But the British Government, in a vain endeavour to obtain the confidence of the Powers, have not hesitated to commit a crime, equally cruel and more shameless, in full sight of the world and of history. It is just as well that I am so young that my opinions do not matter and may be revised and altered without difficulty if necessary. For in this matter I thoroughly agree with the Opposition and I cannot help hoping that the Nemesis which waits on evil actions may reduce & humble the perpetrators of such a crime.

Among the leaders of the Tory party are two whom I despise and detest as politicians above all others—Mr Balfour & George Curzon. The one—a languid, lazy lackadaisical cynic; the other the spoiled darling of politics—blown with conceit—insolent from undeserved success—the typification of the superior Oxford prig. It is to this pair that all the criminal muddles of the last 15 months should be ascribed. Lord Salisbury an able and obstinate man, who joins the brain of a statesman to the delicate susceptibilities of a mule has been encouraged to blunder tactlessly along till nearly every section of the Union party & nearly every cabinet in Europe has been irritated or offended. The result is that abroad we follow the folly that led to that most idiotic of wars, the Crimea, & keep the ring in which the Turk massacres subjects & at home we see the party to whom so much that is precious is confided, reduced by the blunders of its leaders to ruin. So much for politics. It is surprising how easily epithets and indignation arise in the mind, when the sun is hot, has been hot & is daily getting hotter. Just as religion as it approaches the equator becomes more full of ceremony and superstition—so language & ideas here flourish with a floral fertility—which is unknown in more temperate climes. So you must take 50% off this letter when you read it. . . .

Of course it was not just the sun which led to these ebullitions, of which Lady Randolph may well have been a sceptical and usually, as far as is known, an unresponsive audience. Churchill would far rather have been addressing a crowded House of Commons or mass meetings from a public platform. These letters are merely another symptom of his frustration and his mother was the only person to whom he could blow off steam.

In the matter of Crete, however, she was moved to reply:

Lady Randolph to WSC

EXTRACT

18 March 1897   Brooksby
Leicester

. . . I hope you have changed yr mind about Crete—subsequent events must show you that the Concert of Europe were *obliged* to act as they did altho' they certainly were slow in making up their minds. I suppose after a bit the Cretans will settle down under a form of autonomy & afterwards will become annexed to Greece. . . .

WSC to Lady Randolph

EXTRACT

6 April [1897]   Bangalore

. . . I [am] sorry you do not agree with my views on Crete. Certainly I have seen no reason to alter what I wrote. We are doing a very wicked thing in firing on the Cretan insurgents & in blockading Greece so that she cannot succour them. It will take a lot of whitewash to justify the spectacle of the Seaforth Highlanders fighting by the side of the Bashi Bazouk. I admit the material arguments are rather on the other side. That is bound to be the case, I look on this question from the point of view of right & wrong : Lord Salisbury from that of profit and loss.

Besides it does not appear to me that we are being dragged by the nose by the European Powers into this action. Rather does it look as if we took the lead. We have more ships & more men on the spot and generally appear to be taking a very leading part. So what? In a most atrocious crime, where France & Germany have hesitated, we have rushed in. I am quite sure the people of England do not approve of the use to which their fleets and armies are being put—and the Government will most certainly have to answer for their conduct.

Lord Salisbury is a strong man & a clever man. He is not running the risk of so much unpopularity for nothing. He does not wish the Russians to get to Constantinople and with this object he is willing to crush the Greeks & Cretans or anyone else whose interests do not coincide with his. The Turkish Empire he is determined to maintain. He does not care a row of buttons for the sufferings of those who are oppressed by that Empire. This is not only wrong but foolish. It is wrong because it is unjustifiable to kill people who are not attacking you—because their continued existence is inconvenient : and because it is an abominable action, which prolongs the servitude under the Turks of the Christian races.

It is foolish because, as surely as night follows day—the Russians are bound to get Constantinople. We could never stop them even if we wished. Nor ought we to wish for anything that could impede the expulsion from Europe of the filthy Oriental.

After all, we do not live in Crimean War days, nor need we repeat the follies of the past. Russia must have Constantinople. It is the birthplace of her religion & the aim of her ambitions. 'Were I a Russian as I am an Englishman I would never rest till I saw the Russian eagle floating over St Sophia—never! never! never!' (Pitt on the American Colonies adapted). We shall be mad if we attempt to bar the just aspiration of a mighty people. I would sooner face an avalanche. Seventy millions of people without a warm water port. Is it rational?

But what is Russia doing in Crete? Of all the powers she alone has not the required troops and appears to cooperate most loyally. I do not trust her. Such rectitude would not be human. She cannot be acting in good faith. Every atrocity and every disturbance smooths her path to Constantinople. Is it conceivable she is acting disinterestedly. Never will I believe it.

Our Machiavellian Government had better be careful lest they find themselves even out done in vice. There are no lengths to which I would not go in opposing them were I in the House of Commons. I am a Liberal in all but name. My views excite the pious horror of the Mess. Were it not for Home Rule—to which I will never consent—I would enter Parliament as a Liberal. As it is—Tory Democracy will have to be the standard under which I shall range myself.

1. Reform at home. Extension of the Franchise to evry male. Universal Education. Equal Establishment of all religions. Wide measures of local self-government. Eight hours. Payment of members (on request). A progressive Income Tax. I will vote for them all.

2. Imperialism abroad.

East of Suez Democratic reins are impossible. India must be governed on old principles. The colonies must be federated and a system of Imperial Defence arranged. Also we must combine for Tariff & Commerce.

3. European Politics.

Non Intervention. Keep absolutely unembroiled— Isolated if you like.

4. Defence.

The Colonies must contribute and hence a council must be formed. A mighty navy must keep the seas. The army may be reduced to a training depot for India with one army corps for petty expeditions.

5. To maintain the present constitution of Queen—Lords —Commons—& the Legislative union as at present established.

There! that is the creed of Tory Democracy. Peace & Power abroad—Prosperity & Progress at home—will be the results. . . .

*   *   *   *   *

When he sailed for India, Churchill embarked on that process of self-education which was to prove so serviceable a substitute for the opportunities which he had neglected or rejected in his formal education. His letters to his mother show that he was already reading, while at Aldershot, Gibbon and Fawcett. There is no information available of what he read on the voyage out on the S.S. *Britannia;* but within a few months of his arrival at Bangalore he was making insatiable demands upon his mother for more books. During his first spell in India (September 1896—April 1897) his mother sent him at his request 12 volumes of Macaulay (8 of History and 4 of Essays); 27 volumes of the *Annual Register;* and 2 volumes of Adam Smith's *Wealth of Nations.*

He frequently commented on the authors whom he read : 'Macaulay', he wrote to Lady Randolph on 21 January 1897, 'is easier reading than Gibbon and in quite a different style. Macaulay crisp and forcible, Gibbon stately and impressive. Both are fascinating and show what a fine language English is since it can be pleasing in styles so different.'

He was well aware of the influence that Gibbon and his other reading exercised upon his style of writing. 'The voyage', he wrote in one letter to his mother, 'may be made by literature both profitable and agreeable', and then he crossed these words out, commenting 'what a beastly sentence.' 'I suppress with difficulty', he added, 'an impulse to become sententious. Gibbon & Macaulay, however much they may improve one's composition of essays or reports, do not lend themselves to letter writing.'

* * * * *

For some months the financial worries with which Churchill and his mother had been so beset before his departure for India made no appearance in their correspondence. Churchill explains in *My Early Life* how on arrival in India in those days, all the cavalry officer had to do was to hand over his uniform and clothes to the dressing-boy, his ponies to the syce and his money to the butler, 'and you need never trouble any more.' True, the extra allowance paid to cavalry officers in India had increased his Army pay to about £300 a year; and his allowance from his mother, paid quarterly, was now £500 a year; but this was never enough :

All the rest, [he recalled in *My Early Life*] had to be
borrowed at usurious rates of interest from the-all-too
accommodating native bankers. Every officer was warned
against these gentlemen. I always found them most
agreeable; very fat, very urbane, quite honest and
mercilessly rapacious. All you had to do was to sign little
bits of paper, and produce a polo pony as if by magic.
The smiling financier rose to his feet, covered his face
with his hands, replaced his slippers, and trotted off con-
tentedly till that day three months. They only charged
two per cent a month and made quite a good living out
of it. . . .

For the time, then, his financial affairs appeared to be in
a tranquil state. The calm was deceptive :

Lady Randolph to WSC

EXTRACT

26 February 1897   35A Gt Cumberland Place

Dearest Winston,
    It is with very unusual feelings that I sit down to write
to you my weekly letter. Generally it is a pleasure—but this
time is quite the reverse. The enclosed letter will explain
why. I went to Cox's this morning & find out that not only
you have anticipated the whole of yr quarter's allowance
due this month but £45 besides—& now this cheque for
£50—& that *you knew* you had nothing at the bank. The
manager told me they had warned you that they would not
let you overdraw & the next mail brought this cheque. I
must say I think it is *too* bad of you—indeed it is hardly
honourable knowing as you do that you are dependent on
me & that I give you the biggest allowance I *possibly can*,
more than I can afford. I have told them at Cox's not to
apply to me in future as you must manage yr own affairs.
I am not responsible. If you cannot live on yr allowance
from me & yr pay you will have to leave the 4th Hussars. *I
cannot* increase yr allowance. . . .

Yr mother
J R C

Churchill tried to make peace with his mother as best he could; he paid her £30 of the £45 which she had advanced on his behalf, and promised the rest when 'my ship comes home.' He blamed it all on 'that stupid Cox' with whom, however, he continued to bank amicably for the rest of his life. Lady Randolph was obviously desperately worried:

Lady Randolph to WSC

5 March [1897]   35A Gt Cumberland Place

Dearest Winston,

I was glad to get yr nice letter telling me of yr work as Brigade Major. What an extraordinary boy you are as regards yr business affairs. You never say a word about them, & then spring things upon me. If you only told me when you were hard up—& why—perhaps I shld not be so angry. But I don't believe you ever know how you stand with yr account at the Bank. I marvel at their allowing you to overdraw as you do. Neither the Westminster or the National Bank will let me overdraw £5 without telling me at once. Dearest this is the only subject on which we ever fall out. I do wish you wld try & reform—if you only realised how little I have, & how impossible it is for me to get any more. I have raised all I can, & I assure you unless something extraordinary turns up I see ruin staring me in the face.

Out of £2,700 a year £800 of it goes to you 2 boys, £410 for house rent & stables, which leaves me £1,500 for everything—taxes, servants, stables, food, dress, travelling & now I have to pay interest on money borrowed. I really fear for the future. I am telling you all this darling in order that you may see how impossible it is for me to help you—& how you must in future depend on yrself. I make out that you get about £200 pay, which makes yr income for the present £700 a year. Of course it is not much & I can quite understand that you will have to deny yrself many things if you mean to try and live within it. But the fact is, you have got to do more than try. Now when you receive

189

this write me a sensible letter & tell me that I shall be able to count on you.

With best love, Yr Loving Mother
J R C

Let me know exactly how you stand.

And when a week later another creditor came presenting a cheque which had apparently been dishonoured, she wrote with the double object of encouraging financial probity and discouraging him from returning to England:

Lady Randolph to WSC

EXTRACT

18 March [1897]   Brooksby
                                                  Leicester

. . . I seem only to write disagreeable things, but will you attend to the enclosed & explain it to me. I am sending the man the £11 he asks, but about yr dishonoured cheque I know nothing. My darling boy, you can't think how all this worries me. I have so many money troubles of my own I feel I cannot take on any others. You know how dearly I wld love to help you if I could—& also how much I wld like to have you come home—but quite apart [from] the advisability of such a step for such a short time, think of the expense. Every creditor you possess in England will be down upon you, & as far as I can make out you won't have a penny until May & I daresay that is forestalled—of course I can't coerce you & if you have made up yr mind to come, you must, but remember the consequences. I am sure that yr brother officers won't encourage you to come. Yr friend Major Kincaid-Smith wrote me a very kind letter about you—but he deprecated yr coming home. I really think there is a good chance of yr getting to Egypt & in any case you are gaining much military experience in India & showing that you can work & do something. Darling I lay awake last night thinking about you & how much I wanted to help you—if only I had some money I wld do so. I am so proud of you & of all yr great & endearing qualities. I feel sure that if you live you will make a name for yrself but I know to do it you have to be made of stern stuff—& not mind sacrifice & self denial. I feel I am reading you a lecture & you will vote my letters a bore—but you know that I do not mean it in that way. . . .

He had determined, despite his mother's opposition, to return home for leave.

While on board ship on his way home he planned to read more *Annual Registers*. Six of them he had read and 'carefully annotated besides', at Bangalore; they still survive. Most people make use of the *Annual Register,* that admirable institution, of which Edmund Burke was the first editor. Few have read the volumes consecutively in order to gain a comprehensive knowledge of British politics. Churchill was one of the few. Feeling the need for a more detailed knowledge of contemporary English politics and their background, he had written to his mother early in 1897 : 'Will you send me Hallam's *Constitutional History*. Also do you think you can find out for me—from some able politico or journalist—how and where I can find the detailed Parliamentary history (Debates, Divisions, Parties, cliques and caves) of the last 100 years.'

'I hope you have received the books I have sent you,' Lady Randolph wrote on 11 March 1897, '& are duly grateful—for I find the *Annual Register* costs 14/- a time—& as you asked for a 100 ! you will not be surprised if I don't send them all—particularly as I have them in the library. However I have ordered from 1870 to be sent 2 vols at a time.'

He had failed to profit by the expensive formal education which his parents had provided for him : he now prepared to do it for himself. Four of the *Annual Registers* which his mother sent him, for 1874–5–6–7, contain carefully thought-out pencil notes, which are still legible today, pasted in at the appropriate place in the text. He expresses clear, logical and sometimes unfashionable opinions on a variety of issues.

On Gladstone's protest against the new Tory government's

decision to reverse a measure introduced by the previous Liberal administration Churchill commented: 'I should detest the idea that our laws were unalterable like those of the Medes and Persians.' On the Public Worship Regulation Bill to prevent 'the advance of ritualism' he wrote: 'If a Church is "established" and receives recognition from the Government . . . it is obvious that the Government should be able to insist on effective control.' And on the refusal of Lord Northbrook, Viceroy of India, to prohibit the export of grain from India during the famine of 1873–4: 'Lord Northbrook was right in refusing. . . . I should have thought that famine prices would immediately attract the grain without any law being necessary. I am opposed to any interference by Government with private trade.'

In the *Annual Register* for 1875 Churchill noted, in a comment on the new coercion laws for Ireland: 'The chief, indeed some think the only duty of government, is to afford efficient protection to life and property and in the discharge of that duty they may fairly claim the largest powers. The contention that partial and special legislation is an insult to the Irish people is unfortunately unanswerable. The removal of that insult rests with them.' On a bill to establish an intermediate High Court immediately below the House of Lords he wrote: 'I like to see modern principles clothed with the picturesque garments of the past. . . . I am inclined to think that the House of Lords is unsuited for the duties of a judicial court, and should prefer a tribunal on the lines suggested. I should very much like to see the functions of a court of appeal extended to criminal cases.' The Court of Criminal Appeal was established in 1907.

Churchill supported the Artisans' Dwellings Bill, introduced to give local authorities compulsory powers to carry out slum clearance and improvements. 'I affirm the principle that Governments have nothing to give away and hence have no right to be generous: but every class is interested in the extinction of a plague spot.' When Mr Henry Fawcett, the Liberal economist whose works Churchill had already read, opposed the measure on the ground that it was 'class legislation'—'we do not frame Acts of Parliament to enable noblemen to obtain suitable dwellings'—Churchill commented: 'Mr Fawcett's arguments might have claimed the applause of the cavalier parliament or the Oxford Union but such nonsense should not be spoken—still less listened to in the 19th century.'

In 1876, during the debate on the purchase of the Suez Canal shares, Mr Robert Lowe, formerly Gladstone's Chancellor of the Exchequer, attributed press support for the deal to self-interest. A 'spirited policy', he said, 'however expensive it might be to others, was sure to be dear to the newspapers.' Churchill noted indignantly : 'This is ridiculous. Exciting times cost the newspapers much more in telegrams, correspondents etc than they gained in increased circulation.' This was somewhat naive of Churchill at a time when Northcliffe was striding forward to corrupt newspapers. Though Churchill had not perceived it, war and rumours of war were grist to the printing houses of Pulitzer, Hearst and Northcliffe : they were to coin money through these disasters, and Churchill was to be well rewarded for his war correspondence.

On the budget introduced in 1876 by Sir Stafford Northcote, which raised Income Tax by a penny to 3d, but which also raised the line of tax exemption from £150 to £200 : 'I am strongly in favour of exemptions from this tax. Income earned by present work should also be more advantageously dealt with than inherited incomes. Small incomes should not be taxed at all, say under £250 per annum, and only partially if under £500. After that, progressively.' Not only was he an early advocate of differentiation between 'earned' and 'unearned' income, but he also seems to have prognosticated surtax, which was not introduced until 1915 with almost destructive effect, finally reaching 80 per cent of income.

On the question of women's franchise, to which he early held an objection which was to persist, particularly when his only son was nearly kidnapped by the suffragettes, but which he later embraced since three-quarters of the women voted for him, he wrote :

On the grounds that it is contrary to natural law and the practice of civilized states—that no necessity is shown —that only the most undesirable class of women are eager for the right—that those women who discharge their duty to the state—viz marrying & giving birth to children—are adequately represented by their husbands

193

—that those who are unmarried can only claim a vote on the ground of property, which claim on democratic principles is inadmissible—that every kind of hysterical fad would gain strength—that religion would become much more intolerant—that priests and parsons would obtain much more power on the ground that it is only the thin end of the wedge—I shall unswervingly oppose this ridiculous movement.

If you give women votes you must ultimately allow women to sit as members of Parliament. True the Civil Servants and Clergymen have votes & don't sit. But they are few & their votes cannot coerce the community. If once you give votes to the vast numbers of women who form the majority of the community, all power passes to their hands.

He favoured compulsory vaccination, and described its opponents as indulging in the least justifiable of mischievous fads. Of the Deceased Wife's Sister Bill of 1877 he wrote : 'There is no natural impediment of consanguinity, and therefore no reason against legalising such marriages'. Only six years later, under the influence of Lord Hugh Cecil, he was to take a different view (see Vol. II).

Churchill expressed himself in favour of capital punishment. 'Is it a great deterrent?' he asked. 'I think so. Perhaps it is because the sentence is irrevocable, because the actual penalty is and must remain unknown.' He must have been thinking, in the last sentence, of a possible after-life. Referring to the recent substitution of public executions by private executions he added : 'No difficulties should be placed in the way of any (in moderate numbers) who may wish to see the sentence carried out. Justice in every form should not shrink from publicity. The last expiation which she exacts from man should not be hidden from the eyes of his fellow creatures.' A few years before he died Churchill told his grandson Winston that he was still in favour of capital punishment in public as he thought that instead of being secretly hanged in a hut the murderer or traitor ought to be allowed to address a crowd as in the case of the first Marquis of Montrose.

On the franchise he wrote : 'I would extend the franchise to the whole people not by giving votes to the ignorant and

194

indigent, but by raising those classes to the standard when votes may safely be given.' So on elementary education :

> Material comforts should precede mental culture. I am inclined to think that we have been precipitate in adopting universal compulsory education. It is however a step in the right direction—and it is impossible to recede now. I am therefore in support of any and every measure which tends to completing a somewhat dangerous experiment. It will obviously be incumbent on the State to provide—*if required*—a meal for children under education. This is unsound economy—but it is a necessary outcome of the violation of the principle previously stated—that 'material comfort should precede mental culture'.

Thus Churchill recorded his thoughts early in 1897 on the issues of 20 years before. At this time he had seen no action; and his mother was vexed at his return to England on leave. But from these comments on the *Annual Register* we can see that his mind was working, that it was actively engaged in philosophical, economic and political matters. He had not yet read many books : he was hacking it all out for himself. No one, not even his mother, suspected the daemon that was within him, nor foresaw the adventurous and triumphant days and years that lay ahead. He alone possessed the secret, the trust and the clue to his destiny.

10

FRONTIER WARS

CHURCHILL, AS IT HAS already been shown, had dedicated himself to

> 'Seeking the bubble reputation
> Even in the cannon's mouth.'

He was to pursue this course for several years. No other avenue to fame, fortune and Parliament was open to him. Of course, if he had had the money and the opportunity to go into Parliament he would already have left the army; but no glittering legacy hung over his head and he could not at this stage detect any method of paying his debts and acquiring an independent income. He was soon by slow degrees to find a way—the sword and the pen. He early believed that he ought to do business at the top, and he never hesitated to call upon his mother to work on her influential friends, such as the Duke of Cambridge, the Prince of Wales, Sir Edgar Vincent, Lord Salisbury, Sir Evelyn Wood, Lord Kitchener, Lord Cromer and Sir Bindon Blood as the occasion required. People were soon to start attacking him for being 'pushy' and even as a 'medal-hunter'. This sort of talk did not discourage him or deflect him from his purpose. He put up with the flouts and jeers because in his view he was not seeking easy advancement in his profession through influence, but only an opportunity to expose himself to the fire of any enemy of England who happened to be available at the moment. He was tireless and unremitting in his pursuit : what he sought was fame, glory and reputation, and for their sake he was happy to put his life at stake.

So ardent was he in this approach to life that he was even prepared to take part, if only as a witness, in other people's wars. He had already done so in Cuba. Now he wished to go as an observer and report on either side the threatened war between Greece and Turkey over the question of Crete. His earlier excoriating of the Turks and of the diplomacy of the Great Powers he was prepared to swallow in the cause of action. He sailed from Bombay in the *Ganges* on May 8; but within three days of sailing the Greeks were suing for peace, and long before he reached Brindisi the 'war' was over. Disappointed in his expectations of military adventure he travelled back via Naples, where he 'did' Pompeii; Rome and Paris, where he paused to see his younger brother Jack; and then home to participate in the 'delights of the London season' as a minor and expensive compensation for the lost campaign.

Churchill did not allow himself to be completely seduced by the enticements of a London season. He sought, during his three months' leave which he was enforced to spend in England, an opportunity of making his first public speech. Now, soon after his arrival in England, he had got in touch with Captain FitzRoy Stewart, a Galloway connection who was Secretary of the Conservative Central Office. He indicated that he would welcome an early opportunity of becoming a candidate. FitzRoy Stewart suggested he might like to make a speech at some Tory function. Churchill wrote in *My Early Life* : 'It appeared there were hundreds of indoor meetings and outdoor fêtes, of bazaars and rallies —all of which were clamant for speakers. I surveyed this prospect with the eye of an urchin looking through a pastrycook's window. Finally we selected Bath as the scene of my (official) maiden effort.' FitzRoy Stewart wrote to Mr H. D. Skrine, in whose park a rally of the Primrose League was to be held shortly, asking him to allow this 'clever young man' to address the meeting. Mr Skrine acquiesced. Monday 26 July 1897 was the date, and Claverton Manor, now the American Museum, near Bath, was the scene of this auspicious event.

After exchanging the customary courtesies Churchill spoke about the Workmen's Compensation Bill which was at that time before Parliament. 'When the Radicals brought in their Bill and failed, they called it an Employers' Liability Bill. Observe how much better the Tories do these things. They call this Bill the Workmen's Compensation Bill, and that is a much nicer name. . . . I do not say that workmen have not been treated well in the past by the kindness and consideration of their employers, but this measure removes the question from the shifting sands of charity and places it on the firm bedrock of law. . . . So far,' Churchill told his audience, 'the Bill only applies to dangerous trades.' Radicals, and Liberals—'always liberal with other people's money'—asked why it was not applied to all trades. 'This,' said Churchill, 'was just like a Radical, just the slapdash, wholesale, harum-scarum policy of the Radical. It reminds me of the man who, on being told that ventilation was an excellent thing, went and smashed every window in his house. That is not Conservative policy. Conservative policy is essentially a tentative policy, a look-before-you-leap policy, and it is a policy of don't leap at all if there is a ladder. . . . British workmen have more to hope for from the rising tide of Tory Democracy than from the dried-up drain-pipe of Radicalism.' He referred to a strike of engineers : 'One of the questions which politicians have to face is how to avoid disputes between Capital and Labour. I hope that ultimately the labourer may become a shareholder in the profits and may not be unwilling to share the losses of a bad year because he shared the profits of a good one.' And he concluded with a reference to the Primrose League :

In 1880 the Tory party was crushed, broken, dispirited. Its great leader, Lord Beaconsfield, was already touched by the finger of Death. Its principles were unpopular; its numbers were few; and it appeared on the verge of extinction. Observe it now. That struggling remnant of Toryism has swollen into the strongest Government of modern times. And the great Liberal party which in 1882 was vigorous, united, supreme, is shrunk to a few discordant factions of discredited faddists, without numbers, without policy, without concord, without cohesion, around whose necks is bound the millstone of Home Rule. In all this revolution of public opinion the Primrose League has borne its share. It has kept pegging away, driving the principles of the Tory party into the heads of the people of this country, and, though the task has been heavy and the labour long, they have had in the end a glorious reward. . . .

There was some comment in the evening and the weekly newspapers on this maiden speech, accompanied by speculation as to how soon Churchill might seek an entry into

Parliament. Most of the comments were favourable. *The Lady* wrote on 5 August 1897 :

> An auspicious debut on the platform was made the other day by Mr Winston Churchill, elder son of the late Lord Randolph Churchill. He spoke at a large Primrose League meeting, and delighted his audience by the force and mental agility he displayed. Mr Churchill, who is ony twenty-three, aspires to a seat in Parliament. He is in the 4th Hussars at present, and is strikingly like his late father in features and colouring.

Having jumped this fence he went to stay at Deepdene with Duchess Lily and her husband Lord William Beresford for Goodwood Races. The ardour with which he broke away at the first opportunity from these gay and colourful events is well recorded in *My Early Life* :

> . . . I was on the lawns of Goodwood in lovely weather and winning my money, when the revolt of the Pathan tribesmen on the Indian frontier began. I read in the newspapers that a Field Force of three brigades had been formed, and that at the head of it stood Sir Bindon Blood. Forthwith I telegraphed reminding him of his promise, and took the train for Brindisi to catch the Indian Mail. . . .

A year before, Churchill had made friends with Sir Bindon Blood at Deepdene and had extracted from him a promise that if ever he commanded another expedition on the Indian frontier he would allow Churchill to accompany him.

The urgency with which he left is shown in a letter to his mother written from the steamship *Rome* off Aden on August 7 and posted there the following day. He had left behind his polo sticks, he had forgotten to return to old Mr Skrine one of his Primrose League badges, Bain the bookseller had not had time to send him Lord Beaconsfield's and Mr Gladstone's speeches and there were one or two bills which remained unpaid. And when he got to India he remembered that he had intended to take out Peas, his littel dog, 'and in the hurry and bustle of getting off—of course I forgot him'.

In the hope of reputation on a battlefield this impecunious subaltern had sacrificed three weeks of his costly and enjoyable leave and had urgently travelled back to India by the most expensive route. At each port of call, instead of a telegram of welcome from Sir Bindon Blood there was nothing but a forbidding silence. Even when he arrived back with his regiment in the Bangalore cantonment there was no news. It seemed to him that he had hurried back at much expense and with no reward in sight. A few days after his return to Bangalore he wrote to his mother :

WSC to Lady Randolph

E X T R A C T

17th August 1897   Bangalore

. . . I have heard nothing more from Sir Bindon Blood. I cannot think he would willingly disappoint me and can only conclude that someone at Headquarters has put a spoke in my wheel. I still have some hopes—but each day they grow less. It is an object lesson of how much my chances of success in the army are worth. I had the most complete assent of my colonel as well as his official recommendation forwarded six months ago. However as all this must be relegated to the past soon—I will not dilate on my disgust. . . .

There was a letter in the post to him from Upper Swat :

General Sir Bindon Blood to WSC

22 August 1897   Camp Mingaora
                                                    Upper Swat

My dear Churchill,

I had to fill up my personal staff when I started, and I have not been able to manage a billet for you as yet. I should advise your coming to me as a press correspondent, and when you are here I shall put you on the strength on the 1st opportunity. Fincastle was arranged for in this way, and is now attached to the Guides *vice* an officer killed in action.

Army Head Qrs make all appointments except personal

staff and are very jealous of their patronage. I have hardly managed to get any of my pals on my staff—though I have asked for several. However if you were here I think I could, and certainly would if I could, do a little jobbery on your account.

Yours in haste
B. Blood

To his mother he wrote from the train as it was travelling through India :

WSC to Lady Randolph

EXTRACT

29 August [1897]   In the train near Dhond
                                              and later near Itarsi

... The telegram which I sent you yesterday requires some explanation—though I most sincerely hope you will have done what I asked without awaiting it. Sir Bindon Blood wrote to me a letter saying that he had had to make up his staff etc—but that if I could come up as a correspondent (the only excuse possible) he would seize the first opportunity of putting me on the strength of the Malakand Field Force. I accordingly with much difficulty have obtained a month's leave and starting last night shall in four days arrive at Nowshera, from whence I hope to join the General. To go as correspondent, it is necessary to have a special pass and this is in some cases refused if the paper is not of sufficient importance. I hope most strongly I shall not arrive at Nowshera to find you have taken no steps. If I do I shall then have to wire to some Indian paper with possible failure.

... Dearest Mamma before this letter reaches you I shall probably have had several experiences, some of which will contain the element of danger. I view every possibility with composure. It might not have been worth my while, who am really no soldier, to risk so many fair chances on a war which can only help me directly in a profession I mean to discard. But I have considered everything and I feel the fact of having seen service with British troops while still a young man must give me more weight politically—must add to my claims to be listened to and may perhaps

201

improve my prospects of gaining popularity with the country. Besides this—I think I am of an adventurous disposition and shall enjoy myself not so much *in spite of as because* of the risks I run. At any rate I have decided— and having taken a hand I shall do my best to play a good game. . . .

THE NORTH-WEST FRONTIER

So far as is known, he had not yet begun his intensive study of Napoleon, whose life was to fascinate him for many years, and of whom he long perpended writing a biography. But like Napoleon he already had a belief in his star. Of course, as he incessantly and spectacularly exposed himself to the fire of the enemy and remained unscathed, this early expression of his belief was progressively fortified. There are records which show that within the next three years, in three different continents, he asserted to three very different people his ardent conviction that he would one day be Prime Minister of England. Once in India to another officer, the second time in South Africa to the son of a station-master, and the third time to his namesake, the distinguished American novelist whom he met when the latter took the chair for him when he was lecturing in Boston in 1900.

*   *   *   *   *

Lady Randolph had acted upon her son's urgent request to find a paper for whom he could be a correspondent. She drew a blank with *The Times*. The editor, Mr Buckle, wrote to her regretting that he had already appointed a correspondent (Lord Fincastle) to Sir Bindon Blood's headquarters. She was more fortunate with the *Daily Telegraph*, though she succeeded in obtaining only half the fee which Churchill had expected : 'Old Lawson [proprietor of *The Daily Telegraph*] answered a letter I wrote him by telegram saying "Tell him to post picturesque forcible letters." I have no doubt if you get a chance of sending any that they will be well paid—of course they must be attractive.'

Meanwhile, however, in order to justify his presence at Sir Bindon Blood's headquarters he had acquired accreditation to the *Pioneer,* a paper printed in Allahabad which had printed much of Rudyard Kipling's early writing. Churchill's agreement was to cable 300 words a day.

The Daily Telegraph published the first of fifteen 'letters' from Churchill on October 6, and Lady Randolph hastened to allay her son's anticipated displeasure :

Lady Randolph to WSC

EXTRACT

7 October 1897   [Edinburgh]

. . . I read yr letters for the D.T. to Ld Minto who thought them excellent—but begged me not to sign yr name. He

203

said it was very unusual & might get you into trouble. The 1st one appeared yesterday headed 'Indian Frontier—by a young officer.' . . .

Churchill was in no way mollified by her action.

WSC to Lady Randolph
EXTRACT

25 October [1897]   [Bangalore]

My dearest Mamma,

I saw in the week's papers that arrived yesterday the first three of my letters to the *D.T.* I will not conceal my disappointment at their not being signed. I had written them with the design, a design which took form as the correspondence advanced, of bringing my personality before the electorate. I had hoped that some political advantage might have accrued.

However I left the decision in your hands and you have decided—not for the first time—upon a negative course. I will only add that if I am to avoid doing 'unusual' things it is difficult to see what chance I have of being more than an average person. I was proud of the letters and anxious to stake my reputation on them. They are I believe of some literary merit.

As I am deprived of all satisfaction on this account, I mean to solace myself financially. I will not accept less than £10 a letter and I shall return any cheque for a less sum. I particularly asked for that amount *'au moins'* and when I think of the circumstances under wh. those letters were written, on the ground in a tent temperature 115° or after a long day's action or by a light which it was dangerous to use lest it drew fire—when I was tired and hustled and amid other adverse circumstances—I think they are cheap at the price.

He did not mind so much about the fee : what he minded was that his mother had exercised the option which he had given her of suppressing his name. Why? On 'the advice of a soldier'.

After spending a few days at Sir Bindon Blood's Headquarters, Churchill had been invited by Sir Bindon to attach himself to Brigadier-General P. D. Jeffreys' Brigade, which was to go on a punitive expedition into the Mamund Valley. Here on 16 September 1897, Churchill took part in his first real action as a combatant. In his newspaper despatches and later in his account *The Story of the Mala-kand Field Force*, he was suitably modest and even self-effacing as to his role. He revealed his true thoughts to his mother :

WSC to Lady Randolph
[In pencil]

19 September [1897]   Camp Inayat Kila
Private

Dearest Mamma,
    The enclosed 3 letters to the *Daily Telegraph* will tell you a good deal of what happened here. Please do what-ever you think fit with them. I am tired of writing as these long letters take several hours. But I must give you some account of my personal experiences on the 16th. I started with the Cavalry and saw the first shot fired. After half an hour's skirmishing I rode forward with the 35th Sikhs until firing got so hot that my grey pony was unsafe. I proceeded on foot. When the retirement began I remained till the last and here I was perhaps very near my end. If you read between the lines of my letter you will see that this retire-ment was an awful rout in which the wounded were left to be cut up horribly by these wild beasts. I was close to both officers when they were hit almost simultaneously and fired my revolver at a man at 30 yards who tried to cut up poor Hughes' body. He dropped but came on again. A subaltern—Bethune by name—and I carried a wounded Sepoy for some distance and might perhaps, had there been any gallery, have received some notice. My pants are still stained with the man's blood. We also remained until the enemy came to within 40 yards firing our revolvers. They actually threw stones at us. It was a horrible business. For there was no help for the man that went down. I felt no excitement and very little fear. All the excitement went out when things became really deadly. Later on I used a rifle which a wounded man had dropped and fired 40 rounds with some effect at close quarters. I cannot be certain, but I

think I hit 4 men. At any rate they fell. The regiment was fairly on the run and only stopped at the bottom by want of breath. Then I went about with a friend of mine, a subaltern in the Buffs. But, after this first thing, all else was tame. The skirmishing did not even excite me, though the young officers of this regiment were highly delighted at a few bullets that whistled or kicked up the dust close by and considered each a tremendous escape. It was a very nice regiment and works well but they have not yet seen what it means to be well punished.

Altogether I was shot at from 7.30 [a.m.] till 8 [p.m.] on this day and now begin to consider myself a veteran. Sir Bindon has made me his orderly officer, so that I shall get a medal and perhaps a couple of clasps.

We fought again yesterday. But this time things were well managed and loss was only 7. [September] 16th was biggest thing in India since Afghan war. There will be more tomorrow, but I think the worst is over. When I think what the Empire might have lost I am relieved.

I hope you can make out this scrawl dearest Mamma— tell Jack details. In my novel I develop the idea that a 'politician' very often possesses mere physical courage. Military opinion is of course contrary. But at any rate whatever I do afterwards, no one can say anything against me on this score. I rode on my grey pony all along the skirmish line where everyone else was lying down in cover. Foolish perhaps but I play for high stakes and given an audience there is no act too daring or too noble. Without the gallery things are different.

Ever your loving son
WINSTON

Two weeks later Churchill was involved in another engagement:

WSC to Lady Randolph

[In pencil]

EXTRACT

2 October [1897]   Inayat Kila

My dearest Mamma,

Since I last wrote to you—we have had another severe action. Agrah—30th September—I was under fire for five hours—but did not get into the hottest corners. Our loss was 60 killed and wounded—out of the poor 1200 we can muster. Compare these figures with actions like Firket in Egypt—wh are cracked up as great battles and wh are commemorated by clasps & medals etc etc. Here out of one brigade we have lost in a fortnight 245 killed and wounded and nearly 25 officers. I hope you will talk about this to the Prince and others—as if any fuss is made, they may give a special clasp for Mamund Valley. This has been the hardest fighting on the frontier for forty years. I have been attached as a matter of extreme urgency—to 31st Punjaub Infantry. A change from British cavalry to Native Infantry! Still it means the medal and also that next time I go into action I shall command a hundred men—and possibly I may bring off some '*coup*'. Besides I shall have some other motive for taking chances than merely love of adventure.

Today and yesterday I have fever. 103° and an awful head—but I hope to be alright tomorrow. We expect another action on the 5th—Sir Bindon Blood is coming up himself and bringing two more batteries and two fresh Battalions. The danger and difficulty of attacking these active—fierce hill men is extreme. They can get up the hills twice as fast as we can—and shoot wonderfully well with Martini Henry Rifles. It is a war without quarter. . .

All his life Churchill thought that military service was an essential ingredient of a political career. When he came to a powerful station he never cared much—though he sometimes had to condone it—for putting ministers into his government or shadow cabinet who had not exposed themselves to the fire of the enemy in either of the two world was. In later life, notably the 1945 election, he naïvely supposed that good war records would encourage the electorate to vote for candidates who possessed them. He persuaded those with such records (many of them generally against their better judgement) to stand for Parliament. Those who had gained the Victoria Cross or the DSO were almost invariably unsuccessful.

Churchill's hope of medals was to be disappointed. He did not get the VC or the DSO; apart from the campaign medal, he had to make do with a mention in despatches. The citation read : 'And finally he [Brigadier-General Jeffreys] has praised the courage and resolution of Lieutenant

W. L. S. Churchill, 4th Hussars, the correspondent of the
Pioneer newspaper with the force who made himself useful
at a critical moment.'

Churchill wrote to his mother on December 9 : 'I do not
suppose any honour or dignity which it may be my fortune
in life to deserve or receive will give me equal pleasure . . .'

Later Churchill explained his true motives in a letter to
his mother. It was not military glory but to get into
politics :

WSC to Lady Randolph
EXTRACT

26 January 1898 [Bangalore]

. . . In politics a man I take it, gets on not so much by what
he *does*, as by what he *is*. It is not so much a question of
brains as of character & originality. It is for these reasons
that I would not allow others to suggest ideas and that I am
somewhat impatient of advice as to my beginning in
politics. . . .

On his return to Bangalore with his grey pony after his
service with the Malakand Field Force, Churchill laid aside
his half-completed novel, *Savrola*. Instead, he started the
first of the many books he was destined to write in the intervals of a crowded life. He wrote *The Story of the Malakand Field Force*.

WSC to Lady Randolph
EXTRACT

10 November [1897] [Bangalore]

. . . I have been incited to it in some way as a means of re-
pairing the non-signature of my letters. It is a great undertaking but if carried out will yield substantial results in
every way, financially, politically, and even, though do I
care a damn, militarily. . . .

After a fortnight of intense activity he received a set-
back :

24 November [1897]   [Bangalore]

. . . I am working very hard at the book and am daily receiving facts and letters from the frontier concerning it. I
hear Ld Fincastle is also writing one and has received the
pictures I had hoped to obtain. A great nuisance this as the
subject is so small that there is not room for two books on
it. He has not treated me with much consideration in the
matter as he knew I was contemplating writing and might
at least have informed me that he wanted to tell the tale.
Had he done so I would have given way as the novel filled
& still fills my mind. As it is—I have got so far—and the
book promises so well—that I do not mean to give in. It
will of course make all the difference which comes out first.
I want you therefore to approach the publishers on the
subject and write to me. I hope to send the MS home in six
weeks at the latest. It need not be sent out later for cor-
rections—as I am having it typewritten. . . .

Churchill worked hard :

WSC to Lady Randolph

31 December [1897]   [Bangalore]

My dearest Mamma,
    Herewith the book. It has by a great effort been finished
a week earlier than I had expected. Maps & a photograph
of Sir Bindon Blood for frontispiece, I hope by next mail,
but do not delay publication on their account.
    I have hurried vy much & it is possible there are still a
few slips and errors of writing in the MS. I cannot have the
proofs sent out here as that would take too much time. I
want you therefore to ask Moreton Frewen if he will undertake the work of revising and correcting them for me. I
shall be vy grateful indeed if he will. I enclose some notes
as to publication & as to the points I want whoever revises
to look out for.
    Now dearest Mamma I don't want anything modified or
toned down in any way. I will stand or fall by what I have

written. I only want bad sentences polished & any repetitions of phrase or fact weeded out. I have regarded time as the most important element. Do not I beg you lose one single day in taking the MS to some publisher. Fincastle's book may for all I know be ready now.

As to price. I have no idea what the book is worth but don't throw it away. A little money is always worth having. I should recommend Moreton's treating with the publishers, it is so much easier for a man. If the book runs to a second edition, I shall add another three or four chapters on Buner which is now impending. I have wired to Blood to take me again on this new advance. I do not expect to go. Allow nothing to prevent the publication of this book. I have taken great pains—nor do I think the result altogether unworthy.

Lady Randolph, on the advice of no less an authority than Mr Arthur Balfour, entrusted the book to A. P. Watt, the literary agent, who found in Longmans a ready publisher.

The first edition ran to 2,000 copies at home and another 2,000 abroad. Altogether 8,500 copies were published in the nine months between March 1898 and January 1899.

But even as he was finishing his book, Churchill showed himself keen to hurry off to other scenes of action. He did not think that the risks he had run with the Malakand Field Force had gained him the reputation which he believed he had deserved. Three months after he returned to dull regimental soldiering at Bangalore the Tirah Campaign, also on the Afghan frontier, was already under way. It had opened inauspiciously. Churchill was still burning for distinction. To seek a new opportunity for reputation he was prepared to sacrifice his leave and spend money which he could not afford in making a four-day train journey from Bangalore to Calcutta, which was then the capital of India. He spent sixty interesting but abortive hours in Calcutta, and then had to return to Bangalore with sadness and frustration in his heart.

Though abortive, his visit to Calcutta was enjoyable. He stayed with the Viceroy, Lord Elgin, under whom he was later to serve as Under-Secretary at the Colonial Office; he dined with the Commander-in-Chief, Sir George White, with whom he was to dine again, under quite different circumstances, at Ladysmith two years later; and he rode a horse which he was lent in the local point-to-point.

While Churchill was seeking to earn a reputation for courage on the North-West frontier, he was constantly on the alert with a view to finding a Parliamentary opening.

WSC to Lady Randolph

E X T R A C T

17 November [1897]   [Bangalore]

. . . You must keep your eye on the political situation. Although I know & hear nothing out here, it is evident to me that a very marked reaction against the decision of the last general election has taken place. These numerous bye elections might, had I been in England, have given me my chance of getting in. However my experience out here has been of greater value and interest than anything else would be, or perhaps can ever be. Of course should a vacancy occur in Paddington—you must weigh in for me & I will come by the next ship. They would probably elect me even if I could not get back in time. I suppose Ld Salisbury's retirement is now only a matter of months. There might be sweeping changes after that. Chamberlain would not be likely to tolerate Balfour [as] PM unless in the Lords, and would the Londonderry type of Tory allow Chamberlain to dominate even more than at present? Should a split occur, I should remember that a tory democrat is a tory first and a democrat after. The reactionary remnant might always be whipped up. . . .

Lord Salisbury, who had become Prime Minister for the first time as long ago as 1885, had formed his third administration in June 1895; a considerable Unionist victory at the general election had followed. A number of by-elections during the Christmas recess early in 1898—notably the defeat of Churchill's cousin, Ivor Guest, at Plymouth— suggested that the Government's popularity was declining. Nevertheless, Lord Salisbury was to fight—and win— another general election and did not consider it necessary to retire until July 1902.

On his return to Bangalore Churchill found disquieting news. His mother's financial affairs had got into such a state that she felt obliged to seek a fresh loan amounting altogether to £17,000 with which to pay off a series of minor loans and also to clear some pressing debt. The security for such a loan was to be life insurance policies on both her life and on Winston's. What was now required was that Winston should guarantee at least the premiums on these life insurance policies amounting in all to £700 per annum which would also cover the interest on the loans. Lady Randolph did not trouble to inform her son of these important financial transactions but merely caused the solicitors Lumley & Lumley to send to Churchill the necessary forms for signature.

Churchill loved his mother dearly and wished to help her. But he was not prepared to be stripped of his modest competence in this way. He wrote to her.

WSC to Lady Randolph
EXTRACT

28 January 1898   [Bangalore]

. . . Speaking quite frankly on the subject—there is no doubt that we are both you & I equally thoughtless—spendthrift and extravagant. We both know what is good—and we both like to have it.

I rather wish you had written me a letter on the subject—to explain things to me—as I may be quite wrong in my conceptions of the affair. I hope you will not mind my writing in a candid manner. I sympathise with all your extravagances—even more than you do with mine—it seems just as suicidal to me when you spend £200 on a ball dress as it does to you when I purchase a new polo pony for £100. And yet I feel that you ought to have the dress & I the polo pony. The pinch of the whole matter is we are damned poor. . . .

After he had made these remonstrances, Churchill signed the necessary documents that Lumley & Lumley had sent him. He did so, however, only on the condition that Jack should share the burden of £700 a year if and when he came into his own money.

*   *   *   *   *

Towards the end of February 1898, Churchill went to Meerut for the Polo Tournament, in which he distinguished himself. The 4th Hussars beat the 5th Dragoon Guards, but lost in the second round to the famous Durham Light Infantry, the only Infantry Regiment ever to win the Regimental Polo Tournament and to do so three years running. But Churchill's restless mind was not on polo : it was still with the nagging campaign that was being waged on the Northern frontier in Tirah. Constantly he was devising means of joining it. At Meerut he was staying with Sir Bindon Blood and it was there that he conceived the idea of going to Peshawar, the railhead for the Tirah expedition, to see if he could not find employment at Headquarters there. As he explains in *My Early Life,* there was a considerable element of risk attached to this enterprise. Though Meerut was 1,400 miles north of Bangalore, it was still 600 miles short of Peshawar. His leave expired three days after the final match of the tournament—the three days it would take the polo team to return to Bangalore. So if he took train to Peshawar, which would take him a day and a half, and found no employment there, he would be two, if not three, days late returning to Bangalore.

Characteristically, Churchill decided to take the risk. On March 1898, Churchill was able to report success :

WSC to Lady Randolph

7 March [1898]   Camp Ali Musjid
                                                    Khyber Pass

My dearest Mamma,

But for my telegram the address might astonish you. I came on to Peshawar after the Polo Tournament as I told you I proposed to do. I went to see Sir Wm Lockhart in the hopes of being allowed to go and see General Hamilton —but without any expectation of employment. To my astonishment—I have been taken on his (Sir Wm's) staff as Orderly Officer. The appointment has not yet been sanctioned from Army Head Quarters—but I should think it extremely unlikely, in view of Sir William's approaching command [*as Commander-in-Chief, India*], that any obstacle will be raised. If it should be sanctioned I shall wire to you.

The success which has attended my *coup* is in some measure I feel, deserved. But I have received a most remarkable assistance from Captain Haldane—the general's

ADC. I have never met this man before and I am at a loss to know why he should have espoused my cause—with so strange an earnestness. Of this I shall learn more later. But in the meanwhile I am greatly interested. He is a very clever, daring, conscientious & ambitious fellow—his influence over the general is extraordinary. Indeed I think he has pulled the wires all through this war and is in great measure responsible for its success or failure. He is extremely unpopular and takes no pains to cultivate friends in the force. My idea is that my reputation—for whatever it may be worth—has interested him. Of course you will destroy this letter and show it to no one. For though I am under a considerable obligation to this officer I cannot say that I approve of a system which places the reins of power in the hands of so young and unknown a man. I fear this is the explanation of much. However, destroy this and repeat to none—or I may be found a fool as well as an ingrate.

Ever your loving son
WINSTON S. CHURCHILL

The key to his success was, as he indicated in his letter and as he generously pointed out in *My Early Life*, 'remarkable assistance from Captain Haldane.' Aylmer Haldane was at that time serving as a Captain in the Gordon Highlanders. A member of a closely knit and brilliant Scottish family—Richard Burdon Haldane, later to be Secretary of State for War and Lord Chancellor, was a cousin of his—he had soon made his mark as a staff officer in India. Churchill recalls in *My Early Life* how he had been warned that Haldane had immense influence—'in fact, they say throughout the Army, too much.' We do not know what it was about the young Churchill that led to Haldane's benevolent attitude towards him. For apart from ambition, they neither of them seemed to have much in common : 'He is indiscreet—over-bearing—irritating [in] manner—possessed by a great desire to confer favours—but in some ways a remarkable man—and works like a machine', Churchill wrote to his mother on March 31. Earlier he had said : 'Haldane and I get on capitally. He is not as clever as I thought originally—but I think an able fellow. He likes me and in spite of the disparity in age, we talk unreservedly.' Haldane was twelve years older : that he got on well with Churchill is proved not only by the fact that he took all steps to ensure the success of Churchill's attachment to Sir William Lockhart's staff, but also by the way he unburdened intimate details about his unhappy married life to the young subaltern. Churchill 'kept up' with Haldane after he left the Tirah Field Force; as will be seen, they were to meet again in new and more hazardous surroundings not long afterwards.

Churchill soon found that there was no war and not likely to be one : 'Of course I do hope for a fight, but I do not delude myself,' he wrote to his mother :

WSC to Lady Randolph

EXTRACT

18 March [1898]   Camp Peshawar

. . . Both sides are sick of it. . . . Though I now fear fighting is all over—[this] cannot be a bad business. I shall possibly get an extra clasp on my medal. It counts in my record of service and as an extra campaign. But the chief value lies elsewhere. I now know all the generals who are likely to have commands in the next few years. Sir William Lockhart will always give me an appointment with any Field Force and I have now a great many friends in high places —as far as soldiering is concerned.

Churchill wrote a letter for publication to Lord Charles Beresford, Admiral and MP, the flamboyant brother of Lord William Beresford. This was a defence of those serving in India and an attack on those who under cloak of anonymity in newspaper articles and letters to Members of Parliament were attacking the conduct of the campaign. 'I have asked him to publish it,' Churchill explained to his mother on March 31, 'signed by me—and as if by an indiscretion. It is an indirect method which in this case is more suitable. The letter will establish my position with the Indian military authorities on unshakeable foundations. They are extraordinarily sensitive of Press Criticism and welcome the slightest favourable comment.' This letter was duly published in *The Times* on 3 May 1898, but *The Broad Arrow,* the organ of the military Establishment in London, purported to read into it a subtle attack on the military authorities and offered the severest strictures on the presumptuous young subaltern.

Undoubtedly Churchill had brought upon himself a good deal of hostility, both in Simla, where the Indian Army mandarins held court, and at the War Office. Even Lord Roberts had refused to help Churchill to get to the front, and Churchill was genuinely shocked and hurt. Churchill had asked his mother to approach Lord Roberts, who was at this time commanding the forces in Ireland, on the grounds of his father's friendship with—and considerable services to—the Field Marshal. Only a few years before Lord Roberts had been pleased to accompany Lord Randolph to Harrow. Now Churchill commented : 'I don't understand Lord Roberts' refusal. A good instance of ingratitude in a fortunate and very much overrated man.'

Even in the midst of the excitements and new surroundings of Sir William Lockhart's Headquarters at Peshawar, Churchill was able to write that he was thinking of his book, *The Story of the Malakand Field Force,* 'more than of anything else'. 'I have not yet received the proofs or the volume,' he wrote to his mother on March 18, 'but I am sure it has been managed as well as it could possibly have been.' The correction of his proofs had been entrusted to Moreton Frewen, his uncle, who on the strength of a slender work on bimetallism was regarded as the literary member of the family. He had two nicknames : 'Mortal Ruin' and 'Silver Tongue'. On March 21 the proofs arrived at Peshawar.

WSC to Lady Randolph

EXTRACT

22 March [1898]   Peshawar

My dear Mamma,

I add this letter to tell you that the 'revised proofs' reached me yesterday and that I spent a very miserable afternoon in reading the gross & fearful blunders which I suppose have got into the finished copies. In the hope of stopping publication I have wired to Longmans, but I fear I am already too late. Still I may catch the Indian edition, in which the absurdities would be most laughed at.

I blame no one—but myself. I might have known that no

one could or would take the pains that an author would bestow. The result, however, destroys all the pleasure I had hoped to get from the book and leaves only shame that such an impertinence should be presented to the public—a type of the careless slapdash spirit of the age and an example of what my father would have called my slovenly shiftless habits. . . .

WSC to Lady Randolph

25 March [1898]   Peshawar

Altogether there are about 200 misprints, blunders & mistakes, though some of these, perhaps 100 will only be apparent to me.

I have had an evil presentiment. But I risked mistakes for one reason—to get it published before Lord Fincastle's book.

Whereas, I see his is now already out, and mine when the mail left was still being embellished as I have described.

God forbid that I should blame you my dearest Mamma. I blame myself—and myself alone for this act of folly & laziness which has made me ridiculous to all whose good opinion I would have hoped for.

I writhed all yesterday afternoon—but today I feel nothing but shame and disappointment. You could not be expected to know many of these things—but as far as Moreton is concerned, I now understand why his life has been a failure in the city and elsewhere.

In view of all this the letter of thanks he wrote to Moreton Frewen was a masterpiece of restraint and deserves to be quoted :

WSC to Moreton Frewen

(Copy: Leslie Papers)

EXTRACT

2 April 1898   Camp Peshawar

My dear Moreton,
    Many thanks for your letter of the 7th March. I have read the advance copy of the book and I see that you have

taken a great deal of trouble in the matter and have modified a good many of my statements—perhaps judiciously. I am very grateful to you for your kindness in all this matter. It is a very invidious task to come between an author and his proofs—and I felt this fully when I asked you to undertake the business of revision. I agree with you as to the signs of haste and indeed reading the book a second time in print I have found many passages I would gladly alter.

There are two or three unfortunate slips as

> [page] 30 Chitral wall for Chitral road
> page 165 The Koh-i-mohr . . . . a splendid peak
> *in*visible alike from Peshawar and Malakand.
> page 203 fulcrums for fulcra.

This was in my MS. And when I noticed it I thought of writing but did not as I thought you would see it. I fear Mr Welldon will be very much shocked.

The book has been very well brought out by Longmans and the maps are excellent with only two mistakes noticeable.

If it reaches a second edition I shall make some extensive alterations as you suggest.

Once more thanking you let me pass the subject. . . .

In fact the book was received with enthusiasm everywhere—except for *The Broad Arrow,* which commented sourly on the fact that a young cavalry officer should be permitted to shift the burden of monotonous duty at Bangalore on to other shoulders 'in order to obtain preferential treatment at the front'. The weird punctuation was the one criticism that most discerning writers made. The review that Churchill was probably most pleased with was that in the *Athenaeum* :

The operations of the Malakand Field Force have yielded two excellent books [*the other by Lord Fincastle*]. That now before us is a literary phenomenon. Lieut Winston Spencer Churchill, named, if we mistake not, after the father of the first Duke of Marlborough, omits, indeed, the family hyphen from his name, but has evidently much of the genius of his uncle, of his father, and of their best known progenitor. May he become as great a soldier as the last, and a straighter politician ! *The Story of the Malakand Field Force* (Longmans) needs only a little correction of each page to make its second edition a military classic. As it stands, it suggests in style a volume by Disraeli revised by a mad printer's reader. Disraeli's books all showed signs of the influence of Bolingbroke and of Burke; Mr Churchill may be only a reader of Burke and of Disraeli, but in many passages these writers speak again, and the application of Burke's style in particular to the affairs of war yields here and there passages worthy of Napier's great history—the model of military literature. Yet one word is printed for another, words are defaced by shameful blunders, and sentence after sentence ruined by the punctuation of an idiot or of a school-boy in the lowest form. . . .

The Prince of Wales wrote. Churchill wrote to his mother (May 10), 'he professes himself pleased with the book. I have answered dutifully. The cuttings are vy civil but undeserved. The book as it stands is an eyesore and I scream with disappointment and shame when I contemplate the hideous blunders that deface it. I never had any doubts that the style was good and that the ideas were pleasing. But such slovenly work is a dreadful disgrace. Literary excellence is what I aim at. However there is plenty of time—barring accidents. . . .' Had he known that the Prince of Wales was sending a copy of the book to his sister, the Empress Victoria of Germany, his good opinion of himself and of the Prince might well have been even enhanced, for as he said he was 'Tory enough' to be flattered by such things.

Mr Welldon also wrote to Churchill, which gave him great pleasure. 'If the work reaches a second edition,' he told his mother, 'you must telegraph to me. I will then ask Welldon to revise the punctuation as I am rather ignorant in this respect & have alas made one bad grammatical mistake in the misuse of the Present Participle. . . .'

One of the first results of the success of *The Story of the Malakand Field Force* was a series of invitations from magazine editors and publishers to write articles or books. The publishing house of James Nisbet and Co wrote to ask if he would write a life of the great Duke of Marlborough and whether he would consider writing a life of Lord Randolph. He liked the idea of writing the life of Marlborough —as a 'memoir'. He did not wish to poach on his cousin Sunny's preserves, Churchill told his mother (May 10). 'At the same time I think it would produce something that would ring like a trumpet call.' To the suggestion that he should write the life of Lord Randolph he replied that he thought the time had not yet come when such a life could be written, 'and if ever I attempted it I should make it a labour of years.'

The idea of writing, now that he had achieved this success with his first book, appealed to him immensely :

WSC to Lady Randolph

EXTRACT

25 April 1898   Bangalore

. . . This literary sphere of action may enable me in a few years to largely supplement my income. Indeed I look forward to becoming sooner or later independent. We shall see. I have in my eye a long series of volumes which I am convinced I can write well.

1. A life of Garibaldi.
2. A short & dramatic History of the American Civil War.
3. A volume of short stories called 'The Correspondent of the *New York Examiner*.'

(The one I sent you last mail would be included—of the others there are about five, blocked roughly).

I hope, if I live, to produce something that may remain, and if on looking into Garibaldi—of whose wonderful career no good account exists—I find that the materials are congenial—I may perhaps make a classic. *The Story of the M.F.F.* took but 5 weeks to write. But I will take 3 years over the others.

Ian Hamilton, to whom he had entrusted an article for the *United Services Magazine*, gave a word of warning. He wrote from the ship that was to take him from India to England :

25 April 1898   SS *Shamron*

My dear Churchill,

Your kind letter and the magazine article. The latter is of great though unequal power. I see what they mean about your punctuation. You have a habit of putting a comma in between the relative and its subject which is unusual. But punctuation is a matter of fancy after all & this does not matter a d——, one way or the other. You have in you the raw material for several successful careers. But altho' art is long, life is short and, whatever your ambition, be sure you lose no time in getting on to the direct and recognised track which leads up to it. The admirable Crichton—many-sided sort of career leads to dispersion of effort, indefiniteness of aim and ultimate disappointment and defeat. Rather select your line of country forthwith and break in and curb all your talents to be merely subsidiary appendages to help you towards your goal. It would be satisfactory to achieve the combination of Marlborough, Napier and Pitt, but in the existing specialized era, such dreams are of the idlest texture. Briefly then I hold that you should decide now, and either stand for Parliament on the very first occasion or else determine to be a soldier and leave politics alone until you can approach them from the fixed & serene basis of a seat in the House of Lords. I will certainly pay my respects to Lady Randolph if they allow me to stay long enough in town. Your MS I will post to her in London; it will only be 24 hours later than if I posted it on the ship. May we meet again, and soon, when the bugles are blowing and drums are beating and khaki is the colour we wear.

Yours very sincly
IAN HAMILTON

While he had been travelling long distances to and from Calcutta, fruitlessly as it seemed, to join the Tirah campaign, even while he was enjoying his fugitive delights there and again on his return to Bangalore he was still maturing his long-considered project of somehow or other getting to a much bigger war—the re-conquest of the Sudan. Since 1896 Sir Herbert Kitchener, the Sirdar of the Egyptian Army, had been advancing by short stages up the Nile, building a railway as he went along. His force of Egyptians, with a stiffening of English units, grew more powerful as the railway became longer.

10 January 1898   Bangalore

. . . Oh how I wish I could work you up over Egypt! I know you could do it with all your influence—and all the people you know. It is a pushing age and we must shove with the best. After Tirah & Egypt—then I think I shall turn from war to peace & politics. If, that is, I get through all right. I think myself I shall, but of course one only has to look at Nature and see how very little store she sets by life. Its sanctity is entirely a human idea. You may think of a beautiful butterfly—12 million feathers on his wings, 16,000 lenses in his eye—a mouthful for a bird. Let us laugh at Fate. It might please her. . . .

2 February 1898   [Bangalore]

. . . As to Egypt: I beg you to continue to try from every side. My plans have crystallized since I knew the advance was not till the autumn. I shall take my 3 months leave June 15 to Sept 15—and go to Egypt—as a Correspondent if they will allow—failing all other capacities—but I hope you will be able to get me attached—at any rate temporarily. I shall go if I am alive—and I think I shall prevail ultimately. . . .

As it happened Lady Randolph already had a plan to spend part of the winter in Egypt. It was thus easy for her to comply with her son's urgent request. Churchill, unaware of his mother's plan, flattered himself that her expedition was undertaken solely in his interests. Naturally he was ecstatic in his thanks:

222

EXTRACT

16 February 1898   [Bangalore]

. . . Your telegram reached me on Saturday—and I can
assure you I feel vy grateful indeed to you for going to
Egypt. It is an action which—if ever I have a biographer—
will certainly be admired by others. I hope you may be
successful. I feel almost certain you will. Your wit & tact &
beauty should overcome all obstacles. . . .

Like Antony and Napoleon before him, Churchill
ardently aspired for action on the Nile.

On April 8, Kitchener put 16,000 Dervishes to flight at
the Atbara. Churchill was not slow to hear of this and to
see the military significance especially in so far as it concerned his own fortunes:

WSC to Lady Randolph

EXTRACT

13 April [1898]   Bombay

. . . It was evident from the moment that the Dervishes
evacuated Metemmah and Shendy and moved round the
Egyptian left flank with a view to threatening & possibly
assailing Sir Herbert Kitchener's communications—that a
battle was imminent.

The Dervishes were 'formed to a flank' i.e. had their line of retreat in prolongation of their front. For an army to be beaten in such a strategic position is for it to be destroyed. This has happened many times in military history. We all expected a battle therefore—but when it did not come off —Sir B.B. concluded that the Egyptian troops must have been considered worthless and that the Sirdar did not feel strong enough to seize the glorious opportunity presented. He said 'in two days more we shall see'. The next morning we got the news.

I need not tell you how bitter my own feelings were to think I had not been there. Still my conscience is easy and as I was actually on field service at the time, I cannot complain.

I do not think this will alter the prospects of an autumn campaign, tho it may diminish the resistance to be encountered. The Nile will not rise before it is ready, and I am quite easy in my mind that even July would be time enough. We shall see. If I am too late and all is over I can only conclude that perhaps Fate intervened because Chance would have been malicious had I gone.

His brother Jack, who was then eighteen years old, wrote him what was obviously a discouraging letter about the prospects; his letter unfortunately does not survive. However Churchill's reply is extant :

WSC to Jack

EXTRACT

9 May [1898]   Government House
                                          Ootacamund

. . . I do not at all agree with you that the Atbara is the end of the Soudan campaign. Much more severe fighting will ensue—especially at Omdurman. I hear they are making great preparations at Woolwich—for high explosive shells & 5 inch rifled guns—to breach the fortress—which does not look as if all were over.

It seems good fighting—short and sharp. But I don't expect it is any more exciting & less dangerous than the frontier. At Atbara—16,000 men—lost 500 killed &

wounded (60 killed). On 16th Sept in Mamund valley 1000 men—lost 150—(of whom 50 killed) or four times as heavy a proportion. Also the Egyptian fight lasted 28 minutes. I was under fire exactly 13 hours on the 16th. However I look forward with much interest to see both kinds. . . .

11

THE RIVER WAR

NOTHING WAS CERTAIN. Yet Churchill, impecunious as he was, took up his three months' leave and sailed from Bombay on June 18. He arrived in London in early July. At once he animated his mother to pull any strings that had not yet been pulled. By this time many friendly agents were already at work. His mother was doing all she could : Lady Jeune was intriguing with Sir Evelyn Wood, the Adjutant General of the Forces. But none of this seemed to be of avail.

Churchill now recognized that all the best endeavours of his mother with Kitchener and those of Lady Jeune with Sir Evelyn Wood had miscarried. He was beginning to feel that he had wasted his time when, out of the blue, there arrived a potential life-line inspired by memories of the past. Lord Salisbury, then Prime Minister and Foreign Secretary, had chanced to read *The Story of the Malakand Field Force*. Evidently he was not put off by the misprints and poor punctuation which had so distressed the author. He invited him to come and see him. Churchill recounts the story admirably in *My Early Life* :

> The Great Man, Master of the British world, the unchallenged leader of the Conservative Party, a third time Prime Minister and Foreign Secretary at the height of his long career, received me at the appointed hour, and I entered for the first time that spacious room overlooking the Horseguards Parade in which I was afterwards for many years from time to time to see much grave business done in Peace and War.
>
> There was a tremendous air about this wise old Statesman. Lord Salisbury, for all his resistance to modern ideas, and perhaps in some way because of it, played a greater part in gathering together the growing strength of the British Empire for a time of trial which few could foresee and none could measure, than any other historic figure that can be cited. I remember well the old-world

courtesy with which he met me at the door and with a
charming gesture of welcome and salute conducted me to
a seat on a small sofa in the midst of his vast room.

'I have been keenly interested in your book. I have
read it with the greatest pleasure, and, if I may say so,
with admiration not only for its matter but for its style.
The debates in both Houses of Parliament about the
Indian frontier policy have been acrimonious, much
misunderstanding has confused them. I myself have been
able to form a truer picture of the kind of fighting that
has been going on in these frontier valleys from your
writings than from any other documents which it has
been my duty to read.'

I thought twenty minutes would be about the limit of
my favour, which I had by no means the intention to
outrun, and I accordingly made as if to depart after that
period had expired. But he kept me for over half an hour,
and when he finally conducted me again across the
wide expanse of carpet to the door, he dismissed me in
the following terms, 'I hope you will allow me to say
how much you remind me of your father, with whom
such important days of my political life were lived. If
there is anything at any time that I can do which would
be of assistance to you, pray do not fail to let me
know. . . .'

Churchill jumped at the opportunity. Where petticoat
influence had failed, he would succeed. He wrote to Lord
Salisbury :

WSC to Lord Salisbury

(Salisbury Papers)

18 July [1898]   35a Great Cumberland Place

Dear Lord Salisbury,

I am vy anxious to go to Egypt and to proceed to Khartoum with the Expedition. It is not my intention, under any
circumstances to stay in the army long. I want to go, first,
because the recapture of Khartoum will be a historic event :
second, because I can, I anticipate, write a book about it
which from a monetary, as well as from other points of
view, will be useful to me.

Sir Evelyn Wood has tried his best—so he assures me—on my behalf. My mother has exerted what influence she can for two years. Even HRH has allowed his name to be used as a recommendation. All have failed.

I therefore venture to ask you to help me in the matter. I am convinced that if you will write a letter to Lord Cromer and say that on personal grounds you wish me to go—the affair will be immediately arranged. Either I should be attached to the Expeditionary Force direct, or allowed to proceed to the front as correspondent of some, perhaps insignificant, paper and after a few casualties be appointed to fill a vacancy—as I was on the N.W. Frontier.

I am loth to afflict you with this matter. Yet the choice lies between doing so, and abandoning a project which I have set my heart on for a long time. I feel that you will not be unwilling to help me, if that can be done without hurt to the public service and I venture to think that no hurt will result, but rather benefit. The affair is after all of extreme insignificance to any but me.

I beg you will believe me, Yours very sincerely
WINSTON S. CHURCHILL

Lord Salisbury asked Lord Cromer, who for so many years had been the political master of Egypt, to write to Kitchener : 'But I am afraid I cannot advise you to rely too confidently on the result of his letter,' warned the Prime Minister in his reply to Churchill. In the event, the intervention of these distinguished personages was not necessary. Churchill relates in *My Early Life* :

Two days later I received the following laconic intimation from the War Office :

'You have been attached as a supernumerary Lieutenant to the 21st Lancers for the Soudan Campaign. You are to report at once at the Abbasiya Barracks, Cairo, to the Regimental Headquarters. It is understood that you will proceed at your own expense and that in the event of your being killed or wounded in the impending operations, or for any other reason, no charge of any kind will fall on British Army Funds.'

It was the death of a young officer in the 21st Lancers, Lieutenant P. Chapman, that created the vacancy which provided Churchill with his opportunity. Only one thing it seems now stood between Churchill and his goal: the necessary leave from the Indian Army authorities to take part in the Sudan Campaign. Characteristically, he decided not to wait for this leave to be given, but on the contrary to depart at once in case an adverse order might arrive from India. Instead of travelling more speedily by P & O via Brindisi, or more comfortably by Australian Lloyd via Trieste, Churchill opted for a third route, slower and more uncomfortable than either, one that would place him out of communication with the Indian military authorities as soon as possible. Once he was in Egypt it would be impossible for them to recall him; indeed they would hardly know where he was. Thus he travelled to Marseilles and there caught the Messageries Maritimes Paquebot *Sindh*— 'a filthy tramp—manned by these detestable French sailors' as he described it to his mother.

* * * * *

While he crossed the Mediterranean he must, despite his excitement about the voyage and his anxiety as to whether he would be intercepted by an order to return, have had time to reflect on what was for him an important public speech, only the second of his career. He made this twelve days before he left London at Bradford, his father's old stamping-ground.

WSC to Lady Randolph

15 July [1898]   Bradford

My dearest Mamma,

The meeting was a complete success. Personally, I was intensely pleased with the event. The keenness of the audience stirred my blood—and altho I stuck to my notes rigidly I certainly succeeded in rousing & in amusing them. They burst out of the hall & pressed all round the carriage to shake hands and cheered till we had quite driven away.

The conclusions I form are these—with practice I shall obtain great power on a public platform. My impediment is no hindrance. My voice sufficiently powerful, and—this is vital—my ideas & modes of thought are pleasing to men.

It may be perhaps the hand of Fate, which by a strange

229

coincidence closed one line of advance and aspiration in the morning and in the evening pointed out another with an encouraging gesture. At any rate my decision to resign my commission is definite.

> With best love, Your ever loving son
> WINSTON

His speech had provoked praise from some unexpected sources. For instance—Haldane, the Liberal philosopher and future Secretary of State for War, wrote to Lady Randolph :

R. B. Haldane to Lady Randolph

15 July 1898   House of Commons

Dear Lady Randolph,
   Contrary to my habit—I asked for a *Morning Post* to-day—I read the speech at Bradford—I thought it very good—broad in tone—fresh & vigorous—I hope he will soon be in the House, for there is in his voice something of the strong quality of one that is—alas—still—to the loss of all of us, & of you most of all.

> Yours vy sincerely
> R. B. HALDANE

A great sense of destiny, of power and of greatness was already deeply impregnated in Churchill. He was, by this time, markedly egocentric and self-expressive. This alienated many of his contemporaries and to a lesser extent those who were older than he was and who had known his father and were fascinated by the thought that he would prove to be a serviceable successor. Already by this time he had become an object of conversation and controversy. It was facile to say that he was trading on his father's reputation, that he pulled all the strings he could and made use of all the influence which he had inherited. But none could gainsay his courage or the ardour of his ambition. All this, however, did not make him very popular. He was still living in the twilight of a Victorian era in which many of his activities were regarded by older people as 'ungentlemanly'.

* * * * *

No message from the Indian authorities intercepted him. When he reached Luxor on August 5, he permitted himself a sigh of relief : 'As there has been no cancelling order and a fortnight has already passed, I think I may now conclude with certainty that "silence has given consent."'

THE ADVANCE UP THE NILE

Very few personal letters of Churchill's during this campaign survive. He took his military duties seriously and often found it difficult to write his despatches for the *Morning Post,* who had contracted to pay him £15 a column. We must, therefore, for the next few weeks, rely principally upon these despatches and the account he gave of his travels and adventures in *The River War*. This book, which was published in two volumes fifteen months after the recapture of Khartoum, is still regarded by many good judges of literature as one of the best books he ever wrote. It has been reprinted several times. Here are a few extracts which chronicle his journey from the barracks at Abbasiya, where he had reported, until he joined Kitchener's forces a few miles short of Khartoum.

Atbara. Early on the morning of the 16th, while the stars were yet in the sky, the convoy and its escort started. . . . I remained behind, having to hand over surplus stores, and intending to catch up the column in the evening at its first camp, about fifteen miles away. The business I had to do consumed more time than I had anticipated, and it was not until the sun was on the horizon that the little ferry steamer *Tahra* landed me again on the west bank. I made inquiries about the road. 'It is perfectly simple,' they said. 'You just go due south until you see the camp-fires, and then turn towards the river.' This I proceeded to do. I had gone about a mile when the sun sank and the world went into darkness. The bushes by the Nile were thick and thorny, and to avoid these I struck into the desert, steering due south by keeping my back to the Pole star. I rode on at a trot for nearly two hours, thinking all the time that it would be a welcome moment when I sat down to dinner, and above all to a drink. Suddenly, to my dismay, the sky began to cloud over, and my guiding-star and the pointers of the Great Bear faded and became invisible. For another hour I endeavoured to pursue my old direction, but the realisation that I was out of my bearings grew stronger every moment. At last the truth could be no longer disguised. I was lost. No dinner, no drink; nothing for the pony; nothing to do but wait for daylight!

One thing seemed clear in the obscurity. It was futile

to go on at random and to exhaust the animal on whom alone depended my chance of catching up the troops. So I selected a sandy spot behind a rock and, passing the reins round my waist, endeavoured to sleep. Thirst and the fidgeting of the pony effectually prevented this, and philosophic meditation was my sole and altogether insufficient consolation. Although the sky remained clouded, the night was hot. The view in every direction was concealed by the darkness, but the barrenness of the desert was none the less apparent. The realisation of its utter waste and desolation grew. A hot, restless, weary wind blew continuously with a mournful sound over the miles and miles of sand and rock, as if conscious of its own uselessness : a rainless wind over a sterile soil. In the distance there was a noise like the rattle of a train. It was more wind blowing over more desert. The possibility of Dervishes was too remote to be considered; but as the night wore on, the annoyance at missing a needed dinner and the discomfort of my position were intensified by another sensation—a horrible sensation of powerlessness, just like that which a man feels when his horse bolts and will not be stopped.

At about half-past three in the morning the clouds cleared from one part of the sky and the glorious constellation of Orion came into view. Never did the giant look more splendid. Forthwith I mounted and rode in his direction, for at this season of the year he lies along the Nile before dawn with his head to the north. After two hours' riding the desert scrub rose into higher bushes, and these, becoming more frequent and denser, showed that the Nile was not far off. Meanwhile the sky in the east began to pale, and against it there drew out in silhouette the tracery of the foliage and palm-trees by the river's brink. The thirsty pony pricked up his ears. In the gloom we brushed through the thorny bushes, spurred on by a common desire. Suddenly the undergrowth parted, and at our feet, immense and mysterious in the growing light, gleamed the Nile. I have written much of the great river. Here it thrusts itself on the page. Jumping off my horse, I walked into the flood till it rose above my knees, and began eagerly to drink its waters, as many a thirsty man has done before; while the pony, plunging his nose deep into the stream, gulped and gulped in pleasure and relief, as if he could never swallow enough. Water had been found; it remained to discover the column.

After much riding I reached their camping-ground, only to find it deserted. They had already marched. There was a village near by. Once it had consisted of many houses and had supported a large population. Now only a few miserable people moved about the mud walls. War and famine had destroyed nine-tenths of the inhabitants. I selected one of the remainder, whose *tarboush*, or fez, proclaimed him a man of some self-respect, and perhaps even of some local importance. and applied to him for breakfast and a guide. He spoke nothing but Arabic : I, only one word of that language. Still we conversed fluently. By opening and shutting my mouth and pointing to my stomach, I excited his curiosity, if not his wonder. Then I employed the one and indispensable Arabic word, *Backsheesh!* After that all difficulties melted. From a corner of the mud house in which he lived he produced a clean white cloth full of dates. From another corner some *doura* satisfied the pony. From an inner apartment, which smelt stale and acrid, three women and several children appeared. The women smiled amicably, and began to wait on me, handing me the dates one by one in fingers the dark skin of which alone protected them from the reproach of dirt. The children regarded the strangely garbed stranger with large eyes which seemed full of reflection, but without intelligent result. Meanwhile the lord of these splendours had departed with a wooden bowl. Presently he returned, bearing it filled with fresh, sweet but dirty milk. This completed a repast which, if it would not gratify the palate of the epicure, might yet sustain the stomach of the traveller.

I next proceeded to ask for information as to the column. With the point of my sword I drew on the red mud wall the picture of a Lancer—grotesque, disproportioned, yet, as the event proved, not unrecognisable. The women laughed, the man talked and gesticulated with energy. Even the children became excited. Yes, it was true. Such a one had passed through the village early that morning. He pointed at the sun and then to the eastern horizon. But not one—many. He began to make scratches on the wall to show how many. They had watered their horses in the river—he lapped vigorously from his hand—and had gone on swiftly. He pointed southwards, and made the motion of running. Then he gazed hard at me, and, with an expression of ferocious satisfaction, pronounced the word 'Omdurman.' He was of the Jaalin, and, looking at the ruins and the desolation around, I could not wonder that he rejoiced that the strong and implacable arm of civilisation was raised to chastise his merciless enemies. I replied to his speech by repeating with considerable solemnity the word *Backsheesh,* and at this, without more ado, he put on his boots and a dirtier blue shirt, picked up his broad-bladed sword, and started. But I will not be wearisome with a further account of my wanderings in the riparian bush, or of the other meals of dates and milk I was forced, and indeed fain, to eat. In the evening I caught up the column at its camp, and washed away the taste and recollection of native food and native life with one of the most popular drinks of the modern world.

THE APPROACH TO OMDURMAN

Merreh Hill. Trotting out on the morning of the 31st, as the light strengthened, we soon reached the hill of Merreh, and while the horses were being watered, I climbed to the top to view the scene. The sun had just risen, and the atmosphere was clear. A wonderful spectacle was displayed. The grand army of the Nile

235

marched towards its goal : a long row of great brown masses of infantry and artillery, with a fringe of cavalry dotting the plain for miles in front, with the Camel Corps—chocolate-coloured men on cream-coloured camels—stretching into the desert on the right, and the white gunboats stealing silently up the river on the left, scrutinising the banks with their guns. Far in rear the transport trailed away into the mirage, and far in front the field-glass disclosed the enemy patrols. Behind the moving army a long thread of wire made an Empire share its quarrel; before it a long account awaited settlement. . . .

For all his preoccupations Churchill did have time to send back some philosophical reflections :

WSC to Lady Randolph

24 August 1898   Wad Hebeshi
                                                 before Shabluka

. . . Within the next ten days there will be a general action - —perhaps a vy severe one. I may be killed. I do not think so. But if I am you must avail yourself of the consolations of philosophy and reflect on the utter insignificance of all human beings. I want to come back and shall hope all will be well. But I can assure you I do not flinch—though I do not accept the Christian or any other form of religious belief. We shall see what will happen; and in that spirit I would leave the subject. Nothing—not even the certain knowledge of approaching destruction would make me turn back now—even if I could with honour. . . .

When Churchill's squadron of the 21st Lancers joined up with the main army at Shabluka a week before the battle of Omdurman he wrote :

WSC to Lady Randolph

EXTRACT
26 August 1898   N. of Shabluka

. . . F. Rhodes [Colonel Frank Rhodes, Correspondent of *The Times*] vy kind and amiable. He talked to Sirdar about me. Kitchener said he had known I was not going to stay in army—was only making a convenience of it; that he had disapproved of my coming in place of others whose professions were at stake & that E. Wood had acted wrongly and had annoyed him by sending me. But that I was quite right to try my best. Taken in conjunction with his letter to you you can see that whatever his knowledge of war may be his acquaintance with truth is rudimentary. He may be a general—but never a gentleman. Perhaps however I shall meet him. I have however not pressed for an introduction since hearing. If I live he will recognise that it might have been worth while to impress me with his ideas on Egypt & the Sudan. As it is I shall form my own. . . .

This arrogant quip proved to be an omen of better relations between the two men in the distant future.

* * * * *

Only a few days after writing the letter of August 26 quoted above, on September 1, Churchill was destined by an unusual chance to come face to face with the Sirdar himself. This incident is vividly described in *The River War*:

. . . The great army, however, still advanced majestically, pressing the cavalry back before it; and it was evident that if the Khalifa's movement continued, and in spite of it being nearly one o'clock, there would be a collision between the main forces before the night. I was sent back to describe the state of affairs to the Sirdar.

To make certain of the position of the Expeditionary Force before starting in search of it, I climbed the black hill of Surgham and looked around.

From the summit the scene was extraordinary. The great army of Dervishes was dwarfed by the size of the landscape to mere dark smears and smudges on the brown of the plain. Looking east, another army was now visible—the British and Egyptian army. All six brigades had passed the Kerreri Hills, and now stood drawn up in a crescent, with their backs to the Nile. The transport and the houses of the village of Egeiga filled the enclosed space. Neither force could see the other, though but five miles divided them. I looked alternately at each array. That of the enemy was, without doubt, both longer and deeper. Yet there seemed a superior strength in the stolid battalions, whose lines were so straight that they might have been drawn with a ruler.

The urgency of my message allowed only a momentary view. But the impression produced by the sight of two armies thus approaching each other with hostile intent —for the Arab advance was very rapid—was so tremendous, that I found it necessary, lest my excitement should be apparent, to walk for a quarter of a mile before delivering my account.

The Sirdar, followed by a dozen Staff officers, was riding a few hundred yards from the *zeriba*. He had not yet seen the Dervish army, and was at the moment going to the hill of Surgham to take a general view. Nevertheless, he invited me to describe the situation as seen from the advanced squadrons. This I did, though neither at such length nor perhaps with such facility as seen in these pages. The swift advance of the enemy brought the moment very near. They were now but four miles away. In an hour, if they continued their movement, the action must begin. All the results of many years of preparation and three years of war must stand upon the issue of the event. If there had been a miscalculation, if the expedition was not strong enough, or if any accident or misfortune such as are common in battles were to occur, then utter ruin would descend upon the enterprise. The Sirdar was very calm. His confidence had been communicated to his Staff. 'We want nothing better,' they said. 'Here is a good field of fire. They may as well come to-day as to-morrow'. . . .

After completing his brief verbal report to the Sirdar, Churchill rode back to the *zeriba* where a large body of troops was encamped. They had been told to stand to arms at 2 p.m. It seemed likely at the time that the Dervish army would atack them that afternoon or possibly during the night.

There was no attack by the Dervish army that afternoon. Many of Kitchener's troops had made long marches and needed rest. All units, including the 21st Lancers, who had been on patrol and reconnaissance all day were with-

drawn inside the vast crescent-shaped *zeriba* with its back to
the Nile. There were many in the Army who thought that
this was a dangerous posture in which to leave this vast
expeditionary force during the night. Perhaps the Dervishes would attack under cover of darkness, and vast
confusion might be caused. The numerous horses, mules
and camels might stampede and the Dervishes, despite the
accurate fire of highly trained British troops, might con-
ceivably break into the *zeriba*. Churchill, inexhaustible in
his quest for information and knowledge, chose to peram-
bulate the outside of the *zeriba* after dark. It is clear that
Kitchener's decisions were much debated in the camp that
night. Churchill came to the conclusion that Kitchener
had clung to a true decision; but in any case by dawn
Kitchener's decision had been vindicated by events. The
Dervishes feared the dark, and they did not attack.

Before first light the 21st Lancers were sent out to the
high ground which divided the two armies in order to
report on the enemy's movements. To quote again from
The River War :

Even before it became light several squadrons of
British and Egyptian cavalry were pushed swiftly forward
to gain contact with the enemy and learn his intentions.
The first of these, under Captain [Everard] Baring [*a
brother of Hugo*], occupied Surgham Hill, and waited
in the gloom until the whereabouts of the Dervishes
should be disclosed by the dawn. It was a perilous undertaking, for he might have found them unexpectedly
near.

As the sun rose, the 21st Lancers trotted out of the
zeriba and threw out a spray of officers' patrols. With
one of these it was my fortune to be sent to reconnoitre
Surgham Hill. We galloped forward, and as we did not
know that the Egyptian squadron and its officer had
already looked over the ridge, we enjoyed all the excitement without any of the danger, and were also elated
by the thought that we were the first to see what lay
beyond. As there had been no night attack, I had expected that the Dervish army would have retired to their
original position or entered the town. I rejected the idea
that they would advance across the open ground to
attack the *zeriba* by daylight, as it seemed absurd.

Indeed, it appeared more probable that their hearts had failed them in the night, and that they had melted away into the deserts. But these anticipations were immediately dispelled by the scene which was visible from the crest of the ridge.

It was a quarter to six. The light was dim, but growing stronger every minute. There in the plain lay the enemy, their numbers unaltered, their confidence and intentions apparently unshaken. Their front was now nearly five miles long, and composed of great masses of men joined together by thinner lines. Behind and to the flanks were large reserves. From where I stood they looked dark blurs and streaks, relieved and diversified with an odd-looking shimmer of light from the spear-points.

After making the necessary reports I continued to watch the strange and impressive spectacle. As it became broad daylight—that is to say, about ten minutes to six—I suddenly realised that all the masses were in motion and advancing swiftly. Their Emirs galloped about and before their ranks. Scouts and patrols scattered themselves all over the front. Then they began to cheer. They were still a mile away from the hill, and were concealed from the Sirdar's army by the folds of the ground. The noise of the shouting was heard, allbeit faintly, by the troops down by the river. But to us, watching on the hill, a tremendous roar came up in waves of intense sound, like the tumult of the rising wind and sea before a storm. In spite of the confidence which I felt in the weapons of civilisation—for all doubts had dispersed with the darkness—the formidable aspect of this great host of implacable savages, hurrying eagerly to the attack of the *zeriba*, provoked a feeling of loneliness, which was shared, I think, by the rest of the little patrol. Partly to clear the mind of such unnecessary emotions, and also with the design of thereafter writing this account, I moved to a point on the ridge which afforded a view of both armies.

The British and Egyptian force was arranged in line with its back to the river. Its flanks were secured by the gunboats lying moored in the stream. Before it was the rolling sandy plain, looking from the slight elevation of the ridge smooth and flat as a table. To the right rose the rocky hills of the Kerreri position, near which the

Scenes from Life

Second Lieutenant Winston S. Churchill
4th Hussars, 1895

Lord and Lady
Randolph, 1874

Winston and his
mother, 1876
The first known
photograph

Jenny, with Jack and Winston, about 1881

Harrow, 1888-9. Winston is at the left.

Rev. J. E. C. Welldon,
Headmaster of Harrow

Pamela Plowden, 1892

Winston, 1900

**Two drawings by Lady Granby
(later Duchess of Rutland)**

The Armoured Train: the day after the action

Winston S. Churchill
1898.

Attached to 21st
Lancers: In Cairo, 1898

Lord Randolph, 1893.

Head of the Family,
after the death of his father

Member for Oldham

Egyptian cavalry were drawn up—a dark solid mass of men and horses. On the left the 21st Lancers, with a single squadron thrown out in advance, were halted watching their patrols, who climbed about Surgham Hill, stretched forward beyond it, or perched, as we did, on the ridge.

By a singular piece of historical good fortune the 'necessary reports' to which Churchill referred have survived. He took it upon himself in view of the urgency of the matter to address two written reports scribbled in pencil direct to the Sirdar, and a copy to his commanding officer, Colonel Martin. The duplicates do not survive, but the top copy, addressed to the Sirdar, was preserved by his Deputy Asistant Adjutant-General, Captain Sir Henry Rawlinson.

These are the two somewhat crumpled messages which Rawlinson had preserved :

WSC to Sir H. Kitchener

Date Sept 2 1898

No I
From   Lieut Churchill
Place   Left Advd Patrol 21st L.
To   Sirdar
Place   near Omdurman

Duplicate to O.C. 21st Lancers

Dervish army, strength unchanged, occupies last night's position with their left well extended. Their patrols have reported the advance and loud cheering is going on. There is no *zeriba*.

Nothing hostile is between a line drawn from Heliograph Hill to Mahdi's tomb, and river. Nothing is within three miles from the camp.

Signature WINSTON S. CHURCHILL
Lieut 4th Hussars
attd 21st Lancers

And half an hour later :

From Lieut Churchill
To Sirdar   *Desp* 6 hr. 20 min.

About $\frac{1}{4}$ Dervish army is on their right which they have
refused at present. Should this force continue to advance it
would come the South side of Heliograph hill.

Most of the Cavalry are with this force.

> Duplicate to Col Martin
> > *Signature* W I N S T O N S. C H U R C H I L L
> > Lieut 4th Hussars

Churchill wrote lively accounts of the Battle of Omdurman both for the *Morning Post* and later in *The River
War*. Of even greater interest are two letters he wrote—the
first to his mother two days after the battle on September 4
and another to Ian Hamilton on September 16. These were
written while the battle was still vividly in his mind.

4 September 1898   Khartoum
                                        and be damned to it.

My dearest Mamma,

I hope that this letter will not long precede me—certainly not more than a fortnight. You will have been
relieved by my telegram which I sent off at once. I was
under fire all day and rode through the charge. You know
my luck in these things. I was about the only officer whose
clothes, saddlery, or horse were uninjured. I fired 10 shots
with my pistol—all necessary—and just got to the end of it
as we cleared the crush. I never felt the slightest nervous-
ness and felt as cool as I do now. I pulled up and reloaded
within 30 yards of their mass and then trotted after my
troop, who were then about 100 yards away. I am sorry to
say I shot 5 men for certain and two doubtful. The pistol
was the best thing in the world. The charge was nothing
like as alarming as the retirement on the 16th of Sept last
year. It passed like a dream and some part I cannot quite

242

recall. The Dervishes showed no fear of cavalry and would not move unless you knocked them over with the horse. They tried to hamstring the horses, to cut the bridles—reins —slashed and stabbed in all directions and fired rifles at a few feet range. Nothing touched me. I destroyed those who molested me and so passed out without any disturbance of body or mind.

Poor Grenfell—with whom I made great friends and with whom and Molyneux I always lived and eat—was killed and this took the pleasure and exultation out of the whole affair, as far as I was concerned. Dick Molyneux too had a bad sword cut and a wonderful escape. Jack Brinton a slash across his shoulder. I heard at midday of Colonel Rhodes being wounded and at night of poor Hubert Howard being killed. He had ridden out our charge unhurt and it was indeed the irony of fate to kill him with a friendly shell. These things—and at the time they were reported as worse—made me anxious and worried during the night and I speculated on the shoddiness of war. You cannot gild it. The raw comes through. The metaphors are mixed but expressive.

I am just off with Lord Tullibardine to ride over the field. It will smell I expect as there are 7,000 bodies lying there. I hope to get some spears etc. I shall write a history of this war. Colonel F.R. is going to edit it and will give me all his photos. He is a brave gallant man. Nothing depresses him. Oh, there is such a lot to tell that it is useless my trying to write it now that the post is going off.

I will send 3 *M.P.* [*Morning Post*] letters during the next 3 days. And now I shall get back alive in all human probability and will tell you all about it myself.

I have told Molyneux to come & see you. We made great friends. He is a brave and cheery friend. Our losses are worth thinking of. Out of 20 officers and 280 men and horses we lost 5 officers, 70 men and 135 horses killed and wounded in 120 seconds. [*Corrected casualty figures are given in the next letter.*] Pursuit another seven. Meanwhile, arrange me some good meetings in October, Bradford & Birmingham. Sunny will help.

Your loving son
WINSTON

16 September 1898   In the train
Sudan Military Ry

. . . I had a patrol on 2nd Sept and was I think the first to
see the enemy—certainly the first to hear their bullets. Never
shall I see such a sight again. At the very least there were
40,000 men—five miles long in lines with great humps and
squares at intervals—and I can assure you that when I
heard them all shouting their war songs from my coign of
vantage on the ridge of Heliograph Hill I and my little
patrol felt very lonely. And though I never doubted the
issue—I was in great awe.

Then they advanced and I watched them, fascinated
and of course scribbling messages perpetually to the Sirdar
and O.C. 21st Lancers. Their cavalry patrols which consisted of five or six horsemen each made no attempt to
drive me back and I waited until one great brigade of perhaps 2000 men got to within 400 yards. I didn't realize
they could shoot and thought they were all spearmen. Then
they halted for a quarter of an hour and treated me and
my 7 Lancers with complete disdain. Foolishly I dismounted 4 and opened magazine into the brown of them.
Thereat they sent out 20 Riflemen and began to make very
close practice. Finally I had to gallop and as we did so I
did not hear less than 30 bullets. Luckily—(you know how
capricious Fortune is)—we never had a man touched. If
we had it would have meant others.

I then sent the patrol behind the hill and went up to the
top myself. I dismounted but my grey pony was a target
and it got too hot for me to stay although the scene was
worth looking at. Various frantic people—Adjutant
trumpeters etc then arrived and brought me back to my
Squadron. But I assumed so very lofty a position—pointing
out that no one was even hurt (and they admitted the value
of the information) that I was allowed to go off again. I
attributed the fact that we had no casualties to my 'experience' etc. It was really due to the Almighty's amiability.
For candidly the fire was for the time being as hot as any-

thing I have seen—barring only those 10 minutes with the 35th Sikhs—a year ago today.

Then the whole attack developed and they cleared the cavalry into the *zeriba* and we listened for an hour to 20,000 rifles, near 60 guns and 20 maxims without seeing much. Watered and fed etc. A few bullets—all high as good cover down by bank. At 8.30 the attack weakened and we were bustled out of the *zeriba* to left flank. We halted on the old ridge and messed about with carbines for a quarter of an hour. Beyond the ridge thousands of Dervishes could be seen, as I thought fugitives—'meet to be cut up'. I made use of the expression 'supine apathy' here.

At 8.40 we mounted and rode slowly towards these crowds. I was confident that we should spear them till we could not sit on our horses. But between us and the distant fugitives was a single line of 150 men. We all thought these spearmen. They let us get within 250 yards in silence. We proposed—at least I think this was the idea—to move round their flank and slip a squadron at them and then on to the better things beyond. The ground looked all right and besides we did not intend doing anything from that direction.

We trotted in column of troops across their front from right to left. As we did so the enemy got down on their knees and opened a very sharp fire. There was a loud brisk crackle of musketry. The distance was too short for it to be harmless on so big a target and I realised that there were only two courses open viz : Left wheel into line and gallop off—coming back for wounded—a bad business; & Right wheel into line and charge. I think everybody made his own decision. At any rate while the trumpet was still jerking we were all at the gallop towards them. The fire was too hot to allow of second lines—flank squadrons or anything like that being arranged. The only order given was Right Wheel into Line. Gallop & Charge were understood.

I went through the first 100 yards looking over my left shoulder to see what sort of effect the fire was producing. It seemed small. Then I drew my Mauser pistol—a ripper —and cocked it. Then I looked to my front. Instead of the 150 riflemen who were still blazing I saw a line nearly (in the middle)—12 deep and a little less than our own front of closely jammed spearmen—all in a *nullah* with steep sloping sides 6 foot deep & 20 foot broad.

After the Frontier I thought—capital—the more the merrier. I must explain my position. I was right troop leader but one. I saw we over-lapped. I was afraid we would charge into air. I shouted to Wormald 7th Hussars (an excellent officer) to shoulder and we actually struck the enemy in a crescent formation. Result of our shoulder was this—my troop struck the *nullah* diagonally and their decreasing slope enabled us to gallop through not jump it. Result we struck—faster and more formed than the centre troops.

Opposite me they were about 4 deep. But they all fell knocked A.O.T. [arse over tip] and we passed through without any sort of shock. One man in my troop fell. He was cut to pieces. Five or six horses were wounded by back handers etc. But otherwise unscathed. Then we emerged into a region of scattered men and personal combats. The troop broke up and disappeared. I pulled into a trot and rode up to individuals firing my pistols in their faces and killing several—3 for certain—2 doubtful—one very doubtful. Then I looked round and saw the Dervish mass reforming. The charge had passed through knocking over nearly half. They were getting on their legs again and their Emirs were trying to collect them into a lump again. I realised that this mass was about 20 yards away and I looked at them stupidly for what may have been 2 seconds. Then I saw two men get down on their knees and take aim with rifles—and for the first time the danger & peril came home to me. I turned and galloped. The squadron was reforming nearly 150 yards away. As I turned both shots were fired and at that close range I was grievously anxious. But I heard none of their bullets—which went Heaven knows where. So I pulled into a canter and rejoined my troop—having fired exactly 10 shots & emptied my pistol—but without a hair of my horse or a stitch of my clothing being touched. Very few can say the same.

I am glad to have added the experience of a cavalry charge to my military repertoire. But really though dangerous it was not in the least exciting and it did not look dangerous—at least not to me. You see I was so confident we would open them and hunt them and the realisation of our loss did not come to me until we reformed and I saw the wounded etc. It was I suppose the most dangerous 2 minutes I shall live to see. Out of 310 officers & men we lost

246

—1 officer and 20 men killed—4 officers & 45 men wounded and 119 horses of which 56 were bullet wounds. All this in 120 seconds!

I am in great disfavour with the authorities here. Kitchener was furious with Sir E. Wood for sending me out and expressed himself freely. My remarks on the treatment of the wounded—again disgraceful—were repeated to him and generally things have been a little unpleasant. He is a great general but he has yet to be accused of being a great gentleman. It is hard to throw stones at the rising sun and my personal dislike may have warped my judgment, but if I am not blinded, he has been on a certainty from start to finish and has had the devil's luck to help him beside. . .

12

RETURN TO INDIA

As soon as the battle was over Churchill was keen to
return to England and go from there to India to take part
in the Inter-Regimental Polo Tournament. He arrived back
in England early in October. At this time he received
another letter from the Prince of Wales. Some months
before the Prince had written : You have plenty of time
before you, and should certainly stick to the Army before
adding MP to your name.' Churchill's answer does not survive, but the Prince of Wales wrote back :

Prince of Wales to WSC

6 October [1898]   Mar Lodge
                                                    Braemar

My dear Winston,

Many thanks for your letter received today and for
having taken in such good part the remarks I made in my
previous letter. I fear in matters of discipline in the Army I
may be considered old fashioned—& I must say that I think
that an officer serving in a campaign should not write letters
for the newspapers or express strong opinions of how the
operations are carried out.

Your writing a book with an account of the campaign is
quite another matter—& I feel sure you will write it as
a history & not with military criticism which so young an
officer as yourself, however clever you may be, should avoid
as a matter of discipline.

I can well understand that it must be very difficult for you
to make up your mind what to do, but I cannot help feeling
that Parliamentary & literary life is what would suit you
best as the monotony of military life in an Indian station
can have no attraction for you—though fortunately some
officers do put up with it or else we should have no Army
at all !

Believe me, Yours very sincerely
ALBERT EDWARD

I shall be delighted to accept the new edition of *The Malakand Field Force* which you kindly propose sending me.

Churchill went to Marlborough House two weeks later to dine with the Prince of Wales.

Pending his return to India for his final spell and to take part in the Polo Tournament he made full use of the military laxity which at that time permitted a serving officer to make political speeches. He made three, at Rotherhithe, Dover and Southsea. Churchill, like so many other politicians of his day, had an exaggerated idea of the influence of the newspaper press. Though he did not trim his sails to their winds, he always sought to keep on good terms with newspaper proprietors. He was already friends with Oliver Borthwick, the son of Lord Glenesk the proprietor of the *Morning Post,* and he made friends with Alfred Harmsworth, later Lord Northcliffe. 'Harmsworth is very civil and will report the speech at Dover well', Churchill wrote to his mother on October 21. In the same letter he reported that at dinner the day before, given by Ernest Cassel, he sat next to Moberly Bell, the Manager of *The Times.* 'We get on capitally' Churchill reported with some pride.

Churchill became involved at an early stage with some of the controversies that surrounded the conduct of the Omdurman campaign. On October 19, the Editor of *Concord,* a pacifist magazine, had written to the *Westminster Gazette* deploring the massacre of Dervishes at Omdurman, both during and after the battle, as 'deliberately planned and executed in cold blood.' He cited in support of his contention, among others, 'Lieutenant Churchill's account of how the enemy was "destroyed, not conquered by machinery", and of the terrible scenes on the battlefield afterwards'. Churchill in his spirited reply, declined to enter into a discussion of 'the legitimacy of the practice of killing the wounded.' 'The ethics of human destruction', he wrote in his letter to the Editor of the *Westminster Gazette* on October 24, 'must necessarily be somewhat obscure. Neither rhetoric nor hysteria will help us to determine them.' Churchill confined his argument with the Editor of *Concord* to the allegation that the Dervish loss was caused by the unnecessary blood-thirstiness of the British and Egyptian forces.

Had 'The Editor of *Concord*' been present in the *zeriba* on the morning of September 2, and had he seen 40,000 savages advancing with hostile intent, he would not have protested against the soldiers opening fire. He would as a reasonable man have perceived that if the spearmen came to close quarters with the troops, a far greater slaughter would take place than actually occurred —a slaughter in which he himself might have been unfortunately included. Once fire was opened the loss of the Dervishes was mechanical. There was a hail of bullets. The Dervish advance continued, and, in the interests of the Peace Preservation Society, it was necessary that the hail of bullets should also continue. The courage of the enemy was their destruction. When they had had enough they withdrew.

'The Editor of *Concord*' preaches principles with which few will not sympathise. But he should be logical; judging by his literary vehemence, he appears to be a most pugnacious peace maker : a man who disapproves so entirely of physical force that he would employ physical force to prevent it. He should also be just. It will be open to him, if he is dissatisfied with the war on the Nile, to attack the Ministry responsible for that war. They will probably be able to justify their action to the satisfaction of the majority of the electorate. But I submit, that it is unfair as well as irrational to attribute cruelty and bloodthirstiness to soldiers who, placed in a position where they have to defend their lives, use the weapons with which they are armed with skill, judgement, and effect.

Though at this time Churchill sought to soft-pedal the issue, subsequent disclosures forced him to be more outspoken. For instance, he wrote to his mother after he had gone back to India—(26 January 1899) : 'I shall merely say that the victory at Omdurman was disgraced by the inhuman slaughter of the wounded and that Kitchener was responsible for this.'

Before he left for India he wrote to his steady love, Miss Pamela Plowden, with whom he plainly had had words and controversy :

28 November [1898]   35A Great Cumberland Place

My dear Miss Pamela,

I am going to India on Friday : I want to come and see you before then.

The book is getting on magnificently and I am quite satisfied with what is thus far completed. Gordon was an extraordinary character. General, fanatic & wit. A vy rare combination. I met a young lady the other day who is I think—I judge only from the standpoint of reason—nearly as clever & wise as you. I certainly had much the worst of it in an argument on a purely philosophical subject. Hence I rank her one above Plato. I wonder if I arouse your curiosity. I hope so for then you may ask me to come to see you. Were I wise I would not allay it—by telling you that she is less beautiful.

One thing I take exception to in your letter. Why do you say I am incapable of affection? Perish the thought. I love one above all others.

thought . I love one above all others . And I shall be constant . I am no fickle gallant capriciously following the fancy of the

And I shall be constant. I am no fickle gallant capriciously following the fancy of the hour. My love is deep and strong. Nothing will ever change it. I might it is true divide it. But the greater part would remain true—will remain true till death. Who is this that I love. Listen—as the French say—over the page I will tell you

Yours vy sincerely
                        WINSTON S. CHURCHILL

Churchill was obviously in love with this beautiful girl
whom he had met in India two years before. But such were
his ambition and his slender means that he was not yet prepared to commit himself. This letter was cool, distant and
provocative. He was obviously far from settled in his mind
as to his course of action. After all, he was only on the eve
of his twenty-fourth birthday; he had no money, nor had
Miss Plowden, and he was still thinking ferociously about
his future.

On his way to India he wrote to his mother :

WSC to Lady Randolph

11 December [1898]   S.S. *Shannon*
                                              off Aden

My dearest Mamma,
    I daresay you will expect a letter—though in truth there
is nothing to tell. We have had a vy rough passage down
the Red Sea—of all places—and I have not enjoyed myself
excessively. I have however made good progress with the
book. Three very long chapters are now almost completed. The chapter describing the fall of Khartoum
Gordon's death etc is I think quite the most lofty passage I
have ever written. The only thing which has pleased me
apart from the pleasure of writing is that there are two
copies of *The Malakand Field Force* on board which are
very regularly read.
    Please send without delay the *Annual Registers* of 1884,
1885 & 1886. I want them.

                                    Ever your loving son
                                         WINSTON

In all probability he would not have returned to India at
all except for the lure of the polo :

WSC to Lady Randolph

EXTRACT

11 January 1899   Bangalore

. . . I am going next week to Madras to play polo and shall
stay at Government House. The week after that Jodhpore
                        252

where we all stay practising for the Tournament with Sir Pertab Singh. Then Meerut for the Inter-Regimental Tournament, where I stay with Sir B. B. & after that Umballa for the Championship—a very pleasant six weeks. Then home and the more serious pleasures of life. . . .

His next letter to his brother shows how the splendid plan nearly miscarried :

WSC to Jack

EXTRACT

9 February 1899 [Jodhpore]

. . . I am staying with Sir Pertab Singh for a week before the Inter-Regimental Tournament. All the rest of our team are here and everything smiled until last night—when I fell down stairs & sprained both my ankles and dislocated my right shoulder. I am going to struggle on to the polo ground this afternoon—but I fear I shall not be able to play in the Tournament as my arm is weak and stiff & may come out again at any moment.

Churchill played with his right upper arm strapped tightly to his side so that his shoulder would not come out again but giving him only a restricted arc in which to swing his stick. Notwithstanding this, success attended the 4th Hussars—and Churchill—in the first two rounds.

*　*　　*　　*　　*

Curzon had succeeded Lord Elgin as Viceroy on 6 January 1899, and not long afterwards, on his way back from the Inter-Regimental Polo Tournament, Churchill stayed for a week with the Viceroy in Calcutta. All his previous hostility evaporated under the impact of the Curzon charm :

EXTRACT

2 March 1899   Calcutta

. . . Everything is vy pleasant and I have found him very delightful to talk to. His manners are wonderful. All the aggressiveness wh irritated me at home is gone. They have both won everybody's heart. But I fear he works too hard —nearly eleven hours every single day—so his secretary tells me. And you would be shocked to see how Lady C is changed. I was vy pained to see her. She has had a sharp attack of fever and will not I think stand the climate which will spoil the whole thing. She sends all sorts of messages to you and speaks with great affection for you. . . .

Churchill obviously made a good impression during his stay in Calcutta. Lady Curzon wrote to Lady Randolph on 14 March 1899 : 'People in India have an immense opinion of Winston & his book. You hear his praises so often I know Jennie—but you can never hear them too often can you ! Lockhart & Sir Wm Nicholson, and Bindon Blood as you know and Welldon all swear by him & make no limitations as to how far he will go.'

*   *   *   *   *

Before he had left England, Churchill had once again taken in hand his novel which had languished for more than a year, its composition having been interrupted by three military campaigns and two books about them. He had sent the typescript to his grandmother, asking for her to comment, particularly on the character of the heroine Lucile. The old Duchess replied :

29 November [1898]   Castlemead
                                          Windsor

Dear Winston,

You have set me a difficult task in the question you ask
me to answer! There is so much that is clever and graphic
in your Novel and you describe very well, the fighting and
horrors of the Barricades. At the same time there is a want
of interest in the plot and I quite agree with you that Lucile
is a weak and uninteresting personality. It is clear you have
not yet attained a knowledge of Women—and it is evident
you have (I am thankful to see) no experience of Love!
Now as to the policy of publishing the Book I can see no
objection to it. It cannot injure your reputation in a literary
Point of View for the faults are those of youth and inexperi-
ence and not Want of Ability, 250£ is not to be despised
and to my mind you have earned it.

                                          Affectly
                                    GD MOTHER

The outline of the heroine Lucile was sketched for him
by his aunt Leonie. But it seems he did not have time or
opportunity to improve, as he had hoped, the character of
Lucile, for almost immediately *Macmillan's Magazine*
offered £100 for the serial rights which Churchill gladly
accepted. 'It is a great compliment it's being serialised' he
wrote to his mother on 1 January 1899, 'very good and only
the successful novels are serialised'.

*   *   *   *   *

A letter from Churchill to Aylmer Haldane written on the
train between Bombay and Bangalore reveals that even
though Churchill had avowedly only returned to India in
order to play in the Polo Tournament, the least prospect of
military adventure caused him to send cables to his friends
on the frontier. The letter also reveals that his longing for
medals remained undiminished.

18 December [1898]   in the train near Wadi

My dear Haldane,

I am leaving the army in April. I have come back merely
for the Polo Tournaments. I naturally want to wear my
medals while I have a uniform to wear them on. They have
already sent me the Egyptian one. I cannot think why the
Frontier one has not arrived. Young Life Guardsmen on Sir
B. Blood's staff in Buner have already got theirs. Do try
and get mine for me as soon as possible. Otherwise it will
never be worn. I come in either as attd to 31st P.I. in Malakand Field Force or on Sir William's staff. The latter would
of course be the best place to figure in. Will you try and get
the medals sent me—there is only the general clasp—so that
there should be no great difficulty.

Yours very sincerely
WINSTON S. CHURCHILL

A few weeks after arriving back in India, Churchill's
plans for completing *The River War* received a serious set-
back. Major Watson, 'on whom I counted for a great deal
of important information,' who had been aide-de-camp to
Kitchener during the campaign, had been forbidden by the
Sirdar to supply him with any information. But if anything,
this seemed to make Churchill all the more determined.
'This will cause delay but it shall not prevent me from
writing the account,' he told his mother on January 26. It
was one more black mark against Kitchener. 'I am duly
appreciative of the civility', he remarked drily.

What the set-back meant was that he would have to
spend some days in Cairo on his way home from India; and
indeed this proved a very worth-while visit—so much so
that he extended his stay in Cairo by a week.

At first he had found little to say in favour of Kitchener :
'The book grows rather in bitterness about K,' he had
written to his mother on 29 December 1898; 'I feel that in
spite of my intention it will be evident no friend has written
it. I expect they had just about had enough of him when he
went back to his Soudan. A vulgar common man—without

much of the non-brutal elements in his composition.' But after a few days in Cairo he wrote on March 30 :

WSC to Lady Randolph

EXTRACT

30 March [1899]   Savoy Hotel
                                                   Cairo

. . . A great many of my more acrid criticisms of the Sirdar I shall tone down or cut out. I have quite got over any feeling of resentment and I do not wish to profit by the reaction which has set in against him. Major Watson by a lucky chance is in Cairo so that whatever information he was not allowed to give me by writing, I may procure from him by word of mouth. I lunched yesterday with Lord Cromer and he afterwards did me the honour of talking to me about the Soudan, its past and its future with reference to my book for more than two hours and a half.

What I then learned makes it necessary to considerably modify the earlier chapter dealing with the Gordon episode. I feel that it will be impossible for me to sacrifice all the fine phrases and pleasing paragraphs I have written about Gordon, but Cromer was very bitter about him and begged me not to pander to the popular belief on the subject. Of course there is no doubt that Gordon as a political figure was absolutely hopeless. He was so erratic, capricious, utterly unreliable, his mood changed so often, his temper was abominable, he was frequently drunk, and yet with all he had a tremendous sense of honour and great abilities, and a still greater obstinacy. Pray do not mention this otherwise than as coming from me because my conversation was naturally private. . . .

Lord Cromer, indeed, turned out to be of great help to Churchill in putting *The River War* into historical perspective.

Churchill's ambition, of which much has already been written, was never hidden from his friends and acquaintances, nor did he delude himself about it. In one of his rare political comments from India, Churchill told his mother :

EXTRACT

11 January 1899   [Bangalore]

. . . Joe C. [Chamberlain] is losing ground a good deal. I
feel it instinctively. I know I am right. I have got instinct
in these things. Inherited probably. This life is vy pleasant
and I pass the time quickly and worthily—but I have no
right to dally in the pleasant valleys of amusement. What
an awful thing it will be if I don't come off. It will break
my heart for I have nothing else but ambition to cling
to. . . .

Churchill's decision to send in his papers and resign his
commission was courageous, even audacious. He was
trained for no other profession save the Army. Here it
would be a long time before he could gain advancement
and earn a competence. How would he ever be able to pay
off his debts and acquire an income sufficient to sustain a
parliamentary career? He had high hopes of some financial
return from *The River War*; but this was still uncompleted
and there is no record that he had received any advance for
it. Doubtless he had already aspired to write his father's
Life, but the decision was not in his hands. He had not yet
approached his father's literary trustees; when he did they
were somewhat sceptical of his fitness for the task.

Nonetheless he returned to England full of hope and pro-
jects. He was always ready to run risks on the field of battle,
in politics, and in his own personal finances. Fortune does
not always favour the brave : Churchill in later life had his
ups and downs. But fortune was with him in his youth and
again in what for most men would have been regarded as
old age.

13

BOER WAR

ON HIS ARRIVAL in London from Cairo at the end of April
Churchill decided to get on with the battle of life as quickly
as possible.

Already he was being waited on by deputations of
notables from Conservative Constituency Associations who
sought to persuade him to stand as their candidate at the
election, which was expected to take place within the next
eighteen months.

Churchill had, it seems, consulted a fashionable palmist,
Mrs Robinson, who had claimed to see favourable omens in
his hand. Certainly his entry into active politics could
scarcely have been more unexpected. He tells in *My Early
Life* how he had been sounded out by Mr Robert Ascroft,
one of the two members for Oldham, which was in those
days a two-member constituency, to become his 'running
mate' at the next election, as the other Unionist member,
Mr James Oswald, was ailing. In the event it was Mr
Ascroft who died suddenly on 19 June 1899. It was thought
expedient to ask Mr Oswald to resign at the same time.
Mindful of their late member's wishes the Oldham Conservative Association immediately turned to Churchill.

Leading members of the local Tory and Liberal parties
had hoped to arrive at some accommodation whereby they
would return, unopposed, one Tory and one Liberal member; but these ideas were quickly thrown aside by the
enthusiastic rank-and-file supporters of both sides. So
Churchill's fellow Conservative candidate was Mr James
Mawdsley, the General Secretary of the Lancashire branch
of the Amalgamated Association of Cotton Spinners. The
late Mr Ascroft had, it was believed, owed his success to the
fact that he had been for some years the trusted solicitor to
this Trade Union and it was considered to be a shrewd
move towards securing the Labour vote to invite Mr
Mawdsley to stand. Thus the Scion and the Socialist, as
they were dubbed, fought the seat together. They issued

separate election addresses. Churchill in his election address emphasized measures against what he described as 'the lawlessness in the Church'. There were measures before Parliament at this time to deal with ritualism and extreme High Church practices in the forms of worship being carried on by some of the clergy of the Church of England.

For some time Lord Salisbury's Government had had on its hands the Clerical Tithes Bill, a measure intended to benefit the clergy of the Church of England and the Church Schools. This Bill was quickly nicknamed by the Radicals the Clerical Doles Bill and it at once aroused the opposition of Nonconformists everywhere and of Methodists in Lancashire in particular. From the outset, Churchill and his supporters realized that this Bill would greatly diminish his prospects of success. 'This Clerical Tithes Bill Balfour has foolishly introduced', Churchill wrote to his cousin, the Duke of Marlborough on June 29, 'is simply playing the deuce with the Lancashire electors.' Churchill, it will be remembered, had never shown himself deeply committed on religious matters and the niceties of ecclesiastical partisanship often escaped him.

As he was to relate in *My Early Life* : 'As I was ignorant of the needs which had inspired it and detached from the passions which it aroused, the temptation to discard it was very great. I yielded to the temptation'. Just three days before polling he announced in reply to a question at his meeting at the Primitive Methodist School, Washbrook, that if he had represented Oldham when the House of Commons divided on the Clerical Tithes Bill the previous week he would, out of consideration for the views of his constituents, have voted against the Bill. His announcement was greeted with loud cheers; but later Churchill was to admit that it had been a frightful mistake. 'It is not the slightest use defending Governments or parties unless you defend the very worst thing about which they are attacked'.

Opposing Churchill and Mawdsley were two outstanding candidates : Mr Alfred Emmott and Mr Walter Runciman. Emmott's family had been mill-owners for several generations and Runciman came from a shipping family. As Churchill wryly remarked: 'My poor Trade Unionist friend and I would have had very great difficulty in finding £500 between us, yet we were accused of representing the vested interest of society, while our opponents, who were certainly good for a quarter of a million, claimed to champion in generous fashion the causes of the poor and needy'. Three of the candidates were to reach Cabinet rank : Churchill and Runciman in 1908; Emmott in 1914. Mr Mawdsley died in 1902.

Churchill was confident that as public speakers and as men 'in all that makes for popularity—in all that ensures attention'—Mawdsley and he were 'far superior to the Radical candidates.' But he had little illusion about the outcome. 'My private impression', he wrote to the Duke of Marlborough on 29 June 1899, 'is that we shall be beaten in spite of Mawdsley, and in spite of everything I can do, and we shall be beaten simply because the Government have brought forward this stupid Bill which can do them no possible good.'

The result was declared late in the evening of July 6 and was as follows :

Emmott (Radical)	. .	12,976
Runciman (Radical)	. .	12,770
Churchill (Conservative)	.	11,477
Mawdsley (Conservative)	.	11,449

The majority of Emmott over Churchill, 1,499. The figures at the previous election were :

Ascroft (Conservative)	. .	13,085
Oswald (Conservative)	. .	12,465
Lee (Radical)	. . .	12,249
Hibbert (Radical)	. . .	12,092

Mr Ascroft's personal popularity had clearly been exceptional; bearing this in mind, the total swing of about two per cent to the Radicals was not disgraceful, and Churchill could afford to take a calm view of the result.

From Balfour, indeed, he received a kind letter of encouragement : 'Never mind', he concluded, 'it will all come right; and this small reverse will have no permanent ill effect upon your political fortunes'. Balfour, thinking of Churchill's switch on the Clerical Tithes Bill, had however remarked in London at this time : 'I thought he was a young man of promise, but it appears he is a young man of promises'. Churchill was not yet twenty-five when he lost the election.

* * * * *

In 1877, England had abortively annexed the Transvaal, not only for political, military and economic reasons but also in the hope that her action would promote a Federation of the different territories in South Africa. The scheme misfired and in 1881 the Boers reasserted their independence after defeating the English at Majuba Hill. This incident apart, however, the English did not, on the whole, interfere with the Boers who had trekked to the interior of South Africa until the discovery of gold on the Witwatersrand in 1886. The Transvaal rapidly became the most industrialized and wealthy land on the African continent. It became a profitable market not only for overseas suppliers but also for farmers and traders of the Cape, and the Transvaal Republic was able to strengthen its armed forces and demonstrate its hostility towards Britain in a variety of ways.

Fortune seekers from all parts of the world flocked to the Rand and it soon became clear to the Boers that these men had little respect for the Boer way of life. As their numbers grew, the Republican authorities progressively made it more difficult for the Uitlanders, as they were called, to acquire the vote and to settle. 'If I grant the franchise', said their President, Paul Kruger, 'I may as well pull the Republican flag down.'

Britain, on the other hand, championed the cause of the Uitlanders, partly because most of them were British and they had genuine grievances, but also because she hoped this would strengthen her influence in the Transvaal. After the Jameson Raid, the Transvaal Republic increased its purchase of arms and rallied opinion in the Cape and other parts of South Africa to its cause. The Orange Free State, for example, formed a military alliance with the Transvaal and leaders like Smuts gave up their British nationality and settled in what was called the South African Republic.

Early in 1899, the Uitlanders on the Rand petitioned the Queen. Whereas previously their cause had been pleaded by the great capitalists and investors in the Rand, now it was the ordinary working man and settler that took matters into their own hands. Sir Alfred Milner, the High Commissioner in Cape Colony, backed their protest : 'The spectacle', he wrote in a famous despatch, 'of thousands of British subjects permanently in a position of helots, constantly chafing under undoubted grievances and calling vainly to Her Majesty's Government for redress does steadily undermine the influence and reputation of Great Britain and the respect for the British Government within the Queen's dominions.' Milner was ordered by the Government at home to negotiate with the Boers on behalf of the Uitlanders and at Bloemfontein Milner met Kruger from May 31 to June 5.

It was the popular view at that time that the Colonial Secretary, Mr Joseph Chamberlain, was impatient and thirsting for a 'showdown'. The documents of the period seem to show on the other hand that it was Milner who was thirsting for aggressive action. The Bloemfontein negotiations broke down and thereafter, despite various other offers by the British Government to the Boers, the two sides edged ever nearer towards war. A final offer to accept the enfranchisement of the Uitlanders on the Boers' original terms was made by Chamberlain on September 8. This was conciliatory enough to win the support of the Cape Dutch and of Boer sympathizers in England; but it was rejected by the Boer Republics within a few days.

Churchill was by now convinced that there would be war, and so was a large body of opinion in England. On September 18 Alfred Harmsworth, proprietor of the *Daily Mail*, telegraphed to Churchill asking him to act as his paper's war correspondent. Churchill immediately telegraphed to his friend Oliver Borthwick of the *Morning Post*, telling him of Harmsworth's invitation. Churchill suggested to Borthwick that he should go to South Africa for the *Morning Post*, after all his earliest backer, in return for expenses, copyright of his work and £1,000 for four months' shore to shore (£250 per month) and £200 a month thereafter. Within hours Churchill's offer was accepted and he told his mother (September 18): 'I am at their disposal'. This was probably the most lucrative contract into which any newspaper war correspondent had entered up to this time; and it served to elevate the scale of journalists' salaries in general.

Before he left London Churchill wrote to the Colonial Secretary, Mr Chamberlain, and went to see him. He was anxious to obtain letters of introduction to important people in South Africa. Chamberlain at first wrote back in a guarded fashion, but when, early in October, war was seen to be inevitable, he showed himself to be rather more enthusiastic :

Joseph Chamberlain to WSC

4 October 1899   Birmingham

My dear Winston,

I have your telegraph & I will write to Milner tonight asking his good offices for the son of my old friend. I am sure he will do all in his power. I shall be in London on Monday but I gather that you leave before then. If so good luck & best wishes!

Yours very truly
J. CHAMBERLAIN

*   *   *   *   *

Churchill never believed that war should be needlessly uncomfortable : he made his dispositions accordingly. There is preserved a list of the stores with which he equipped himself before sailing to South Africa.

Account
to Randolph Payne & Sons,
Importer of Wines, Spirits and Liqueurs
EXTRACT

6 October 1899   61 St James's Street S.W.

	[per dozen]			
6 Bottles 1889 Vin d'Ay Sec	110/-	2	15	0
18 bottles St Emilion	24/-	1	16	0
6 bottles light Port	42/-	1	1	0
6 bottles French Vermouth	36/-		18	0
18 bottles Scotch Whiskey (10 years old)	48/-	3	12	0
6 bottles Very Old Eau de Vie landed 1866	160/-	4	0	0
12 Rose's Cordial Lime Juice	15/-		15	0
6 x 1 dozen cases for same packing, marking etc			10	0
Cartage Dock charges & Insurance			13	0
Sent by S.S. *Dunottar Castle* to South Africa		16	0	0

By this time, of course, Churchill was a civilian and he had no military status. This, he could foresee, might be irksome if opportunity were to present itself for further military glory. He had moreover been at one time promised a place on the staff of General Sir Redvers Buller who was going out to take command of the British forces in South Africa. So that he might be in a position to take advantage of such opportunities if he wished, he wrote before his departure to obtain a commission in the Royal Bucks Yeomanry, accompanying his formal application with a personal appeal to the Honorary Colonel—Lord Chesham. This application, however, was never in fact forwarded, for when he got on board ship he discovered that it might be easier to obtain a Yeomanry commission from the Adjutant of the 9th Yeomanry Brigade which was under the command of his father's old friend Lord Gerard, of the Lancashire Hussars, who was accompanying Sir Redvers Buller as ADC.

Although both Britain and the South African Republic had drafted ultimatums it was the Boer ultimatum calling for the withdrawal of British troops that in fact proved decisive; it was despatched on October 9 and expired on October 11. The first shots were fired at Kraaipan on October 12. Churchill sailed from Southampton in the *Dunottar Castle* two days later on October 14. On the same ship were Buller and his staff, and many war correspondents.

He was very fond in later life of quoting Dr Johnson's famous phrase : 'Being in a ship is being in a jail, with the chance of being drowned'. To be kept prisoner, as it were, in a boat, cut off from all news of the outside world, while a war was actually going on thousands of miles away, was a frustration Churchill found difficult to endure.

For two weeks there was no news.

Then on October 29 they sighted a homeward bound steamer, the *Australasian*, which displayed a black board on which was painted in white 'Boers defeated; Three battles; Penn Symons killed.' Churchill had known Symons in India but it was not his death which cast a gloom over the passengers of the *Dunottar Castle*. It was the news of the three battles and the Boer defeat : the three battles in which they had not participated. It seemed likely, they argued, that it would be all over before they got to Cape Town.

While Churchill was at sea his book *The River War* was in the press. It was to be published in two volumes a week after his arrival in Cape Town. It was generally very well received and was much praised by the literary and military critics of the day. The courage and fearlessness with which he made his criticisms of Lord Kitchener were commented on as much as his presumption and 'cocksureness' in making them. Nearly all the critics united in acclaiming *The River War* as the standard history of the campaign. Only the *Saturday Review*, the weekly to which Churchill himself had three years before contributed on Cuban affairs, carried a notice that was almost wholly hostile: 'Only this astonishing young man,' it wrote on 18 November 1899, 'could have written these two ponderous and pretentious volumes. . . . The annoying feature in the book is the irrepressible egoism of its author. . . . The airs of infallibility he assumes are irritating. . . .'

The initial print of 2,000 copies was soon sold out at 36/- and two further impressions, making another 1,000 copies in all, were published within six months. But it was to be many weeks after the reviews had appeared that Churchill had the satisfaction of reading them; for within ten days of the book's publication, he was a prisoner of war. His capture and escape may well have promoted the sales of this comparatively expensive work.

* * * * *

On October 31, the *Dunottar Castle* arrived in Cape Town and her passengers were left in little doubt that there would still be plenty for them to do. While Sir Redvers Buller and his staff decided to continue their comfortable and leisurely progress in the *Dunottar Castle* to Durban, Churchill and two of his fellow correspondents, Captain Campbell of the Laffans News Agency and J. B. Atkins of the *Manchester Guardian,* had discovered that by taking a train from Cape Town to East London (by way of De Aar), and thence by steamer to Durban, they would arrive three or four days earlier than the General and his staff.

In Durban harbour, near his own coaster's moorings, lay the hospital ship *Sumatra*. There he found a number of old friends among the wounded, one of them Reggie Barnes, his companion in Cuba and fellow polo-player in India. Barnes, who had been shot through the groin in the attack on Elandslaagte, told him of the courageous and successful manner in which the Boers were fighting the war.

It was evident that Buller would not be arriving in Durban for three days and that, after assembling his stores, there would be a considerable delay before the new General Headquarters moved to the front. Churchill and Atkins naturally anticipated these cumbersome activities. At Durban Churchill heard that Ian Hamilton, now a General, had arrived in Ladysmith on the last train before the Boers had advanced and cut the railway line near Chieveley. He decided to go to the front as quickly as he could by rail.

Atkins takes up the story:

Then by train to Maritzburg, where we hired a special train to Ladysmith. Many miles short of Ladysmith, however, we came to a stop—the line was cut; the Boers were across it; Ladysmith was invested. Perhaps it was as well that we failed.

We pitched our tents in the railway yard at Estcourt. We had found a good cook and we had some good wine. We entertained friends every evening, to our pleasure

267

and professional advantage and, we believed, to their satisfaction.

One memorable evening we entertained the officer commanding at Estcourt. While we were dining the clang of field guns being loaded into trucks went on unceasingly; for the officer, as he told us, had decided that the position at Estcourt could hardly be held and that a retirement to better ground nearer Maritzburg was necessary. As dinner proceeded Winston, with an assurance which I partly envied and partly deprecated, argued that Joubert was probably too cautious to advance yet; that he was no doubt delighted with the security of the Tugela River; that it would be a pity to point the way to Maritzburg, and so on. Shortly after our guest had left us the clanging in the trucks, which had ceased, began again. The trucks were being unloaded. Winston gleamed '*I* did that!' he said; but added gracefully, 'We did that!' Whether he did it or not we shall never know. The officer may have acted on fresh information. At least Winston's effort was singular for persuasive reasoning.

Churchill's own account of the journey of the armoured train, first transmitted to the *Morning Post* from Durban and published on 1 January 1900, has remained unchallenged and substantially unaltered over the years. It is reprinted in its entirety in *My Early Life*. Of more interest, in a way, is the official account which was written by Haldane in prison at Pretoria, but which was not despatched until well after Churchill had completed his escape.

Captain Aylmer Haldane to Chief of Staff,
Natal Field Force

(*Royal Archives*)

3 January 1900   Pretoria

Sir,

I have the honour to forward the following report concerning the capture of an armoured train which left Estcourt under my command on the 15th November 1899.

1. On the night of the 14th November, I received verbal instructions from Colonel Long, R.A., commanding at Estcourt, to take a 9-pr muzzle-loading Naval gun and detach-

268

ment, HMS *Tartar*, one company 2nd Bn Dublin Fusiliers, and one company Durban Light Infantry, and with the armoured train reconnoitre in the direction of Colenso, proceeding with caution and keeping out of range of the enemy's guns. The train, which was made up and manned as follows :

> Ordinary truck—gun and detachment,
> Armoured truck—$\frac{3}{4}$ company, 2nd Bn Dublin Fusiliers,
> Engine,
> Tender,
> 2 armoured trucks—1 company, 2nd Bn Dublin Fusiliers; 1 company, Durban Light Infantry,
> Breakdown gang truck,

left Estcourt at 5.10 a.m. and on arrival at Frere Station at 6.20 a.m. I reported that no enemy had been seen. Here I met a party of eight men of the Natal Mounted Police, from whom I learnt that their patrols were in advance reconnoitring towards Chieveley, whither I proceeded after a halt of 15 minutes. On reaching there at 7.10 a.m., I received the following message by telephone from Estcourt, 'Remain at Frere in observation, watching your safe retreat. Remember that Chieveley station was last night occupied by the enemy. Nothing occurred here yet. Do not place reliance on any reports from local residents as they may be untrustworthy', and in acknowledging it stated that a party of about 50 Boers and three wagons was visible moving south on the west side of the railway.

2. I at once retired towards Frere, and on rounding the spur of a hill which commanded the line the enemy opened on us at 600 yards with artillery, one shell striking the leading truck. The driver put on full steam and we ran down the gradient at high speed, and almost immediately on reaching the level three-quarters of a mile from Frere, the breakdown gang truck and two armoured trucks, which preceded the engine were derailed, one of the latter standing partly across the track. The enemy, lying in ambush, had allowed the train to pass Chieveley, and had then placed a stone on the line, which the guard, probably owing to the shell fire, had neither seen or reported.

3. Mr Winston Churchill, special correspondent of the *Morning Post* who was with me in the truck next the gun-truck offered me his services, and knowing how thoroughly I could rely on him, I gladly accepted them, and undertook

took to keep down the enemy's fire while he endeavoured to clear the line. Our gun came into action at 900 yards, but after four rounds, was struck by a shell and knocked over. I recalled the gun detachment into the armoured truck, whence a continuous fire was kept up on the enemy's guns, considerably disconcerting their aim, as I was afterwards informed, killing two and wounding four men.

The Boers maintained a hot fire with rifles, 3–15 pr Creusot guns and a Maxim shell fire, but as the shells struck the engine and truck obliquely the armour-plating was only occasionally penetrated. For an hour efforts to clear the line were unsuccessful, as the trucks were heavy and jammed together, and the break-down gang could not be found, but Mr Churchill with indomitable perseverance continued his difficult task, and about 8.30 a.m. the engine forced its way past the obstructing truck, which, however, again fell forward some inches across the line.

Shortly before this the couplings which fastened the armoured and gun trucks to the engine had been broken by a shell, and when the engine cleared the wreckage they were left behind. Perhaps it was possible to again remove the wreckage and re-couple the trucks to the engine, but as the cab of the latter was now crammed with wounded, who would have been scalded had a shell struck the boiler, as the pipe of the reserve water-tank was torn open and the water rushing out, as the front of the engine was in flames, and because I apprehended lest the enemy, seeing the engine free, should again tamper with the line, I resolved to allow the engine to retreat out of range towards Frere, and withdrawing the men from the trucks, made a run for some houses, 800 yards distant, where I had some hope of making a further resistance. As the enemy had not relaxed his artillery and musketry fire, and there was absolutely no cover, the men became considerably scattered along the line, and in a formation ill adapted to offer resistance. To my disgust, and in direct disobedience of my orders, I saw two men 200 yards in front of me holding up white handkerchiefs. I shouted and ran towards them, but at this moment the Boers, who, unperceived by us, had left the hill on our right rear, and, seeing the signal, had stopped firing, galloped among the retreating soldiers, who remained uncertain what to do, and called upon them to surrender. Under these circumstances, at 8.50 a.m., I, 2nd Lieutenant T. Frankland, 2nd Bn Royal Dublin Fusiliers, and 50 men, were captured; the remainder, on whom the Boers continued to fire, making good their retreat across the railway bridge to Frere Station, whence I understand they and the engine reached the British lines at Estcourt in safety.

4. I venture here with some diffidence, owing to the unfortunate termination of our reconnaissance, to record my acknowledgements of the services of the following :

2nd Lieutenant T. C. Frankland, 2nd Bn Royal Dublin Fusiliers, a gallant young Officer who carried out my orders with coolness.

A.B. Seaman E. Read, HMS *Tartar,* No 6300 Lance-Corporal W. Connell, Privates Phoenix and Kavanagh, 2nd Bn Royal Dublin Fusiliers, who, notwithstanding that they were repeatedly knocked down by the concussion of the shells striking the armoured truck, continued steadily to fire until ordered to cease. Captain Wylie and the men of the Durban Light Infantry, who ably assisted in covering the working party engaged in clearing the line, and who were much exposed to the enemy's fire. I regret I am unable to give exact details of any deserving special mention, but I beg to suggest that Captain Wylie be called upon for a report.

Mr Winston S. Churchill, whose valuable services have already been detailed in the text of this report, and whom, owing to the urgency of the circumstances, I formally placed on duty.

I would point out while engaged on the work of saving the engine, for which he was mainly responsible, he was frequently exposed to the full fire of the enemy. I cannot speak too highly of his gallant conduct.

The driver of the engine, who, though wounded, remained at his post.

The telegraphist attached to the train, who showed a fine example of cheerfulness and indifference to danger.

Lastly, under this heading, I desire to mention the bearing

of all the troops under my command, which, under the trying circumstances of this small affair, was admirable.

5. I understand that the Boers buried four of the killed, and that they have 13 wounded in hospital. Of the 52 taken prisoner, seven, including Mr Churchill, are slightly wounded.

I have the honour to be, Sir, Your obedient Servant

AYLMER HALDANE

Captain, 2nd Bn Gordon Highlanders

Leo Amery of *The Times*, J. B. Atkins of the *Manchester Guardian*, G. W. Steevens of the *Daily Mail*, and Bennett Burleigh of the *Daily Telegraph* all agreed that Churchill had behaved with great gallantry at the armoured train disaster. The more Radical newspapers were inclined to suspect that this was a mutual admiration society among war correspondents but this impression was quickly dispelled by similar tributes from the Natal railway authorities.

Inspector Campbell of the Natal Government Railways sent the following letter to the General Manager of the Railways on behalf of the railway employees who escaped with the armoured train; it was published in the *Natal Witness* on November 17 :

The railway men who accompanied the armoured train this morning ask me to convey to you their admiration of the coolness and pluck displayed by Mr Winston Churchill, the war correspondent who accompanied the train, and to whose efforts, backed up by those of the driver, Wagner, is due the fact that the armoured train and tender were successfully brought out, after being hampered by the derailed trucks in front, and that it became possible to bring the wounded in here. The whole of our men are loud in their praises of Mr Churchill, who, I regret to say, has been taken prisoner. I respectfully ask you to convey their admiration to a brave man.

Many of the reports suggested that Churchill would be recommended for the Victoria Cross.

Numerous accounts are extant of the exact circumstances in which Churchill was captured. His own in *My Early Life,* though not exact in all details, deserves to be cited first.

I had not retraced my steps 200 yards when, instead of Haldane and his company, two figures in plain clothes appeared upon the line. 'Platelayers!' I said to myself, and then with a surge of realization, 'Boers!' My mind retains its impression of these tall figures, full of energy, clad in dark, flapping clothes, with slouch, storm-driven hats, poising on their levelled rifles hardly a hundred yards away. I turned again and ran back towards the engine, the two Boers firing as I ran between the metals. Their bullets, sucking to right and left, seemed to miss only by inches. We were in a small cutting with banks about six feet high on either side. I flung myself against the bank of the cutting. It gave no cover. Another glance at the two figures; one was now kneeling to aim. Movement seemed the only chance. Again I darted forward : again two soft kisses sucked in the air; but nothing struck me. This could not endure. I must get out of the cutting—that damnable corridor! I jigged to the left, and scrambled up the bank. The earth sprang up beside me. I got through the wire fence unhurt. Outside the cutting was a tiny depression. I crouched in this, struggling to get my breath again.

Fifty yards away was a small platelayers' cabin of masonry; there was cover there. About 200 yards away was the rocky gorge of the Blue Krantz River; there was plenty of cover there. I determined to make a dash for the river. I rose to my feet. Suddenly on the other side of the railway, separated from me by the rails and two uncut wire fences, I saw a horseman galloping furiously, a tall, dark figure, holding his rifle in his right hand. He pulled up his horse almost in its own length and shaking the rifle at me shouted a loud command. We were forty yards apart. That morning I had taken with me, Correspondent-status notwithstanding, my Mauser pistol. I thought I could kill this man, and after the treatment I had received I earnestly desired to do so. I put my hand to my belt, the pistol was not there. When engaged in clearing the line, getting in and out of the engine, etc, I had taken it off. It came safely home on the engine. I have it now! But at this moment I was quite unarmed. Meanwhile, I suppose in about the time this takes to tell, the Boer horseman, still seated on his horse, had covered me with his rifle. The animal stood stock still, so did he, and so did I. I looked towards the river, I looked towards the platelayers' hut. The Boer continued to look along his sights. I thought there was absolutely no chance of escape, if he fired he would surely hit me, so I held up my hands and surrendered myself a prisoner of war.

'When one is alone and unarmed,' said the great Napoleon, in words which flowed into my mind in the poignant minutes that followed, 'a surrender may be pardoned.' Still, he might have missed; and the Blue Krantz ravine was very near and the two wire fences were still uncut. However, the deed was done. Thereupon my captor lowered his rifle and beckoned to me to come across to him. I obeyed.

. . . Such is the episode of the armoured train and the story of my capture on November 15, 1899.

It was not until three years later, when the Boer Generals visited England to ask for some loan or assistance on behalf of their devastated country, that I was introduced at a private luncheon to their leader, General Botha. We talked of the war and I briefly told the story of my capture. Botha listened in silence; then he said, 'Don't you recognise me? I was that man. It was I who took you prisoner. I, myself,' and his bright eyes twinkled with pleasure. Botha in white shirt and frock coat looked very different in all save size and darkness of complexion from the wild war-time figure I had seen that rough day in Natal. But about the extraordinary fact there can be no doubt. He had entered upon the invasion of Natal as a burgher; his own disapproval of the war had excluded him from any high command at its outset. This was his first action. But as a simple private burgher serving in the ranks he had galloped ahead and in front of the whole Boer forces in the ardour of pursuit. Thus we met.

*   *   *   *   *

Haldane, who was eventually to rise to the rank of full General, has left in his *A Soldier's Saga,* a first-hand account of Churchill's demeanour immediately after his capture.

. . . At this time we were all feeling, not unnaturally, very disconsolate, but Churchill must have been cheered by the thought, which he communicated to me, that what had taken place, though it had caused the temporary loss of his post as war correspondent, would help considerably in opening the door for him to enter the House of Commons. As we trudged along wearily over the damp veldt he remarked to me that in allotting him what I might call the 'star turn' I had effaced myself, while his work of clearing the line had brought him into prominence and in full view of the Durban Light Infantry and the railway personnel, and that those of them who had escaped on the engine would not fail to make the most of what they had seen when they got back to Estcourt. He added that so far as I was concerned he would at first opportunity publish the facts in his newspaper, to which, while thanking him, I replied that being satisfied that I had done my duty and acted in what I considered the wisest way in the circumstances, no explanation as to what had occurred was necessary. . . .

News of Churchill's capture was cabled speedily all around the world; and though Lady Randolph was in Yorkshire, she was soon informed. The first news reached her from Moreton Frewen : later his communications were to prove more tardy than those from other sources. He telegraphed that there was 'Unpleasant news capture hundred men from armoured train Ladysmith.' The first full account came from the Editor of the *Morning Post* who telegraphed Lady Randolph at her London address; this was forwarded to her in Yorkshire by Jack. The telegram, dated November 16, stated : 'I regret to inform you that Mr Winston Churchill has been captured by the Boers : he fought gallantly after an armoured train in which he was travelling had been trapped.'

*   *   *   *   *

After a march of two days the captives had reached the small railway station of Modderspruit. From there the journey by rail to Pretoria took the best part of 24 hours. On arrival at the Boer capital the officers were taken to the State Model School while the other ranks were imprisoned in a cantonment on a race course. The State Model School was indeed a model. Opened less than three years before, it had just begun its educational functions when they were cut short by being commandeered by the military authorities as a prison. It still remains a fine solid building, worthy of the sturdy Boers, and after the war it served for many years as a school and stands as a historical monument. A plaque commemorating Churchill's incarceration was put up in 1963.

WSC to Lady Randolph

18 November 1899   Pretoria

Dearest Mamma,

A line to explain that I was captured in the armoured train at Frere on the 15th, with some 50 officers and soldiers and some other non-combatants and platelayers and such like. As I was quite unarmed and in possession of my full credentials as a Press correspondent, I do not imagine they will keep me. They have always treated Press correspondents well and after Majuba Hill the *Morning Post* correspondent was released after a few days' detention. You need not be anxious in any way but I trust you will do all in your power to procure my release. After all this is a new experience—as was the heavy shell fire.

Your loving son
Winston S. Churchill

PS Cox's should be instructed to cash any cheques I may draw. Their cheques are the ones cashed here easiest.

W S C

18 November [1899]   Pretoria

Pamela,

Not a vy satisfactory address to write from—although it begins with P. I daresay you know everything that happened and more from the Press. I expect to be released as I was taken quite unarmed and with my full credentials as a correspondent. But I write you this line to tell you that among new and vivid scenes I think often of you.

Yours always
WINSTON S. CHURCHILL

The letter to Lady Randolph reached London on New Year's Day 1900. Churchill had escaped more than a fortnight before. The reader will observe the care with which Churchill had to write in these and subsequent letters partly in order to camouflage the somewhat un-civilian role he had played in the action and partly in order to convey through the censors to the Boer authorities a plausible argument for his release.

On the same day that Churchill wrote these letters he also began an artful correspondence with the Boer authorities in the person of L. de Souza, the Transvaal Republic's Secretary of State for War. This quite possibly might have secured his release, but it was also calculated to conceal the plans already being formed for an escape that would have been far more spectacular than a prosaic release.

WSC to L. de Souza

(*SA Govt Archives*)

18 November 1899   Pretoria

Sir,

1. I was acting as special correspondent of the *Morning Post* newspaper with the detachment of British troops

captured by the forces of the South African Republic on the 15th instant at Frere, Natal, and conveyed here with the other prisoners.

2. I have the honour to request that I may be set at liberty and permitted to return to the British lines by such *route* as may be considered expedient, and in support of this request I would respectfully draw the attention of the Secretary of State to the following facts :

a. I presented my credentials as special correspondent immediately after the British force surrendered and desired that they might be forwarded to the proper authority. This was promised accordingly.
b. I was unarmed.
c. My identity has been clearly established.

3. I desire to state that on my journey from the scene of the action to this town I have been treated with much consideration and kindness by the various officers and other burghers of the Republic with whom I have been brought into contact.

I am Sir, Your obedient servant
WINSTON SPENCER CHURCHILL
Special correspondent, *The Morning Post*, London

General P. J. Foubert to F. W. Reitz
(SA *Govt Archives*)

TELEGRAM
(*Translation*)

19 November 1899   Ladysmith

I understand that the son of Lord Churchill maintains that he is only a newspaper reporter and therefore wants the privilege of being released. From a newspaper it appears entirely otherwise and it is for this reason that I urge you that he must be guarded and watched as dangerous for our war; otherwise he can still do us a lot of harm. In one word, he must not be released during the war. It is through his active part that *one section* of the armoured train got away.

[*Note on telegram* :]

The Government will act accordingly. Thereafter the Commandant-General's Office will be instructed to act accordingly. F.W.R. [Reitz] 22.XI.99.

As to releasing Churchill the local Boer commanders remained adamant.

Captain D. Theron to F. W. Reitz

(*SA Govt Archives*)

(*Translation*)

28 November 1899   Colenso

I should like to state that in the *Natal Witness & Natal Mercury* of the 17th of this month full reports appeared of the active and prominent part taken by the newspaper reporter Winston Churchill in the battle with the armoured train at Frere Station. Churchill called for volunteers and led them at a time when the officers were in confusion. According to *Volkstem* and *Standard & Digger News,* he now claims that he took no part in the battle. That is all lies. He also refused to stand still until Field-Cornet Oosthuizen warned him to surrender. He surrendered only when he aimed his gun at him. In my view Churchill is one of the most dangerous prisoners in our hands. The Natal papers are making a big hero out of him.

On November 30, his twenty-fifth birthday, Churchill wrote two long letters, one to the Prince of Wales, the other to Bourke Cockran. Conscious of the censor who was going to read them, Churchill reiterated in both letters that he regarded his detention as unjustifiable. But while the letter to the Prince gave details of the armoured train action and drew attention to the gallantry of the engine driver, Churchill permitted himself some reflections of a more general nature in the letter to Cockran : 'I think more experience of war would make me religious. The powerlessness of the atom is terribly brought home to me, and from the highest human court of appeals we feel a great desire to apply to a yet higher authority. Philosophy cannot convince the bullet.' And as a postscript : 'I am 25 today—it is terrible to think how little time remains !'

When the decision of the authorities not to release him was conveyed to Churchill at the beginning of December he realized that he would have to avail himself of other means to secure his release from captivity. Nevertheless, partly no doubt to distract the attention of the authorities from his clandestine preparations, he made one more attempt to obtain his release.

WSC to L. de Souza

(SA Govt Archives)

8 December 1899   Pretoria

Sir,

1. I understand that the question of my release rests ultimately with the commandant-general, and I therefore request that my previous application may be forwarded to him so that he may have an opportunity of learning my side of the case.

2. I would point out that I did not fight against the Boer forces, but only assisted in clearing the line from the *debris*. This is precisely what the civilian platelayers and railway staff did. They have since been released.

3. I have now been kept a close prisoner for 24 days.

4. If I am released I will give any *parole* that may be required not to serve against the Republican forces or to give any information affecting the military situation.

I am, Sir, Your obedient servant
WINSTON S. CHURCHILL
Sp correspondent, *The Morning Post*

Joubert remained sceptical; but he seems to have grown weary of the business, and was not prepared to press his objections to Churchill's release any further.

General P. J. Joubert to F. W. Reitz

(SA Govt Archives)

(Translation)

12 December 1899   Volksrust

Referring to the request by Lt Churchill which was forwarded to me, I desire to state that he is entirely unknown to me; and I would not in the least have noticed him if the

British newspapers had not mentioned him as being Lt Churchill, with an account of all the highly appreciated services rendered by him in the British Army for years and on different occasions.

These culminated in the attacks on the armoured train, when, owing to his actions, the engine or a section of the train escaped being captured. It is even mentioned in an exaggerated way that but for his presence on the train, not a single Englishman or soldier would have escaped. After the train was forced to a standstill the officers and men would definitely have fallen into enemy hands had he not directed proceedings in such a clever and thorough way, whilst walking alongside the engine, that the train together with its load escaped capture.

All this became known throughout the world, and I suppose the British Empire, through the newspapers. All this however is denied by Mr Churchill, and I have to accept his word in preference to all the journalists and reporters. If I accept his word, then my objections to his release cease. Seeing that a parole was promised him and that he suggested leaving Africa to return to Europe where he would report and speak only the truth of his experiences —and if the Government accepts this and he does so—then I have no further objections to his being set free, without our accepting somebody else in exchange.

P. J. JOUBERT, Commandant
PS Will he tell the truth? He will also be a chip off the old block.

But, by the time this telegram reached the authorities in Pretoria, its content had become irrelevant to the situation.

14

ESCAPE

WHILE THIS PROTRACTED and seemingly abortive correspondence was passing between Churchill and the Boer authorities, plans for escape had from the earliest been afoot in the State Model School. 'We thought of nothing else but freedom, and from morn till night we racked our brains to discover a way to escape.' The original plan which is described in *My Early Life* in vivid details was one of breathtaking audacity. It involved nothing less than the 60 British officers seizing control of the State Model School by a *coup de main* in the middle of the night; thereafter liberating 2,000 British other ranks who were in a prisoner-of-war cage a mile and a half away on the racecourse; and then, with their aid, seizing control of Pretoria, the Boer capital, together with President Kruger and his Government. This exciting plan had to be abandoned since it was overruled by the senior British officers in the State Model School. Though there is no documentary evidence, the plan was so original and it is described by Churchill with such loving and indeed mouth-watering expectation that the reader may incline to believe that he was its 'true and onlie begetter'.

While the more grandiose plan was being studied and soon abandoned, Haldane and 'Lieutenant' A. Brockie had been maturing their own plans for a joint escape. Brockie, who was in fact a Regimental Sergeant Major in the Imperial Light Horse, but who, on his capture near Ladysmith, had succeeded in passing himself off as a Lieutenant of the Natal Carabineers with the object of being placed in the officers' prisoner-of-war camp, was a Johannesburg man who spoke Afrikaans and a native language also. For this reason he was considered by Haldane essential to his plan of escape. Churchill now sought to attach himself to this enterprise. Haldane was at first reluctant; he considered that Churchill, already a conspicuous and marked man in the State Model School, would have his absence from the camp noticed sooner than others. Eventually Haldane agreed to let Churchill come, but he did not make him privy to every detail of the plan.

The plan that Haldane and Brockie had formulated was to climb out of a circular-shaped latrine in the back yard of the School. The spot was chosen because the electric light did not shine upon it. A sentry normally stood close by, but if he happened to move a few paces away, which he usually did during the dinner hour in order to converse with another sentry patrolling another side of the yard, an attempt to climb over the fencing could be made unobserved.

On December 11 the trio made what proved an unsuccessful attempt. Just before 7 p.m. Haldane and Churchill strolled over to the latrine which abutted on the perimeter of the camp, ahead of Brockie; but after a few minutes' inspection it was plain that there was nothing doing. A sentry was on duty just in front of them. He refused to move. They returned to their quarters.

The following night at the same hour Haldane and Churchill once again went to the latrine. Many accounts, some of them contradictory, have appeared about the exact details of Churchill's escape; in his own contemporary accounts he was compelled to give reports that were necessarily obfuscating in order to protect his comrades in the prison and those who were to help him outside. Churchill's most considered account was not to be put down until 1912 when it became necessary for him to bring an action for libel against *Blackwood's Magazine*, which, having libelled him already in 1900, had incontinently libelled him again. Churchill at that time put on paper his careful recollections of the events. This 1912 memorandum, which has never been published (and the portion in square brackets was not even included in the final version), reads in part :

before the moon rose, Haldane and I both got into the
roundhouse and waited for a chance of climbing over; but
after much hesitation we ~~thought~~ it too dangerous; and
he could not make up our minds to it,
came back to the veranda. Brockie then came up and
asked us why we had not got over. Haldane explained
the difficulty of the sentry's position, and Brockie
said; "You're afraid". Haldane replied: "You can go
and see for yourself". Brockie then went across the
yard, got into the roundhouse, and remained there some
time. Then I said: "I will go back again". I went
across the yard, and at the entrance to the roundhouse
I met Brockie coming out, but we dare not speak to each

. . . Haldane and I both got into the roundhouse and
waited for a chance of climbing over, but after much
hesitation we could not make up our minds to it, we
thought it too dangerous; and came back to the veranda
again. Brockie then came up and asked us why we had
not got over. Haldane explained the difficulty of the
sentry's position, and Brockie said : 'You're afraid'.
Haldane replied : 'You can go and see for yourself'.
Brockie then went across the yard, got into the roundhouse, and remained there some time. Then I said to
Haldane : 'I will go back again.' I went across the yard,
and at the entrance to the roundhouse I met Brockie
coming out, but we dared not speak to each other in the
presence of the sentry, and though he muttered something as he went by, I did not hear what it was. [I had
come to the conclusion that we should waste the whole
night in hesitations unless the matter were clinched once
and for all; and as the sentry turned to light his pipe, I
jumped on to the ledge of the wall and in a few seconds
had dropped into the garden safely on the other side.
Here I crouched down and waited for the others to
come. I expected them to come every minute. My position in the garden was a very anxious one because I had
only a few small and leafless bushes to hide behind, and

people kept passing to and fro, and the lights of the house were burning. Altogether I waited more than an hour and a half in the garden for the others to join me. Twice a man from the house walked along a path within 7 or 8 yards of me.]

Meanwhile Brockie had rejoined Haldane, had agreed with him that the sentry's position made the attempt too dangerous, and both of them went in to the dining room where the evening meal had already begun. They had not abandoned the attempt for the night, and meant to have another try after dinner.

After I had waited about a quarter of an hour, I managed to attract the attention, by tapping gently, of an officer whose name I forget, who had come to the roundhouse for a private purpose, and told him to tell Haldane that I had succeeded in getting over, and that he must come and make the attempt to join me as soon as he could. Both he and Brockie then came back, and I suppose about half an hour after I had got over, Haldane attempted to climb the wall. Whether he made some slight noise, or just through bad luck, the sentry turned round at the moment and he was seen as his shoulders were about level with the top of the wall by the sentry. The sentry immediately challenged him, levelled his rifle at him, and ordered him to come back, which of course he was forced to do. It was very lucky for him that the sentry was a humane man who gave him a chance to come back instead of firing at once, which at that very close range would probably have been fatal. The sentry seems not to have believed that a serious attempt to escape was in progress, and took no further notice of Haldane once he had come down and gone back to the main building though he thenceforward changed his position and stood so as to make it quite impossible for anyone to go over the wall without being seen.

Meanwhile, I was waiting in the greatest anxiety in the garden on the other side, and of course knew nothing of all this. At length I heard someone in the roundhouse trying to communicate with me by tapping, and going close to the wall I had a conversation with Haldane who had come to tell me that he had made his attempt and had been stopped by the sentry; that the position of the sentry now made it quite impossible for

285

him or Brockie to follow that night. This was of course a tremendous blow to me and seemed to make my position absolutely hopeless. I could not climb back in because the wall was higher on the outside than on the in, and there was no ledge to help me. Had I attempted to come back, I should have made a tremendous noise and been instantly detected. If I had walked round to the front of the building and given myself up to the sentry, an instant enquiry would have been made and our loophole of escape would have been effectually closed in the future. On the other hand, to go on alone seemed quite hopeless; Brockie with his knowledge of Kaffir and Dutch had been our only chance of buying food without being detected. How was I alone, without any local knowledge, without even a compass or a map, or any fixed plan what to do except to walk by night and hide by day, to cover 300 miles of wild and hostile country to the frontier? So hopeless did this appear that I would gladly have climbed back again had this been possible. Haldane and I discussed the situation in whispers through the chinks in the corrugated iron fence, he quite agreed with me that it was impossible to come back, and that I must go on alone. It was a great disappointment to him to be left behind, but he bade me good-bye and wished me good luck.

I am sure he thought my chances of getting clear away were practically nil, and I took the same view myself. If I had not believed that I was certain to be recaptured, I should never have run the risks which were necessary to success; but I felt that I would have a run for my money and see how far I could get.

I immediately made up my mind not to attempt to walk through the country by night and hide by day, as we had intended to do had we been three together and with Brockie. I did not feel equal to the physical strain, and I was sure I should be starved out if I tried it. One of the few things we knew was that there was a train to Delagoa Bay each night : we had several times discussed the possibilities of getting into this train, but had rejected it on account of the danger, and chosen instead the alternative of walking. I felt, however, that the train was my only chance, though a desperate one.

I had waited in the garden now for one hour and a

half, and got up without any attempt at concealment and walked straight out at the gate into the road. Passing another sentry who stood in the roadway at a distance of 2 or 3 yards, in full moonlight and electric light. . . .

The incidents of the next few hours are simply chronicled in *London to Ladysmith*, in the *Strand Magazine* of December 1923 and January 1924, and in *My Early Life*. How he, choosing the middle of the road, walked through the streets of Pretoria humming a tune (not whistling, for this was a habit he always deprecated); how he stumbled unconvinced upon the railway to Delagoa Bay in Portuguese East Africa. How he calculated that his best chance of boarding a train would be 200 yards from the station, when the train would not have gathered much steam, on an uphill gradient, when it would be slowing down, and on an outward curve, when he would be hidden from the view of both the engine driver and the guard. How, when a train came along, he clambered on to its couplings and then on to a truck full of empty coal bags, and how he thought it prudent to descend from the train before first light; how he quenched his thirst at a stream; how a few hours later, sheltering from the sun, he had as his sole companion a hungry-looking vulture; and how, when night fell, lost on the veld, and with few resources, he marched resolutely towards the only light he saw.

The house which Churchill approached belonged to John Howard, manager of the Transvaal and Delagoa Bay Collieries at Witbank. It was situated near the railway at Balmoral, seventy-five miles to the east of Pretoria and nearly two hundred miles to the west of the frontier with Portuguese East Africa at Komati Poort. Howard had spent the evening playing cards with some neighbours, who had left him about 1 a.m. It was a warm night and he was lying on his bed still awake, when, about 1.30 a.m., he was roused by a knock at his bedroom door which opened on to the verandah. John Howard recalled in 1923 :

. . . I seized my revolver, and then opened the door. I saw before me a man below medium height, and dripping water from the waist. His hair was red, his eyes blue, and his face inclined to be freckled. He said : 'Are you an Englishman?' and I in turn asked him what he wanted and who he was. He replied : 'I am Dr Bentick. I have fallen off the train and lost my way.'

Personally I believed he was a Boer spy, and keeping him covered with my revolver I ordered him into the dining room. He seemed very much knocked about and agitated, and he was no sooner in the dining room than he sank into a chair that was at the head of the table. I stood at the other end, revolver still in hand. I told him it was an insult to my intelligence to say that he had fallen off his train and lost his way on a bright moonlight night. After a little wordy sparring I said to him, 'You shan't leave this room without my permission. I advise you to play the open game'. You will understand that, believing him to be a Boer spy, I had to be very careful of what I said. His expression at intervals changed, giving place to one of doubt, and eventually determination, when he explained, 'I am Winston Churchill'.

Churchill then made a clean breast of the matter. According to Churchill, Howard locked the door, came over and shook his hand and exclaimed : 'Thank God you have come here! It is the only house for twenty miles where you would not have been handed over, but we are all British here, and we will see you through.'

It seems strange that Howard did not instantly guess the identity of his visitor. Churchill's escape had become known at 9.30 a.m. the previous morning and within a few hours an official of the Transvaal Government had called at the mine and given a description of the escaped prisoner-of-war. Howard, in common with a number of other British subjects in the neighbourhood, had assumed Transvaal citizenship a few years before the war; but because they were of British descent and also because their presence was vital to the running of the mine, they were not called up for service with the Boer army when the war broke out. Now, although as a Transvaal citizen Howard was running a grave risk in harbouring Churchill, he at once started to make plans for the next stage of the escape. He decided to call in a number of his friends and enlist their advice and help. Accordingly, before sunrise, he had assembled John Adams, the secretary of the mine; Dan Dewsnap, the engineer, formerly an Oldham man; and two Scots miners, Joe McKenna, the mine captain, and Joe McHenry. Dr.

Gillespie, the mine doctor, was also brought into their deliberations.

No detailed plan could be concerted that night, but it was decided that Churchill should be secreted at the bottom of a mine, in a stable that had recently been constructed for the pit ponies. Churchill entered the pithead cage with Howard and Dewsnap:

Down we shot into the bowels of the earth. At the bottom of the mine were the two Scottish miners with lanterns and a big bundle which afterwards proved to be a mattress and blankets. We walked for some time through the pitchy labyrinth, with frequent turns, twists, and alterations of level, and finally stopped in a sort of chamber where the air was cool and fresh. Here my guide set down his bundle, and Mr Howard handed me a couple of candles, a bottle of whisky, and a box of cigars.

'There's no difficulty about these,' he said. 'I keep them under lock and key. Now we must plan how to feed you tomorrow.'

'Don't you move from here whatever happens,' was the parting injunction. 'There will be Kaffirs about the mine after daylight, but we shall be on the look-out that none of them wanders this way. None of them has seen anything so far.'

Howard's reference to there being no difficulty about the whisky and cigars because they had been under lock and key plainly implied that the servants would not notice their disappearance: on the other hand he was apprehensive that the servants might notice the disappearance of food.

* * * * *

Nearly thirty-six hours had now elapsed since Churchill's escape and nearly twenty-four since the authorities had discovered his absence. Haldane recalls how Churchill's departure was discovered:

We made up a dummy which, placed in his bed, had such a natural appearance that early on the morning of the 13th it was invited to accept a cup of coffee by a soldier servant. No reply being vouchsafed, the beverage was placed on a chair. But our attempts to defer the evil hour of discovery were speedily frustrated; for a barber of the town, who, watched by a policeman, plied his trade on certain days in the school, came by appointment at 8 a.m. and failing to find his client, roused suspicion in the mind of his escort. These suspicions were conveyed to Dr Gunning [*the civilian administrator of the camp*], who came himself to see what was the matter. I had endeavoured to get rid of the barber by telling him that he was not required that morning, but, unfortunately, he was an inquisitive, persistent fellow, who was unwilling to depart before earning his expected fee. Dr Gunning came and made inquiries about Churchill's whereabouts but obtained no information.

At 9.30 a.m. when the commandant returned a roll was called, and each prisoner's presence carefully noted. The fact of there being an absentee became apparent.

Churchill had left behind him a letter of a saucy character which the authorities were to read after his flight had become known. The envelope, addressed to the Under-Secretary for War, was marked 'p.p.c.'—*pour prendre congé.*

WSC to L. de Souza

(Copy : Mrs O. E. de Souza Papers)

11 December 1899   State School Prison
                                                                Pretoria

Dear Mr de Souza,

I do not concede that your Government was justified in holding me, a press correspondent and a non-combatant, a prisoner and I have consequently resolved to escape. The arrangements I have succeeded in making [in] conjunction with my friends outside are such as to give me every confidence.

But I wish, in leaving you thus hastily and unceremoniously, to once more place on record my appreciation of the kindness which has been shown to me and the other prisoners by you, the Commandant and by Dr Gunning, and my admiration of the chivalrous and humane character of the Republican forces.

My views on the general question of the war remain unchanged, but I shall always retain a feeling of high respect for the several classes of burghers I have met and, on reaching the British lines, I will set forth a truthful and impartial account of my experiences in Pretoria.

In conclusion, I desire to express my obligations to you and to hope that when this most grievous and unhappy war shall have come to an end, a state of affairs may be created which shall preserve at once the national pride of the Boers and the security of the British and put a final stop to the rivalry and enmity of both races. Regretting the circumstances have not permitted me to bid you a personal farewell, believe me

Yours vy sincerely
WINSTON S. CHURCHILL

The Commandant of the camp also had to write to Mr de Souza:

R. W. L. Opperman to L. de Souza

(SA Government Archives)

(Translation)

13 December 1899 Guard Office
State Model School
Pretoria

I have the honour to inform you that one of the prisoners of war escaped during the night (W. S. Churchill, correspondent of the *Morning Post*). During the past 4 or 5 days his behaviour was most unusual. He hardly spoke to any of the other prisoners and dreamily wandered alone around the building.

In my view the only way he could have escaped was by bribing one or more of the guards, because the guards were so placed that it would have been impossible for him to escape without their knowledge.

I have the honour to be
Your Excellency's obedient servant
R. W. L. OPPERMAN

After Churchill's escape a formal enquiry was held by the the Boers into its circumstances. No evidence emerged then or since that bribes were offered or taken. The records are preserved in the State and Leyds Archives. It appears that these guards were somewhat slack in the execution of their duties. One of them, Guard Bodenstein, told the Court of Enquiry that Churchill often slept on the verandah—it being near Christmas time and very warm. Another, Corporal Scheepers, recalled that Churchill would walk around the compound until three or four o'clock in the morning. There was no roll-call. The guards, though they were described as members of the South African Republic Police, were in fact either too old or too young or too unfit for military service. The Commandant, Opperman, had only been at the State Model School for a month. But the most important fact that emerged from the enquiry was that instead of ten men being on duty as was normal and as was expected, there were for some reason only eight men posted around the State Model School at the time that Churchill escaped, thus leaving unguarded what was to be his bolt-hole.

The letter that Churchill had left for Mr de Souza was deliberately misleading. The references to friends outside immediately made the Boer authorities assume that he had accomplices in Pretoria. The warrant for searching houses in Pretoria which was issued by the Magistrate, P. Maritz Botha, shortly after the escape states that 'There is reason to believe that W. Churchill, a prisoner of war who escaped from the building of the Model School, is hidden in a certain house in this town inhabited by certain parties, to be pointed out by Detective Donovan'.

Some English people living in Pretoria were ordered out of the Transvaal altogether on the pretext that they were suspected of having aided Churchill in his escape. Soon descriptions of Churchill were circulated throughout the country; almost as soon false reports about him having been seen and even recaptured came in to the authorities.

The first description of Churchill stated that he was 'about 5 ft 8" or 9", blonde with light thin small moustache, walks with slight stoop, cannot speak any Dutch, during long conversations he occasionally makes a rattling noise [*voggeld* in original] in his throat.' It was not until December 18 that the first photographs of Churchill were issued to the police, and a reward of £25 was set on his head, dead or alive.

General Joubert's reaction on hearing of Churchill's escape was to telegraph to the State Secretary in Pretoria on December 15 : 'With reference to Churchill's escape I [wonder] whether it would not be a good thing to make public the correspondence about the release of Churchill to show the world what a scoundrel he is.'

The news of the escape was soon flashed around the world. Oliver Borthwick wrote to Lady Randolph on December 14 : 'Just received the following from Reuter, "Churchill escaped". The country being free from Boers & knowing his practical turn of mind I have no doubt that he knows what he is about and will turn up with an extra chapter of his book finished in a few days' time at some English encampment. So do not be uneasy.'

His friends must have held their breath fearing recapture on the open veld; but there were not lacking those who, while one of their own fellow countrymen was still on the run, did not scruple to attack him and to encourage the Boers to take reprisals against his fellow prisoners. Thus, the *Daily Nation* (Dublin) of December 16 :

Mr Winston Churchill's escape is not regarded in military circles as either a brilliant or an honourable exploit. He was captured as a combatant, and, of course, placed under the same parole as the officers taken prisoner. He has, however, chosen to disregard an honourable undertaking, and it would not be surprising if the Pretoria authorities adopted more strenuous measures to prevent such conduct.

British officers and troops are not allowed to give their parole—it is indeed laid down that it is their plain duty to escape. It is true—though this was not the point of the *Daily Nation*—that Churchill did not hold a commission and was a civilian war correspondent; he could have given his parole : indeed, he offered it if he were to be released. But since his suggestions were rebuffed, all bets were off. Churchill was not to know that at the very time he was escaping the authorities were considering in a more favourable light the possibility of his release.

Haldane, Brockie and Lieutenant Frederick Neil Le Mesurier of the Dublin Fusiliers were themselves to escape three months later in a singularly imaginative fashion.

293

Churchill took the first opportunity of giving an account of this escape, publishing extracts, in *Ian Hamilton's March*, from the diary of Lieutenant Frankland, who had been in the same room as Churchill and the other escapers. Shortly after Churchill's own escape Haldane had devised a plan for making a tunnel from under his room in the State Model School across the road. A trap-door under their floor revealed below a series of compartments about 24 feet by 4 feet and in one of these they began to dig; but after they had made a shaft of about 6 feet they struck water and try as they might to bale it out the shaft was always flooded in the morning and they had to abandon this particular enterprise. Towards the end of February, however, the officers learned that they were to be moved from the State Model School in two days to a new prison in Pretoria. Haldane, Brockie and Le Mesurier decided that they would 'go to earth now'. They opened the trap-door and disappeared into the compartment below, waiting for the prison to be empty of prisoners and guards when they would merely walk out. This they did on the night of February 26–27. Unfortunately, it soon became apparent that the prison was not to be vacated as soon as they had hoped. Haldane and his two companions, however, refused to give up, and gradually, with the aid of prisoners in an adjoining room, began tunnelling sideways through two cross walls each 2 feet thick until they dug their way into a large end room whose outer wall lay opposite the yard of a house then used as part of the prison. For nineteen days the three men remained underground, being fed all the time by Frankland and one or two brother officers who were let into the secret. Finally on March 16 the State Model School was evacuated and Haldane, Brockie and Le Mesurier were able to make good their escape and reached Lourenço Marques two weeks later, having followed much the same route as Churchill and having indeed been harboured by Mr Howard and his friends at the Witbank colliery.

A further quotation from Churchill's 1912 memorandum is necessary at this point.

My conscience is absolutely clear on the whole episode; I acted with perfect comradeship and honour the whole way through. I would not consent to escape on the 15th

November on the engine while he [Haldane] and others were left behind. I gave up a certain means of escape, with honour and credit, from a scene of disaster, in order to return and fight it out with those who were left behind. I was a party to all the discussions about plans for escape from the very first day of our captivity, and the only reason I did not decide to go with them until about a week before the time, was that I expected to be released by the Transvaal Government as a civilian. After our attempt on the 11th, we were all fully resolved that we must at all costs get over on the night of the 12th. There was no more agreement, or bargain, or stipulation, as to who should go first, or how we should go, than there is among a dozen people in the hunting field who are waiting to take their turn at an awkward gap. When I had got over, I waited for an hour and a half at imminent risk of recapture, for the others to come, and the fact that they were not able to come seemed to me and seemed to them to deprive me of all reasonable chance of escape.

In these circumstances, it is monstrous that any mis-understanding, however honest, for which I am not in the slightest degree responsible, should be allowed to serve as a basis for the abominable charges and slanders of which I have been repeatedly the object. I have no doubt that every word of the above statement will be corroborated by Captain Frankland, of the Dublin Fusiliers who is now at the Staff College. He was taken prisoner with us in the armoured train, and knows the whole circumstances in every detail; and he it was who afterwards rendered a supreme service to Haldane and Brockie by feeding them when they were concealed underground, thus giving up for their benefit his own chance of escape.

Churchill had hoped that Haldane would testify in his action for libel against *Blackwood's Magazine* which was heard before Mr Justice Darling and a special jury on 20 May 1912. Haldane, although he indicated that he would certainly not testify against Churchill, seemed reluctant to testify for him, particularly when it became apparent that the case would be uncontested and that Blackwood's were to apologise. Up till then Haldane, for various reasons, although he did not see very much of Churchill, appeared to be on very good terms with him and had made no complaints about his conduct. But in the year 1924, in his Diary which he re-wrote and amplified in 1935, he set down his account of the affair which shows that he had become embittered and that his grievances had rankled with him.

No one can be sure what would have been Frankland's views at the time Haldane wrote in 1924, for he was killed fighting as a Major on the Gallipoli Peninsula during the First World War. He plainly harboured no resentment against Churchill as late as 1908, for on the occasion of Churchill's marriage he sent him Maxwell's two-volume *Life of Wellington*, handsomely bound in full red morocco with the Churchill arms emblazoned on both of them in gold, and the family motto *Fiel pero desdichado* (Faithful but unfortunate) underneath. A note inserted ran: 'From J. H. C. Frankland in Memory of November 15th 1899'. November 15 was the date of their capture after the armoured train disaster. Haldane's resentment also does not seem to have gone very deep. When his *A Soldier's Saga* was published in 1948 (by Blackwood's) he sent a copy to Churchill with the inscription : 'With the profound admiration of an old Ally'.

* * * * *

It was dark in the mine. When Churchill awoke he felt for his candle but could not find it. He went back to sleep. It was not until the evening that an advancing lantern heralded Howard's return with a chicken and some books; he expressed surprise that Churchill had not lighted his candle. Churchill explained that he could not find it. Howard said : 'You cannot have put it under your mattress'. He then explained that the rats must have got it.

Howard reported that the Boers were making a widespread search for him, and that he must lay quiet for the moment. Churchill was to spend another two nights and days in the mine, and Howard's greatest anxiety was how to feed him without arousing the suspicion of his Dutch and native servants.

On the evening of the third day Churchill was brought up from the mine. His new friends were concerned for his health, and insisted on his taking a walk in the dark. Dr

Gillespie was also summoned: he suggested that Churchill should be found accommodation above ground. So it was decided that he should be hidden in the spare room of the office—a sort of storeroom.

The plan to take train to Delagoa Bay was now being concerted. Mr Charles Burnham, who had also been drawn into the plot, was the local storekeeper, as well as an agent for shipping wool; he had a consignment of bales that was to be put on a train for Lourenço Marques. It was decided to load it on the train leaving Witbank at 11 p.m. on December 19. The idea was that a *cache* should be created among the bales where Churchill could lie in comfort and secrecy.

Churchill was duly smuggled aboard, together with a revolver, two roast chickens, some slices of cold meat, a loaf of bread, a melon and three bottles of cold tea. Fifteen months later eight gold watches, suitably inscribed, were on the way to the Witbank Colliery as a token of Churchill's gratitude to those who had helped him during those six days.

At the last moment Mr Burnham decided, and it was

THE RAILWAY TO FREEDOM

well that he did, to accompany the train himself. Later Burnham was to write to Churchill an account of their journey, of which he naturally had seen a great deal more than Churchill:

Charles A. Burnham to WSC

EXTRACT

8 March 1908   Transvaal & Delagoa Bay Collieries
P.O. Witbank

... My first obstacle to overcome was at Middleburg where they wanted to shunt your truck into a side track and there

297

leave it until next day, a few drinks and a tip to the shunter soon put him in a good frame of mind, and on we went after a short delay.

The next at Waterval-Onder, when the guard told me that your truck would have to remain there as the next train leaving was not a freight train, I did not argue this point with him but dispensed a bottle of Whisky between the Shunter and the guard taking the next train on; when the time came to leave he told me it was all right he had fixed the trucks on to the passenger train.

When we arrived at Kaap Muiden Station the platform was crowded with armed Boers and on looking out of my compartment I noticed an old Boer leaning against the very truck you were in; it struck me at once that I must get him away at all costs. I at once walked up to him and asked if he could direct me to the Buffet which happened to be just opposite. He looked at me in surprise, and then pointed at it saying, 'Why, there is the place'. I simply said 'Oh yes, will you not join me in a cup of coffee?' Although I had never seen him before in my life, he came at once.

All went smoothly and luck had not deserted us at Komati Poort the border Station where the whole train was searched. I happened to be acquainted with the Chief Detective there, by name, Morris; after a short talk with him he gave orders to his subordinates that nothing belonging to me was to be touched and that the wool was to continue on its journey without interruption; at Ressano Garcia the first station in Portuguese territory, I was disappointed at having to leave you behind, as the Station Master there was the only one on the whole journey who was proof against a bribe. I offered him up to £20 to allow the trucks to continue with the passenger train. All I could get from him was a promise that the trucks would be forwarded on within half an hour; on hearing I wished to wait and continue my journey with you on the goods train but this being against their regulations he would not allow, there was nothing else for me to do but to go on with the passenger train and await your arrival at Lourenço Marques. . . .

Churchill had memorized the names of all the stations, and when he saw through slits of the truck that he had reached Ressano Garcia, which he knew to be the first station in Portuguese East Africa, he surfaced from the privacy of his bales and 'sang and shouted and crowed at the top of my voice'. Indeed, he recalls that he was 'so carried away by thankfulness and delight that I fired my revolver two or three times in the air as a *feu de joie*. None of these follies led to any evil results'.

In the goods yard of Lourenço Marques he was met by the admirable Mr Burnham who, while waiting there, had been arrested by a Portuguese official for 'loitering with intent'. He had however been quickly released, and now he guided Churchill discreetly to the office of the British Consul. By this time it was late in the afternoon. At the Consulate he was turned away by a secretary, who not unnaturally did not recognise him; he became so angry and made so much noise that the Consul looked out of the window and came down and asked who he was. Thereafter he was warmly welcomed. 'A hot bath, clean clothes, an excellent dinner, means of telegraphing, all I could want,' he wrote later. 'I devoured the file of newspapers which was placed before me. Great events had taken place since I had climbed the walls of the State Model School. The Black Week of the Boer War had descended on the British Army. General Gatacre at Stormberg, Lord Methuen at Magersfontein, and Sir Redvers Buller at Colenso, had all suffered staggering defeats, and casualties on a scale unknown to England since the Crimean War. All this made me eager to rejoin the army, and the Consul himself was no less anxious to get me out of Lourenço Marques which was full of Boers and Boer sympathisers.' The steamer *Induna* was sailing that night for Durban. These Boer sympathizers might have sought to kidnap Churchill from the neutral territory of Portuguese East Africa. Anticipating this possibility a group of Churchill's fellow countrymen, 'fully armed', spontaneously gathered in the Consulate garden to escort him to the quay and see him safely on board. As it proved, there was no trouble and the *Induna* sailed with Churchill aboard.

On the afternoon of the day after next, December 23, the *Induna* docked at Durban. Churchill arrived to find that he had become world famous overnight. The Black Week of which he had read in Lourenço Marques only served as a sombre backcloth which set off his personal achievement in the most vivid colours. He might well have exclaimed, as Lord Byron did after the publication of *Childe Harold* : 'I awoke one morning and found myself famous.'

The headlines of the world's press screamed the news : telegrams poured upon him : he was hailed in Durban as a popular hero. The most welcome telegram probably only reached him much later. It was from Miss Plowden to his mother, and read : 'Thank God—Pamela.'

* * * * *

Elated by his ovation from the Durban crowd, one of the most loyal communities of the British Empire, and having made a stirring address from the steps of the Town Hall, Churchill took train the same afternoon to Pietermaritzburg where he stayed the night as the guest of the Governor of Natal, Sir Walter Hely-Hutchinson, and from where on the following morning he set out for the Headquarters of Sir Redvers Buller at Chieveley. 'He really is a fine fellow', Buller wrote to Lady Londonderry, 'and I must say I admire him greatly. I wish he was leading regular troops instead of writing for a rotten paper.'

He spent that night, Christmas Eve, in the platelayers' hut a few hundred yards from the place where he had been captured thirty-six days before.

15

LADYSMITH TO LONDON

FROM CHIEVELEY CHURCHILL went up to the forward groups
of Buller's army who were preparing to attack the Boer
positions around the Tugela River near Colenso. From
there he wrote to his mother, on 6 January 1900, that
Buller had given him a Lieutenancy in the South African
Light Horse without requiring him to abandon his status as
a war correspondent. This was most remarkable : it was
largely because of his activities as an officer-correspondent
in the Omdurman campaign that a rule had been established that the two jobs could not be doubled. Churchill
was the first and as far as is known the only individual for
whom it was relaxed. This, he added in his artless way,
'may have been done to qualify me for some reward they
might care to give me'. This expectation was to be disappointed; he had already acquired too many enemies.

In his letter he went on to compliment his mother on her
'enterprise & energy in coming out to manage the *Maine*.'
This was a hospital ship which had been provided as a
gesture of Anglo-American solidarity by a group of well-
wishers in England and New England who raised more
than £40,000 in two months.

Churchill went on in the same letter :

> I have another piece of [news] that will surprise you. Jack
> sailed from England on the 5th and I have obtained him
> a lieutenancy in the S.A. Light Horse too. I feel the
> responsibility heavily but I knew he would be longing to
> come and I think everyone should do something for the
> country in these times of trouble & crisis. I particularly
> stipulated that Cassel should agree, and I hope you will
> not mind.

Jack, who had sailed a few days later than his mother, was
by good fortune able to join Lady Randolph and the *Maine*
in Cape Town; they sailed together to Durban.

Churchill was to remain in South Africa for another six months. He was to be present at a number of skirmishes around the Tugela River, at the battle of Spion Kop, at Hussar Hill and Potgieter's Ferry. He was to be among the first to enter Ladysmith and, later, Pretoria. He was to accompany General Sir Ian Hamilton's campaign through the Orange Free State and the Transvaal, bicycle through Boer-infested Johannesburg, and finally distinguish himself on reconnaissance at the battle of Diamond Hill. All these incidents have been described in detail in Churchill's contemporary despatches to the *Morning Post*, in *London to Ladysmith* and *Ian Hamilton's March*, and in *My Early Life*. These despatches are fortified in a number of letters which survive to his mother, to his brother, to Miss Pamela Plowden and to the Colonial Secretary, Mr Joseph Chamberlain.

Churchill ends the letter of January 6 to his mother : 'I think a great deal of Pamela; she loves me vy dearly'. Four days later, when he had already been in action with Buller's troops in one of the many skirmishes around the Tugela River, he wrote to Miss Plowden :

WSC to Miss Pamela Plowden

(Lytton Papers)

EXTRACT

10 January 1900   Chieveley
                                      Natal

. . . Alas dearest we are again in retreat. Buller started out full of determination to do or die but his courage soon ebbed and we stood still and watched while one poor wretched brigade was pounded and hammered and we were not allowed to help them. I cannot begin to criticise— for I should never stop. If there were any one to take Buller's place I would cut and slash—but there is no well known General who is as big a man as he is and *faute de mieux* we must back him for all he is worth—which at this moment is very little. You will see that my telegrams do not waver or flinch. Nor must anyone in public attack the best men the state can find. I know one great general—but the War Office will not consider him—Sir Bindon Blood—so what is the use of crabbing the man at the wheel.

Ever your loving and devoted
WINSTON

Even when he recounted the story of the abortive battle of Spion Kop he made every excuse for Buller's indecisiveness in his despatches to the *Morning Post*. In a letter to Miss Plowden, written from Durban on January 28, he gave some hint of the dangers he had encountered : 'The scenes on Spion Kop were among the strangest and most terrible I have ever witnessed'. And again : 'I had five very dangerous days—continually under shell and rifle fire and once the feather on my hat was cut through by a bullet. But in the end I came serenely through'.

His faith in his star was one of his recurrent themes. No doubt it was encouraged by communications such as the one he received in March from Captain Percy Scott, the Commander of the cruiser *Terrible*, who had landed and transported four 7-inch naval guns for the defence of Ladysmith :

> I am very proud to have met you, because without any luck you have made a wonderful career. Though I did not shake hands with you before I left PMB [Pietermaritzburg] I feel certain that I shall someday shake hands with you as Prime Minister of England, you possess the two necessary qualifications genius and plod.

Churchill had gone to Durban at the end of January to meet his mother and his brother Jack who were arriving from Cape Town in the *Maine*. Churchill expressed anxiety about his brother. He had taken the responsibility for bringing him out, hoping, that at least the relief of Ladysmith would have been effected before he arrived. 'But now we have the bloodiest fight of the war immediately before us—a supreme effort to break through the Boer lines.'

Churchill's anxiety proved justified sooner than he could have feared. On February 12, in his first action—a minor skirmish during a reconnaissance at Hussar Hill above the Tugela—Jack was shot in the calf by a Boer bullet.

J. B. Atkins, Churchill's fellow war correspondent, commented on Jack's wound: 'It seemed as though he had paid his brother's debts'. Churchill himself wrote, in a letter to Miss Plowden, on February 21 : 'Here is an instance of Fortune's caprice. There was a very hot fire—bullets hitting the ground or whizzing by in dozens. Jack—whose luck was fresh—was lying down. I was walking about without any cover—I who have tempted fortune so often. Jack was hit. I am glad he is out of harm's way *honourably* for a month.'

Slowly, despite the blundering and indecisiveness of the higher command, and at considerable cost in lives, the approaches to Ladysmith were cleared of Boers.

Churchill entered Ladysmith with the first relief column, on the evening of February 28. With him he had brought a box of food which Miss Plowden had sent to him for her brother-in-law, Major Edgar Lafone. Unfortunately Major Lafone was not well enough to enjoy these delicacies and Churchill had to report that he was impelled to eat them himself. That night he dined with the defender of Ladysmith, Sir George White. Next to him sat Ian Hamilton, and next but one General Hunter. 'Never before have I sat in such brave company nor stood so close to a great event.'

With the relief of Ladysmith the war in Natal receded north into the fastness of the Drakensberg mountain range. Churchill remained in Ladysmith for some weeks, attending to personal and political matters. Even before the crossing of the Tugela, while he was hotly engaged in the fighting around Spion Kop, he had received a telegram from the Southport Divisional Conservative Association, inviting him to be adopted as Conservative Candidate at the next election. Churchill had wired back from Spearman's Farm : 'Impossible decide here'. But though he was pressed by the Southport Tories, Churchill decided that his first loyalties, for the moment at any rate, lay with Oldham.

There were also business matters to attend to. Now that he had been taken prisoner and had escaped he considered that the value of his next book, which was *London to Ladysmith,* was far greater than could have been expected when he had originally made a contract with his publishers. 'Make sure that I get two thousand pounds on account of the royalties', he told his mother. Then there were offers to write magazine articles and an offer from a lecture agent in America, Mr Pond, to go on a lecture tour.

*　　*　　*　　*　　*

During his stay in Ladysmith, Churchill was able to read the reviews of his novel *Savrola,* which had been published in New York on February 3 and in London ten days later.

Though it was the third of his books to be published, it was, as we have seen, the first which he had begun: its completion, however, had been delayed by *The Malakand Field Force* and *The River War*. The book bore many signs of immaturity; few of the critics pretended there was much originality, though at least one claimed that it had 'literary merit of a high order' and quite a few drew a parallel with Disraeli.

At this time Churchill received a long and encouraging letter from the Colonial Secretary, Joseph Chamberlain.

Joseph Chamberlain to WSC

2 March 1900   40 Princes' Gardens S.W.

My dear Churchill,

I received your letter of many weeks ago & have kept it ever since on my table. I had no heart to write again as long as the military situation was so unsatisfactory. Now I am full of congratulations—firstly on your good work & clever escape from the Boers; secondly upon the admirable & graphic letters which you have since been sending home; and thirdly & chiefly, on the success which has at last attended our arms.

I read your *River War* with great pleasure, but your next history of an Expedition will be of even greater interest & value.

The lessons of this war are already most important. It has shown that there is no falling off in the bravery & endurance of the rank & file, but our generalship is, I fear, open to some of the criticism which has been so plentifully poured upon it by our foreign critics.

It has also been proved that our extended Empire renders us liable to a strain on our military resources for which we are insufficiently prepared. The whole system must be reviewed after the war, and I hope that one result will be that our War Office will give more attention to the splendid material that we have in our Militia & Volunteers, and will not treat them as they hitherto have done as toy soldiers in peace time & useless in war.

On the whole the Boers seem to have behaved well, to have treated our prisoners & wounded with kindness & to have shown a tenacity & courage beyond all praise.

It has been my conviction all along that they are much less numerous than our people have supposed, but their instinct of self-protection which enables them always to obtain good cover, & their mobility, have assisted them to maintain a successful defence against superior forces.

There has been, even in the worst time of depression, no flinching on the part of the public. On the contrary with each reverse the determination to bring the matter to a final & satisfactory issue has been strengthened. I think this feeling will continue to the end & the Government will have a vast majority at their back in insisting on terms which will for ever prevent a recurrence of this trouble & will place beyond a doubt the supremacy of the British flag in South Africa.

I hope you keep well & wish you continued success & distinction. I was sorry to see that your brother has been wounded, but I hope, like yourself not seriously.

Believe me, yours very truly

J. CHAMBERLAIN

Churchill replied:

WSC to Joseph Chamberlain

(J. Chamberlain Papers)

7 April 1900   In the train near De Aar

Dear Mr Chamberlain,

It was a great pleasure to me to receive and read your letter and I think it vy kind of you to write when you are so busy and I daresay so anxious.

I hope, now that it is over, the nation will not complain of the Ladysmith 'entanglement' for it makes a fine page in English history and besides it is becoming vy clear that the Boers threw away around Ladysmith their best chance of success. Fancy if they had flung their main strength upon the Cape Colony at the very beginning and stood strictly on the defensive at Laing's Nek. The Natal army which was practically the only strong force in S. Africa would have been unable to get at them and meanwhile every Dutchman from the Orange River to the sea would have risen in rebellion. The Boer doctrine that Natal rightly belongs to them has ruined them, or at least has led them into a most serious error.

I have left Natal, I think for good, and am now on my way to join Lord Roberts at Bloemfontein. The situation has in the last fortnight changed considerably for the worse. The Field Marshal did not surround and destroy Oliver's southern commando because, first, his own cavalry were exhausted and secondly, he did not want to break them up behind him, but rather to allow all his enemies to collect in front. The result has been most unfortunate and the campaign consequently prolonged. I earnestly hope that the resolve of the country will not weaken, but I fear that they will regard a new series of misfortunes, such as may vy easily come to us, as an anticlimax. However we all have entire confidence in Lord Roberts. If he cannot carry this war to a prosperous issue, no one else in the British Empire will be likely to succeed. I hear he has had occasion to put Lord Kitchener in his place several times and there is no doubt out here as to who commands the army or whose brain directs its movements.

I cannot of course come home until the end of the war or at least until the Transvaal is in our hands : but I shall hope to find a seat before the dissolution, as I should like to record a vote on many points which will arise both out of the settlement of S. Africa and the disturbance of Pall Mall [*the reorganisation of the War Office*]. I have tried to form my own opinion on the state of affairs and society here without accepting the usual formulas, and in consequence I have many doubts. But I do see three things quite clearly. The Republics must go : we should not treat with their civil government or negotiate with either President except in his military capacity : and it will not be possible to effect a satisfactory settlement by means of an [Afrikaner] Bond Ministry.

Touching this last matter, when we have been freely terminating men's lives, I cannot see why we should hesitate to temporarily abrogate a constitution.

With all good wishes and my best congratulations on the success with which you have dealt with your many bitter enemies,

I remain Yours sincerely
WINSTON S. CHURCHILL

Eager to see more fighting, Churchill applied to join the army which Field Marshal Lord Roberts, newly arrived from England, was preparing for a push through the Orange Free State into the heart of the Boer territory, the Transvaal. Churchill believed he had some claim on his goodwill; moreover he was entitled, in common with all war correspondents, to go to the front. Now, for the second time—just as when three years before Churchill had tried to get up to the frontier in India—the Field Marshal proved niggardly with his favours. For a long time after Churchill had applied to be attached as war correspondent he heard nothing. Then, gradually, it became known to him that Lord Roberts did not wish to have him. Two reasons were advanced. First, that Churchill's presence would annoy Robert's Chief of Staff, none other than Lord Kitchener, who bitterly resented criticism made by Churchill in *The River War*, which had been published the previous November. Secondly, Lord Roberts was displeased with Churchill on account of a criticism he had ventured in one of his despatches of a sermon preached by an army chaplain on the eve of the battle of Vaal Krantz, just after the bloody battle of Spion Kop :

I attended a church parade this morning. What a chance this was for a man of great soul who feared God! On every side were drawn up deep masses of soldiery, rank behind rank—perhaps, in all, five thousand. In the hollow square stood the General, the man on whom everything depended. All around were men who within the week had been face to face with Death, and were going to face him again in a few hours. Life seemed very precarious, in spite of the sunlit landscape. What was it all for? What was the good of human effort? How should it befall a man who died in a quarrel he did not understand? All the anxious questioning of weak spirits. It was one of those occasions when a fine preacher might have given comfort and strength where both were sorely needed, and have printed on many minds a permanent impression. The bridegroom Opportunity had come. But the Church had her lamp untrimmed. A chaplain with a raucous voice discoursed on the details of 'The siege and surrender of Jericho'. The soldiers froze into apathy, and after a while the formal perfunctory service reached its welcome conclusion.

Lord Roberts felt that the Army chaplains had been unjustly treated, and the very fact that learned divines from cathedral closes all over England had instantly volunteered their services in South Africa only seemed to make the matter worse.

Churchill, however, had two friends at court: General Ian Hamilton and General Nicholson, both intimate confidants of Lord Roberts. Their pleas on Churchill's behalf prevailed, and eventually the Field Marshal's private secretary, Colonel Neville Chamberlain—not the same Neville Chamberlain who went to Munich and later conducted Britain into the Second World War: he never served in the armed forces—wrote:

Colonel Neville Chamberlain to WSC

11 April 1900   Bloemfontein

My dear Churchill,

Lord Roberts desires me to say that he is willing to permit you to accompany this force as a correspondent—*for your father's sake*.

Yours sincerely
NEVILLE CHAMBERLAIN

'You will form your own opinion', wrote Churchill to his mother, 'as to the justice of making me accept as a favour what was already mine as a right.'

Roberts continued to ignore Churchill until, nearly six weeks later, the young war correspondent undertook a daring bicycle ride through Boer-held Johannesburg in order to bring to Roberts an important message from Hamilton, and also the first news that Johannesburg was being evacuated by the enemy. Only then did Roberts relent. Churchill had however already softened the ground by relieving the Commander-in-Chief of one of a superfluity of dukes which encumbered his staff. The Radical press had made mock of the fact that Roberts had on his staff the Dukes of Norfolk, Marlborough and Westminster. Churchill took Marlborough off with him on the march with Ian Hamilton.

Churchill first attached himself to the Brigade of Imperial Yeomanry commanded by his old friend and Commanding Officer, Brabazon. It was during the few days he spent with him that he had one of his narrowest escapes in the war—

'Indeed,' he wrote to his mother afterwards, 'I do not think I have ever been so near destruction.' He had gone on an impetuous sortie with Captain Angus McNeill and Montmorency's Scouts, racing a contingent of Boers to an important kopje near Dewetsdorp. They had just dismounted at a wire fence about a hundred yards from the summit and were cutting the wire, thinking they were the first to arrive, when from behind some rocks on the summit itself appeared the heads of a dozen Boers—'Grim, hairy, terrible.' Young McNeill shouted : 'Too late, back to the

WITH BULLER AND HAMILTON

other kopje !' But as Churchill tried to remount, his horse, terrified by the firing, plunged wildly. Churchill lost his stirrup; he tried to jump into the saddle, but the saddle only slipped beneath the animal, which broke away and bolted.

Barely a hundred yards from the enemy, with the rest

of the Scouts two hundred yards away by now and no cover for a mile around, Churchill's position seemed hopeless. But as he ran to dodge the bullets, a scout came riding across his front. Churchill describes the incident in his despatch to the *Morning Post* : 'A tall man with skull and crossbones badge, and on a pale horse. Death in Revelation but life to me !' Churchill shouted to the scout : 'Give me a stirrup.' To his surprise he stopped at once and told him to get up behind him. Churchill ran to him, mounted, and away they rode, out of range of the Boer bullets, but not before the scout's horse had been hit. 'Oh my poor horse,' moaned the trooper. 'Never mind,' said Churchill, 'you've saved my life.' 'Ah,' rejoined the scout, 'but it's the horse I'm thinking about.'

* * * * *

At the beginning of May, Churchill, together with his cousin the Duke of Marlborough, had joined General Ian Hamilton's column, which was to make its way through the Orange Free State into the Transvaal on one flank or another of Roberts's army.

There were only eight small actions in the course of the march, and the four-hundred-mile advance was accomplished in 45 days including ten days of halts *en route*. Simultaneously Lord Roberts was advancing along an approximately similar axis with the main army of some nine divisions. In all, in order to capture Pretoria, a force of more than 200,000 men was brought into action. The Boers, recognizing that they were being overwhelmed by superior numbers, prudently withdrew their forces to the east.

Pretoria was reached on June 5. Churchill and Marlborough galloped ahead of the main force of Hamilton's column. Churchill's first concern was for the prisoners. He knew that the State Model School had been evacuated, but he quickly found his way to the new prison. There the British prisoners, who had during the night before narrowly prevented the Commandant from moving them away, were waiting anxiously. Lieutenant Frankland records :

Presently at about half past eight, two figures in khaki came round the corner, crossed the little brook and galloped towards us. Were they Boers come to order our removal?—the advance scouts, perhaps, of a commando

to enforce the order!—or were they our friends at last?
Yes, thank God! One of the horsemen raised his hat and
cheered. There was a wild rush across the enclosure,
hoarse discordant yells, and the prisoners tore like mad-
men to welcome the first of their deliverers.

Who should I see on reaching the gate but Churchill,
who, with his cousin, the Duke of Marlborough, had
galloped on in front of the army to bring us the good
tidings.

Thus less than six months after his escape Churchill was
back in Pretoria.

While the Army had been marching towards Pretoria,
Mafeking was relieved by two flying columns under the
command of Colonel Bryan Mahon and Colonel H. C. O.
Plumer (the former became a General and C-in-C, Rhine
Army) after a siege lasting 217 days. The London crowds
went mad and the word 'maffiking' has passed into the
language. When, three weeks later, the Boer capital of
Pretoria was captured, it seemed to most people that the
war was over.

WSC to Lady Randolph

EXTRACT

9 June 1900   Pretoria—Again

. . . Now that Pretoria is taken I propose to come home,
although as the line is at present cut by the Boers, and I
may possibly go with General Hamilton to Heidelberg,
there may be some delay in starting. We shall, I think, fight
an action tomorrow, which should have the effect of clearing the country east and north east of Pretoria, and should
I come through all right I will seriously turn my face
towards home . . .
. . . I need not say how anxious I am to come back to
England. Politics, Pamela, finances and books all need my
attention. . . .

The action of which he had warned his mother took
place two days later and took the name of Diamond Hill.
Though the Boer War was to drag on for another two
years this was the last engagement in which Churchill was

to take part; and he displayed his usual spirit. In 1944 Sir Ian Hamilton wrote in his book *Listening for the Drums*:

. . . Winston gave the embattled hosts at Diamond Hill an exhibition of conspicuous gallantry (the phrase often used in recommendations for the V.C.) for which he has never received full credit. Here is the story:—My Column, including Broadwood's cavalry and a lot of guns, lay opposite and below a grassy mound, bare of rocks or trees, not unlike our own South Downs where they meet the sea. The crestline was held by the Boer left. The key to the battlefield lay on the summit but nobody knew it until Winston, who had been attached to my column by the High Command, somehow managed to give me the slip and climb this mountain, most of it being dead ground to the Boers lining the crestline as they had to keep their heads down owing to our heavy gunfire. He climbed this mountain as our scouts were trained to climb on the Indian frontier and ensconced himself in a niche not much more than a pistol shot directly below the Boer commandos—no mean feat of arms in broad daylight and one showing a fine trust in the accuracy of our own guns. Had even half a dozen of the Burghers run twenty yards over the brow they could have knocked him off his perch with a volley of stones. Thus it was that from his lofty perch Winston had the nerve to signal me, if I remember right, with his handkerchief on a stick, that if I could only manage to gallop up at the head of my mounted Infantry we ought to be able to rush this summit. . . .

The capture of Diamond Hill meant the winning of the battle, ending as it did with a general retirement by the Boers; also it meant that it was the turning point of the war. The capture of Pretoria had not been the true turning point but rather this battle of Diamond Hill which proved that, humanly speaking, Pretoria would not be retaken. Persistent efforts were made by me to get some mention made or notice taken of Winston's initiative and daring and of how he had grasped the whole layout of the battlefield; but he had two big dislikes against him—those of Bobs and K. And he had only been a Press Correspondent—they declared—so nothing happened.

A month later, on July 4, Churchill, who had paused in Cape Town to have some interesting talks with the British High Commissioner, Sir Alfred Milner, and also a day's fox-hunting with the Duke of Westminster and Milner, sailed for home in the same ship which had brought him out, the *Dunottar Castle*. In eight months he had managed to make a name for himself both at home and abroad. He had established that reputation for courage to which he so ardently aspired : he had made friends as well as enemies in high places : he had confirmed that he could earn his living with his pen : he had learned to think for himself and—that most blessed of all gifts of the statesman—to form independent views : he had matured and developed and now felt fully qualified to mount a more important stage.

16

OLDHAM AND AMERICA

Churchill landed from the *Dunottar Castle* at South-ampton on 20 July 1900. On the voyage home he had occupied himself with completing his forthcoming book, *Ian Hamilton's March,* which largely consisted of his despatches to the *Morning Post.* His previous book, *London to Ladysmith via Pretoria,* had been published five days before the relief of Mafeking; he was to sell 14,000 copies of this in England, the Colonies and America. *Ian Hamilton's March,* also published by Longmans, was not to come out until October. It sold 8,000 copies.

His mother was not at Southampton to greet him. She was on the point of marrying Captain George Cornwallis-West. He was sixteen days older than Churchill and twenty years younger than Lady Randolph and was the most handsome man of his time. Though his sister was soon to marry the Duke of Westminster, he was, after paying Lady Randolph's debts, to be very hard up. Lady Randolph's new marriage was improvident and unsuitable. It lasted on and off for thirteen years until Cornwallis-West left Lady Randolph to marry Mrs Patrick Campbell, the famous and beautiful actress, so glorified by George Bernard Shaw. Mrs Campbell's description of the married state is worthy to be put upon the record : 'The deep deep bliss of the double bed after the hurly-burly of the *chaise longue'.*

A General Election was in the air. Churchill had no Parliamentary thoughts save of Oldham, where he had been defeated at the by-election a year before by 12,770 to 11,477 : Churchill had been in a minority of 1,293 votes to the Liberals. On his return to Oldham he received what he described in a letter to his brother as 'an extraordinary reception'. 'Over 10,000 people turned out in the streets with flags and drums beating and shouted themselves hoarse for two hours, and although it was 12 o'clock before I left the Conservative Club, the streets were still crowded with people. I don't think the two Radical members are at all pleased with the idea of my standing against them.' Churchill was readopted as the Conservative candidate; and as his running mate they selected Mr C. B. Crisp, a London stockbroker, in place of Mr Mawdsley, the Conservative working-man candidate.

Churchill at once made the necessary preliminary arrangements for the coming election. It had always been thought that the election would take place in October and it was not until September that Parliament was dissolved and that the date of the election was finally established.

Churchill quickly found that he was to be in great demand as a speaker, and that he would have to limit his engagements to helping personal friends. He was determined not to make any mistake over Oldham this time. He wrote to his mother on August 12 from Earl Grey's seat:

WSC to Lady Randolph

EXTRACT

12 August 1900

Howick
Lesbury
Northumberland

. . . I have had an enormous number of invitations to speak for people about the country but have had, steadily, to refuse them, with the exception of Plymouth [*for his cousin Ivor Guest*] on the 17th of this month and Staly Bridge [*for George Wyndham*] on the 28th of September.

I must concentrate all my efforts upon Oldham. I am going to have a thorough campaign from the 20th to the 23rd of this month, speaking at 2 or 3 meetings every night upon the African question, and trotting through Cotton Mills and Iron works by day. . . .

Marlborough, with whom he spent some days at Blenheim, accompanied Churchill on this speaking tour during August. He was also to give him £400 towards his election expenses and £100 per annum towards the expenses of registration in his constituency.

But perhaps the most notable service that Marlborough rendered to Churchill at this time was to provide him, at least temporarily, with a home. Lady Randolph had said that she wanted to let 35A Great Cumberland Place and that after an extended honeymoon she proposed to live at Salisbury Hall near St Albans. As a result, Churchill had to find new accommodation for himself. Marlborough generously handed over to him the unexpired two years of a lease he held on a flat at 105 Mount Street.

Parliament was formally dissolved on September 17 and Churchill began his election campaign in Oldham two days later. 'I prepare myself for defeat', he wrote to Lord Rosebery. 'But yet I cannot quite exclude the hope of victory.'

The campaign was short—shorter even than Churchill had anticipated, for polling day in Oldham was to be October 1. Mr Emmott, the senior Radical member and local mill-owner, was again the most formidable of the other candidates. Mr Runciman, the other Radical member, was a Liberal Imperialist—that is, he belonged to that faction in the Liberal party led by Rosebery, Asquith, Grey and Haldane, that supported the prosecution of the South African war.

Churchill wrote to Mr Balfour asking him to fulfil a vague promise to come over from Manchester and speak for him, but he did not come. At some inconvenience however —his return journey by railway took more than four hours in the middle of the night—Chamberlain came up from Birmingham to speak on behalf of the son of his old adversary and friend. This khaki election has been described as Chamberlain's election, just as the war had come to be regarded as Chamberlain's war.

Churchill was to need all the support he could find. For when the votes came to be counted it was found that the Liberals had retained their overall majority in Oldham. Only because some 400 electors had split the straight party vote in order to make him one of their choices did Churchill prevail by a small margin. The figures were as follows:

Emmott	12,947
Churchill	12,931
Runciman	12,709
Crisp	12,522

Thus Churchill was returned in Runciman's place by 222 votes. The result was announced shortly before midnight and the morning papers of October 2 all carried the announcement; *The Times,* however, contrived to say that Churchill had been defeated, though it made amends the following day with an apology and a leading article that welcomed his arrival in Parliament.

In those days, when polling in the various constituencies was spread over three weeks, the early results could have a considerable influence on the rest of the country, where polling had not yet taken place. A clear gain by the Conservatives from the Liberals at Oldham naturally put the former in good heart, and a telegram of congratulations from Lord Salisbury was received by Churchill that same night. On the following day Arthur Balfour, who had found it impossible to assist in Oldham, asked Churchill to abandon any idea of returning to London and instead begged him to go to Manchester to speak on his behalf. When he arrived at the hall, Churchill recalled, 'the whole meeting rose and shouted at my entry. With his great air the Leader of the House of Commons presented me to the audience. After this I never addressed any but the greatest meetings.'

The Conservatives won a decisive victory, gaining an overall majority of 134. This, it is true, was 18 less than Lord Salisbury's majority in 1895 : but that majority had been whittled away by by-elections to the extent of 12 seats (24 on a division), which was now partly made good at the General Election.

* * * * *

Even while he was still in South Africa, Churchill had been attracted by offers to give lectures on the war and on his experiences. First, there had come the offer from Major J. B. Pond, an American agent. In March Churchill had written to his mother asking her to find out about Pond and to make arrangements. 'I would not go to the United States unless guaranteed *at least* a thousand pounds a month for three months and I should expect a great deal more. Five thousand pounds is not too much for making oneself so cheap. I beg of you to take the best advice on these matters. I have so much need of money and we cannot afford to throw away a single shilling.' The following month came offers to lecture in England. Churchill did not relish the idea : 'But you must remember how much money means to me and how much I need it for political expense and other purposes,' he wrote to his mother, 'and if I can make three thousand pounds by giving a score of lectures in the big towns throughout England on the purely military aspect of the war, it is very hard for me to refuse, but I should like you to ask Mr Balfour and Mr Chamberlain what they may think of such a course and whether it would be likely to weaken my political position if I appeared as a paid lecturer on public platforms in this connection.'

The reply they gave must have been reassuring, for soon after his return to England, Churchill had set about assiduously collecting eminent men to preside at his lectures in the various cities.

Between October 30 and his twenty-sixth birthday, November 30, Mr Christie's lecture agency (the author lectured under the same auspices more than thirty years later) had arranged twenty-nine lectures throughout the kingdom.

In all that month of lecturing in England Churchill's share of the proceeds was £3,782 15s. 5d.

By contrast, the American lecture tour was to prove more exhausting and less rewarding.

In the United States, as in Britain, Churchill had distinguished men to take the chair for him at his meetings— Mark Twain in New York, Winston Churchill, the American novelist, in Boston. In his introductory speech Mark Twain said :

I think that England sinned when she got herself into a war in South Africa which could have been avoided, just as we have sinned in getting into a similar war in the Philippines. Mr Churchill by his father is an Englishman, by his mother he is an American, no doubt a blend that makes the perfect man. England and America; we are kin. And now that we are also kin in sin, there is nothing more to be desired. The harmony is perfect —like Mr Churchill himself, whom I now have the honour to present to you.

EXTRACT

21 December 1900   Hotel Touraine
                                                    Boston

. . . I encountered a great deal of difficulty in starting my
tour properly. First of all the interest is not what Maj Pond
made out and secondly there is a strong pro-Boer feeling,
which has been fomented against me by the leaders of the
Dutch, particularly in New York. However, all is now in
train, but the profits are small compared to England and
so far the result to me as follows :

Philadelphia	£120	
New York	£150	
Newhaven	£ 40	
Washington	£ 50	
Baltimore	£ 35	average about
Boston	£ 66	£50 per lecture
New Bedford	£ 40	
Springfield	£ 30	
Hartford	£ 10	
Fall River	£ 40	

Churchill had spent Christmas in Ottawa as the guest
of Lord and Lady Minto at Government House. By good
fortune or good management, Miss Plowden was there.
Shortly before he had returned from South Africa Lady
Randolph had written to him from England : 'Pamela is
devoted to you and if yr love has grown as hers—I have
no doubt it is only a question of time for you 2 to marry.'
Yet by October it was common talk in London society
that Churchill had 'put off' with Miss Plowden. 'Pamela
was there', Churchill wrote to his mother from Ottawa,
'very pretty and apparently quite happy. We had no painful discussions, but there is no doubt in my mind that she
is the only woman I could ever live happily with.' Lord
Minto reported to Lady Randolph of Winston's visit : 'I
think he ran no risks here—everything seemed to me to be
very tolerably platonic—but I am becoming so humdrum
that it is difficult for me to imagine that anyone ever had
any other feelings than those of Plato.'

Churchill was on his last lectures in Winnipeg when the news arrived of the death of Queen Victoria:

WSC to Lady Randolph

EXTRACT

22 January 1901   [Winnipeg]

... So the Queen is dead. The news reached us at Winnipeg and this city far away among the snows—fourteen hundred miles from any British town of importance began to hang its head and hoist half-masted flags. A great and solemn event: but I am curious to know about the King. Will it entirely revolutionise his way of life? Will he sell his horses and scatter his Jews or will Reuben Sassoon be enshrined among the crown jewels and other regalia? Will he become desperately serious? Will he continue to be friendly to you? Will the Keppel be appointed 1st Lady of the Bedchamber? Write to tell me all about this to Queenstown. (SS *Etruria* leaving New York on the 2nd prox).

I contemplated sending a letter of condolence and congratulations mixed, but I am uncertain how to address it and also whether such procedure would be etiquette. You must tell me. I am most interested and feel rather vulgar about the matter. I should like to know an Emperor and a King. Edward the VIIth—gadzooks what a long way that seems to take one back! I am glad he had got his innings at last, and am most interested to watch how he plays it. ...

The Queen's funeral took place on February 2. A day of mourning was proclaimed throughout the Empire. On that day, Churchill sailed from New York on the SS *Etruria* for England. He had entered a new century and a new reign.

INDEX

328